Cambridge Computer Science Texts. 3

Computer Simulation of Continuous Systems

R.J.ORD-SMITH and J.STEPHENSON

Computing Laboratory, University of Bradford

Cambridge University Press

CAMBRIDGE

LONDON· NEW YORK· MELBOURNE

CAMBRIDGE UNIVERSITY PRESS
Cambridge, New York, Melbourne, Madrid, Cape Town,
Singapore, São Paulo, Delhi, Tokyo, Mexico City

Cambridge University Press
The Edinburgh Building, Cambridge CB2 8RU, UK

Published in the United States of America by Cambridge University Press, New York

www.cambridge.org
Information on this title: www.cambridge.org/9780521098724

© Cambridge University Press 1975

This publication is in copyright. Subject to statutory exception
and to the provisions of relevant collective licensing agreements,
no reproduction of any part may take place without the written
permission of Cambridge University Press.

First published 1975
Re-issued 2011

A catalogue record for this publication is available from the British Library

Library of Congress Catalogue Card Number: 74-12957

ISBN 978-0-521-09872-4 Paperback

Cambridge University Press has no responsibility for the persistence or
accuracy of URLs for external or third-party internet websites referred to in
this publication, and does not guarantee that any content on such websites is,
or will remain, accurate or appropriate.

Contents

Preface

The study of problems by computer simulation forms an important part of many courses given at the University of Bradford to students from a wide range of scientific and engineering disciplines. The text is based on material presented in these lecture courses and should be of interest to both undergraduate and postgraduate students wishing to use computer simulation as an aid to a better understanding of their own subject.

Most texts about analogue and hybrid computing describe how the computers function. However, in this book emphasis is placed upon how such computers, and also how digital computers, are used in the simulation of continuous systems. Their use is illustrated in the text by reference to a number of simple problems and most chapters also contain examples of varying complexity selected from a wide range of scientific and engineering subjects. Many of these are based on questions set in a variety of examinations at Bradford and, where appropriate, examples are also included from B. C. S. examination papers.

The important and expanding technique of digital simulation is described in a single, though lengthy, chapter which can be read in relative isolation from the rest of the text.

The text is intended for students attending courses in Physical Sciences or Engineering at a Technical College or University and pre-supposes only a knowledge of Physics or Applied Mathematics to A level standard. Unlike most texts on analogue and hybrid computing, knowledge of electric circuit theory is not required. However, for those with the requisite knowledge of circuits, an appendix is included in which the functioning of analogue and hybrid units is described. Readers will need a little knowledge of logic to understand applications of parallel logic hybrid computers and will also require some familiarity with digital computing to appreciate fully the material relating to digital simulation and the operation and use of full hybrid computers.

1

Space only allows an introduction to be given to the important application of simulation to control engineering. In this introduction equations are presented in differential form so that all the material and all but two of the examples can be understood by the general reader. However, to clarify for those conversant with control theory, equations are also given in Laplace transform, transfer function form.

The authors would like to thank their colleagues at Bradford who have directly or indirectly helped with the production of this text. In particular we wish to acknowledge the great contribution made by Geoff Brown in producing the digital simulation language BEDSOCS referred to in chapter 8, to Tony Jenkins   for the coach suspension problem in chapter 11 and some of the discussion on optimisation, chapter 10, and also to Bob Butts for implementing many of the hybrid routines referred to in chapter 11.

R. J. Ord-Smith
J. Stephenson

1·Computer Simulation

1.1 Introduction

Simulation is the technique by which understanding of the behaviour of a physical system is obtained by making measurements or observations of the behaviour of a model representing that system. There are many reasons why simulation is valuable. Frequently, simulation studies are made to check and optimise the design of a system before its construction. These studies are of great value in avoiding costly design errors and in ensuring safe designs (e. g. of chemical plants, aircraft). When simulation is used in model building the object of the study is to determine a model which adequately represents a given system.

Models of ships have been used for many years to aid good ship design. Understanding is gained by making measurements on a model. This is what simulation is all about, i. e. experimenting with models.

The word model is closely related in meaning to the word analogue which has been used to describe all types of calculating aid in which there is a close correspondence or relationship between parts of the original system and parts of the calculating aid. An early example of this type of calculating device (in which the analogy is not easy to see!) is the slide rule (seventeenth century). On the slide rule numbers are represented by lengths and multiplication achieved by the addition of lengths.

Network analysers using electric circuit elements have been used since about 1920 to study problems involving differential equation solution, e. g. mechanical vibration problems. An example of this type, called a direct or special purpose analogue is considered below. Comparison of equations (1.1) and (1.2) shows that the behaviour of the two systems is determined by the same basic differential equation. The systems are analogous and there is a one-one correspondence between the elements of the two systems. The analogy is very close. The resistor converts

3

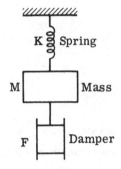

K 🌀 Spring

M | Mass

F | Damper

If x = displacement of mass from its equilibrium position and if friction is proportional to speed then

$$M\frac{d^2x}{dt^2} + F\frac{dx}{dt} + Kx = 0. \qquad (1.1)$$

Fig. 1.1   Mechanical vibration system

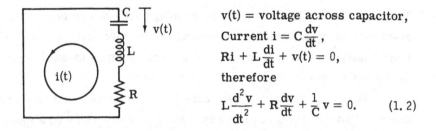

$v(t)$ = voltage across capacitor,

Current $i = C\frac{dv}{dt}$,

$Ri + L\frac{di}{dt} + v(t) = 0$,

therefore

$$L\frac{d^2v}{dt^2} + R\frac{dv}{dt} + \frac{1}{C}v = 0. \qquad (1.2)$$

Fig. 1.2   Analogue electrical system

electrical energy into heat in an analogous way to that in which energy of movement is converted by friction into heat. The inductor and capacitor store electrical energy and the spring and mass mechanical energy. The voltage across the capacitor and the current in the circuit vary in the same way as the position and velocity of the mass.

The effect of variations in M, K and F on the vibrations in the mechanical system can thus be determined by simply observing the effect on the oscillations in the electric circuit of variation in L, C and R.

However, such analogues have serious limitations. Basic amongst these is the need to find analogue elements which exactly simulate the elements of the original system. This is not always easy, e.g. if the friction were $\pm f + ax + bx^2$ it would be difficult to find an electrical element (or combination of elements) having the same characteristic.

General purpose mechanical differential analysers, developed from the wheel and disc integrator invented in 1876 by James Thomson, have been used since about 1930 to study problems involving differential equations. Much of the development was due to Bush and others at M. I. T.

In more recent times (1943 onwards) electronic computers have become the major tool in simulation studies. In computer simulation the system is represented by a set of equations (algebraic, differential and/or logical) which are solved by the computer and the solutions output in tabular or graphical form.

Systems can be broadly grouped into <u>continuous variable</u> or <u>discrete event</u> with some examples overlapping both groups. In continuous systems the model equations include differential equations, e. g. dynamic equations representing the motion of a car wheel or the temperature of a body. These notes describe the various computer techniques (analogue, hybrid and digital) used to study the behaviour of such systems. Discrete event simulation, which lies outside the range of these notes and almost invariably involves use of digital computers, is concerned with the occurrence of discrete events in time and space. An example of this type is traffic flow control in which the arrival of a vehicle is a discrete event.

1. 2   Computer simulation for continuous systems

The general purpose <u>analogue computer</u>, developed at M. I. T. and elsewhere from about 1943, mainly for military applications, comprises various electronic units able to perform mathematical operations on voltages. Each problem variable is represented by a computer variable (voltage) and the computer units are interconnected so that variables are constrained to obey the same differential equations that control the behaviour of the problem variables. The computer independent variable is time and the computer variables vary in time in the same way (but generally at a different rate) as the problem variables vary as functions of the independent variable (frequently time).

The computer contains <u>integrators</u>, summers, multipliers, etc. and the computer 'solves' the problem by integrating the differential equations. The user or programmer joins the units together by inserting plugs joined by wires into various sockets on a patch panel, a process called patching. The solutions are observed and measured by means of oscilloscopes, graph recorders, X-Y graph plotters and data loggers. These measuring instruments are joined to the computer by means of patching wires and plugs.

Modern analogue computers are very fast due to the parallel nature of their construction, i. e. all units operate simultaneously so that all the variables change together in the same way as they do in the problem. Machines are available to solve sets of differential equations tens, hundreds and even thousands of times per second. Speed of solution is unaffected by problem size. The larger the size of system to be simulated, the greater the number of units needed.

In order to make best use of this high speed of solution, digital logic and small digital computers have been added (since about 1960) to the analogue computer to form so called hybrid computers. In such machines the digital section is primarily used to control and monitor the operation of the analogue section and provide program and data storage.

Digital computers also play a completely different role in simulation. Special software has been developed (from 1955) which programmes a computer to solve differential equations by numerical integration. This technique, called digital simulation, offers advantages in accuracy and simplicity over analogue simulation but is very restricted in speed of solution. This speed limitation is caused by the sequential nature of the operations in the central processor of the computer. Numerical integration involves the performing of very many simple arithmetic (and other) operations and although each operation may take a very small time (e. g. 1 microsecond) the sum total of operations needed to solve a reasonable sized problem (20 integrations) will take many seconds. Attempts are being made using a number (~10) of very fast processors operating simultaneously in parallel to improve the speed of solution and so make digital simulation even more attractive than it already is for studying problems involving the solution of differential equations.

1.3 Formulation and solution of problems by simulation

When studying problems using analogue, hybrid or digital simulation, a number of definite steps must be followed from problem formulation to the final solution and conclusion. The actual steps needed do depend on the type and size of problem considered. A typical sequence of steps for a small problem is shown in the following flow chart (Fig. 1. 3).

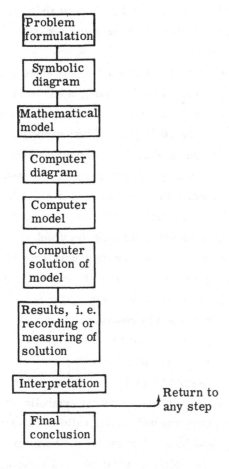

Fig. 1. 3

Notes

(i)   At problem formulation the general problem is considered and objectives specified. This step is often not mathematical; it could, for example, simply be 'given a particular process determine the conditions at which it can be operated most efficiently from the profit viewpoint'.

(ii)   Sometimes the system or process to be studied is represented as a series of blocks, each block corresponding to a certain
element of that system.

(iii)   The mathematical model equations must not only describe
the system but also the objective. Should the equations be found to be
very simple at this stage it may be decided to solve them analytically!

(iv)   The computer diagram shows the units and their interconnections needed to 'model' the system.

(v)   The computer model is essentially a set of variables corresponding to the problem variables, constrained by analogue hardware or
digital software in such a way that they can only vary according to a set
of equations corresponding to those obeyed by the problem variables.

(vi)   When studying certain types of system problems using analogue means, it is possible to go from a symbolic diagram representation
of the system directly onto a computer diagram without ever explicitly
forming system equations in differential form. Each part of the original
system is represented by a block in the symbolic diagram which is simulated by a definite unit (or combination of units) on the computer. The
simulation is said to be direct in this case because of the one-one correspondence between parts of the analogue set up and parts of the original
system. This technique is sometimes used in control problems where
analogue units are designed to simulate the transfer characteristics
corresponding to the blocks in the symbolic diagram.

(vii)   In many cases it is possible to go directly from problem
formulation to mathematical model without introducing a symbolic diagram.

(viii)   The sequence shown does not include any validity checking.
It is essential whenever studying problems by computer methods (or
otherwise) to check the validity of the solutions obtained. Such checks must
relate the   final solution/interpretation directly to the original problem
(or problem equations) in order to be clear of working errors.

(ix)   In some simulation studies the object is to gain understanding
of the problem itself. Once this is done the problem is considered solved
and results in the form of tables, graphs, etc. may not be needed. In
other cases the object of the simulation is to find a model to match some
experimental observations. Once a model is found the problem is solved

and again actual results or recordings may not be (but are likely to be) needed.

1.4   Errors

The accuracy of total problem solution depends on:

(i)   Conformity of the mathematical model equations to the original problem. Errors at this stage can be almost any size. Frequently non-linear systems are approximated to by linear equations (small deflection, perturbation equations). In other cases the problem is not fully understood so that the formulation is not complete.

(ii)   Conformity of the theoretical computer model to the mathematical equations. Errors can be non-existent at this stage if the computer is able (theoretically) to perform the mathematical operations needed. However, some mathematical operations are difficult to simulate, particularly by analogue hardware, and some form of approximation may be needed between computer model and the model equations.

(iii)   Errors in solution of the computer model. These depend in a complex way on the accuracy of the units used and the speed of operation of analogue units or on the step size used in digital integration. Errors may be from 0.01% or less, to 1% or more depending on method, equipment and size and nature of problem.

(iv)   Errors in taking results. Analogue computer solutions must be recorded or measured. Errors depend on type of equipment available and may be from 0.01% for digital voltmeters and data loggers to at least 10% for poor oscilloscopes.

The overall error is a complex function of the problem, computer and recording equipment.

Analogue computers are not high precision devices but are good enough for very many of the problems needed to be studied by computer simulation. In fact, computer and recording errors may be an order less than errors associated with problem formulation.

Digital computers also introduce errors in solution with problems involving differential equations due to integration step length and numerical approximation. In certain cases these errors can exceed those involved in analogue simulation if care is not exercised in the selection of step length and integration technique used.

The total problem solution is no more accurate than the weakest link in the chain (except by lucky error cancellation). Very often the least accurate part (and also the most difficult part of the total study) is the formulation of the mathematical model equations. It is not uncommon to see results of digital simulations given to 4 or more figures when it is known that the model equations only approximately represent the behaviour of the system. Unnecessary, meaningless figures should always be suppressed before publishing results. This is one advantage of presenting results in graphical form. Simple graphs can be read to about the same accuracy as that obtained in many simulation studies involving dynamic systems.

2·Analogue and Simple Parallel Logic Hybrid Computers

2.1 Introduction to analogue computing

A general-purpose ANALOGUE computer essentially comprises a set of units able to perform certain mathematical operations on variable voltages. The user or programmer is able to interconnect these units to form a computer model the variables of which obey specified equations. The basic units and the mathematical relationships obeyed by their input-output variables are shown in Fig. 2.1. They are grouped together under two headings, linear and non-linear.

The input-output variables of LINEAR units obey linear algebraic and differential relationships. When such units are interconnected the variables obey LINEAR CONSTANT COEFFICIENT differential equations. Thus potentiometers, summers and integrators are able, for example, to simulate models of the type:

$$\frac{dv}{dt} + av + bu + cx = 0$$

$$\frac{du}{dt} + ey + f = 0$$

$$\frac{dx}{dt} = v$$

$$\frac{dy}{dt} = u,$$

where a, b, c, e and f are constants and u, v, x and y are variables.

MULTIPLIERS, together with linear units, are needed in the simulation of VARIABLE COEFFICIENT LINEAR differential equations. An example of this type is the equation

$$\frac{d^2y}{dt^2} + a(1 + b \sin wt)y = 0$$

which occurs in the study of the behaviour of a simple pendulum in which the support is subjected to a sinusoidal vertical motion.

11

Unit	Use	Symbol	Equation
LINEAR			
Potentiometer	Multiplication of a variable by a positive constant coefficient ≤ 1	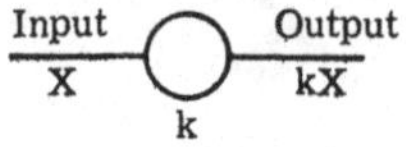 Input X —○— Output kX, k	Output=k. Input where $0 < k < 1$
Inverter	Sign reversing, i. e. multiplication of a variable by -1	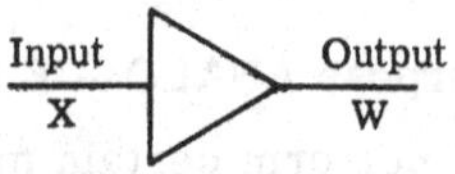 Input X —▷— Output W	-Output=Input $-W = X$
Summer	Summation of number of variables including multiplication by 'gains' 1 or 10	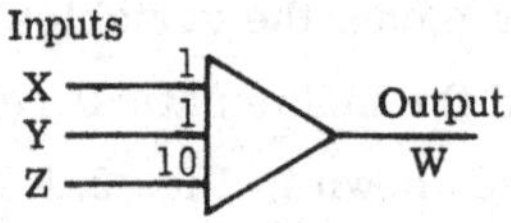 Inputs X(1), Y(1), Z(10) —▷— Output W	-Output='Sum of Inputs' $-W = X+Y+10Z$ (in this case)
Integrator	Integration of a variable with respect to the computer independent variable 'time t'	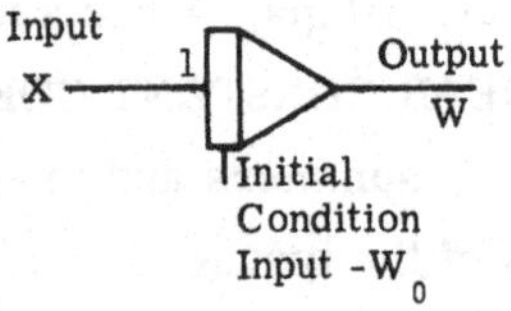 Input X(1) —▷— Output W; Initial Condition Input $-W_0$	$-\frac{d}{dt}$(Output)=Input $-\frac{d}{dt}W=X$ with: Initial value of Output=W_0 = -value of the Initial Condition (I. C.) Input
Summer-Integrator	Summation with integration	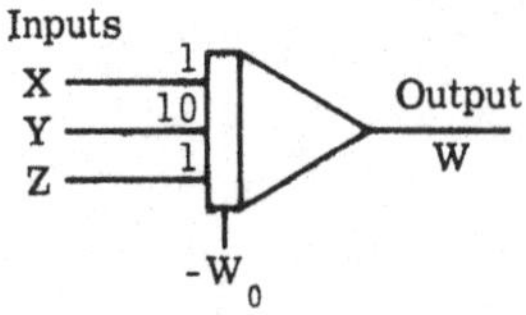 Inputs X(1), Y(10), Z(1) —▷— Output W; $-W_0$	$-\frac{d}{dt}$(Output)= 'Sum of inputs' $-\frac{d}{dt}W=X+10Y+Z$
NON-LINEAR UNITS			
Multiplier	Multiplication of 2 variables (with or without sign change)	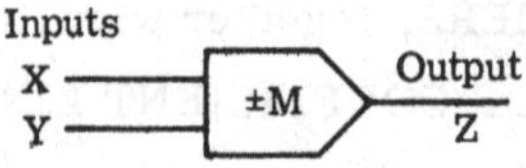 Inputs X, Y —[±M]— Output Z	±Output=product of inputs $\pm Z = XY$
D. F. G. (Diode Function Generator	Generation of functions, e. g. X^2	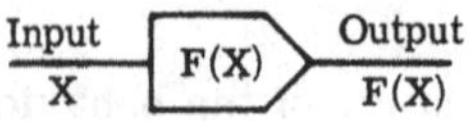 Input X —[F(X)]— Output F(X)	Output=Function of Input Output=F(X)

Fig. 2.1   Table showing basic units

Multipliers and other NON-LINEAR units together with linear units are used in simulations of NON-LINEAR differential equations, e.g. the equation

$$\frac{d^2Q}{dt^2} = aQ - b\frac{d}{dt}(Q|Q|^{0.85})$$

which, under certain conditions, determines the rate flow, Q, of a liquid through a pipe joining two tanks.

All the basic linear units, with the exception of the potentiometer used to multiply a variable by a constant, involve a sign change in their input-output relationship. Each of these units contains a high gain electronic OPERATIONAL AMPLIFIER. Multipliers and other non-linear units also contain operational amplifiers (1, 2 or 3 per unit) but the circuitry is such that sign reversal does not necessarily take place. Collectively all these units containing operational amplifiers are called AMPLIFIER or ACTIVE units to distinguish them from PASSIVE (i.e. non-power amplifying) potentiometers.

Integrator and summer units normally have 6 (or so) inputs, 3 of gain 1 and 3 of gain 10. Multipliers enable division and rooting operations to be carried out.

2.2 Sequence of study

The detailed preparation and solution of a problem by analogue simulation is described in §3. The notes below introduce the general terminology used and the principal features of the technique.

The programmer converts the physical PROBLEM EQUATIONS, i.e. the mathematical model, into a set of MACHINE EQUATIONS by a process of reduction and scaling. In REDUCTION the problem equations are broken down into a set of simple algebraic and first order differential equations, each equation applying to one amplifier unit. Whenever studying problems by simulation it is best to derive the problem equations in the simplest possible form to minimise this need for reduction.

To ensure correct (accurate) operation of the analogue units all the dependent variables (voltages) must lie within a specified range of ±1 MACHINE UNIT (generally ±10 or ±100 volts) of zero. Thus all problem variables (temperature, distance, speed, etc.) must be converted into computer or machine variables the magnitudes of which must not exceed 1 machine unit throughout the computation. This process called AMPLITUDE SCALING is similar to the process in which numbers are converted in digital computers to have values less than one if arithmetic operations are to be performed on numbers in fractional form. (Frequently amplifier units have OVERLOAD indicators (lamps) which show if output variables lie outside the permitted range.) A further object of amplitude scaling is to make the variables be as large as possible without overloads occurring throughout the simulation. This ensures maximum accuracy of operation.

The problem independent variable (generally time) is converted into COMPUTER TIME, i. e. the computer independent variable, by a process called TIME SCALING. The object here is to enable the equations to be solved at a rate suitable for the computer concerned and the recording equipment available.

Once scaled equations are obtained, the programmer ASSIGNS specific units to the equations and produces a SCALED COMPUTER DIAGRAM showing the units, their interconnections and other essential data. The units themselves are interconnected by wires, a process called PATCHING. Patching is normally done 'off line' on a detachable PATCH

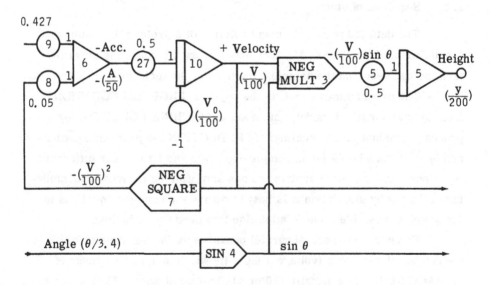

Fig. 2.2 Section of analogue computer diagram

14

PANEL. The units themselves become joined together when this panel is attached to the computer. A typical section of a computer diagram of a problem involving the motion of a projectile could be as shown in Fig. 2.2. The diagram shows the scaled variables at the outputs of units, potentiometer coefficients, the reference numbers of all units used and initial condition (time $t = 0$) information. Unit 10 is used to compute velocity from - acceleration and units 3 and 5 used to compute the height from the velocity by implementing the relationship 'height = ∫ velocity. sin θ. dt', where θ is the angle made by the path of the projectile with the horizontal. The loop formed by units 6, 10 and 7 illustrates the concept of 'feedback'. Velocity information is needed in order to compute the acceleration and the acceleration is used to produce the velocity. The interconnections between the units form 'constraints' forcing the computer variables to vary according to certain equations.

The diagram, Fig. 2.2, shows a connection made to a '-1' reference supply. Both +1 and -1 precision constant REFERENCE supplies are made available on the panel in order that constant values (≤ 1) may be generated, e.g.

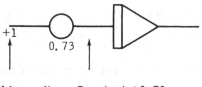

+1 Machine unit   Constant +0.73
reference   machine unit   Fig. 2.3

When the problem is patched and the panel attached to the computer, the computer is switched into a number of static MODES of operation during which the problem is set up and statically checked prior to the actual solution of the model equations.

In the POT SET or PS mode each potentiometer is adjusted so that it multiplies its input by the correct constant coefficient (≤ 1). Various means are provided for setting up potentiometers. In simple machines each POT has to be MANUALLY turned until the correct coefficient is set, this point being determined by a metering system, often a digital

15

voltmeter or DVM. In many large machines most (but not all) of the pots are driven by SERVO control systems and can be set from keyboard inputs or from a digital computer. In some machines fast setting ELECTRONIC pots are provided.

Once the setting up of potentiometers is complete the computer is switched into a STATIC TEST or ST mode in order that the static state of the simulation can be completely checked. In this mode checks are made to ensure that all integrators are operating correctly 'initially' and that all other units are correctly connected and working. Values of variables (constant in this mode of operation) and constants are read using the computer's metering system.

Once these checks are completed the computer is switched into an INITIAL CONDITION or I.C. mode during which time the simulation is constant in its initial time $t = 0$ state. This mode is very similar (in some machines identical) to the ST mode just described; the differences are explained later.

When the computer is switched into the COMPUTE C or OPERATE OP mode the equations are 'solved', i.e. the variables are made to vary from their initial values according to the equations (or constraints) set up. If the computer is switched into the REP OP mode the equations are solved repetitively, i.e. the computer is made to cycle:

Reset (to Initial Values) → Compute → Reset → Compute → Reset → etc.

The time durations of the compute and reset (to Initial Values) periods are set by controls on the computer.

In both the COMPUTE and REP-OP modes the rate at which the equations are solved (essentially by integration) is determined by the TIME SCALE of the integrators used. The time scale can normally be selected, using a common or master time scale control, to be from 1 second to 0.001 or even 0.0001 of a second in factors of 0.1. In the NORMAL SECONDS or SLOW SPEED mode the time scale is 1 second and a 1 machine unit input to an integrator (via a gain of 1) will cause the output to vary at a constant rate of 1 machine unit per second. This is the normal slow speed mode of operation used to achieve maximum accuracy and used when making pen recordings of the solutions. If a

16

smaller time scale is selected (e. g. 0. 001 second) the integrators integrate more quickly (e. g. X1000 normal rate) and the solutions are speeded up accordingly. High-speed operation is particularly useful when observing the behaviour of the computer model repetitively on an oscilloscope display.

The computer has one other important mode of operation, i. e. HOLD H. If the computer, operating in the COMPUTE mode, is switched to HOLD the solution is 'frozen' at that particular instant of time. This is a useful facility in many situations, e. g. it enables the state of all the problem variables to be monitored at a particular time and when graph plotting solutions it enables the recording to be stopped at a certain time so that the pen can be lifted from the paper.

Fig. 2. 4 summarises the effect of mode control on the computer units. In particular it shows how the integrators are connected in these different modes. In the I. C. mode the integrator output equals minus the value of the I. C. input. In the COMPUTE mode an integrator integrates the normal input variables (times -1) with respect to time so that the subsequent output equals the initial output x_0 minus the time integral

Mode	Integrator connection	Integrator output	State of other units
POT SET		Zero	Outputs all zero
ST and IC	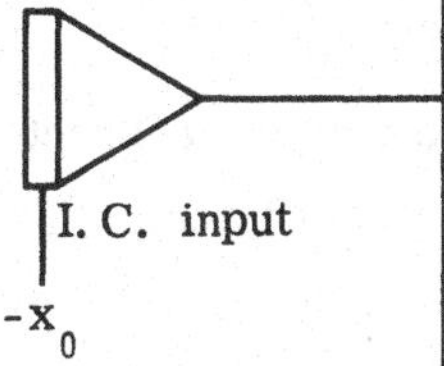 I. C. input $-x_0$	$x = x_0$	Fully operational
COMPUTE OR OPERATE	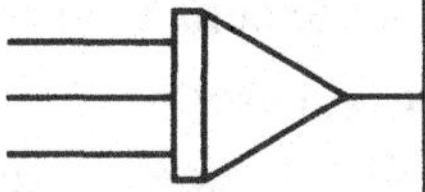	$-\dfrac{d}{dt}$ Output = sum of inputs	Fully operational
HOLD	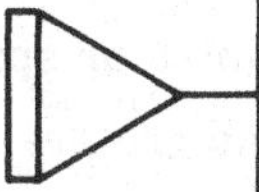	Last value it had before entering HOLD mode	Fully operational

Fig. 2. 4   Table showing effect of mode control

of the effective sum of the inputs from 'time $t = 0$' when the integrators are switched from I. C. to COMPUTE.

i. e.   Output $x = x_0 - \int_0^t$ effective sum of inputs. dt.

The integrator equation is not usually written in this rather clumsy form but in an equivalent neater way:

$$-\frac{dx}{dt} = \text{effective sum of inputs}$$

with initial output $x_0 = -$ initial condition input.

It should be noted that if the effective sum of the inputs to an integrator is zero then the output of the integrator will remain constant.

Miscellaneous Important Notes

(i)   Amplifier units are essentially unidirectional devices. Their outputs are driven by their inputs, as governed by the controlling equation.   This unidirectional property is emphasised by the arrowhead on the computer diagram.   No attempt must be made to force an output to move except under control of the inputs.   In particular, an integrator cannot be made to differentiate by connecting it the reverse way round!

(ii)   As a consequence of (i) above, outputs of amplifier units are never joined together.   Joining two outputs will certainly not produce summation.

(iii)   A potentiometer must be connected the correct way round otherwise it will not multiply by the correct coefficient.

(iv)   The value a potentiometer multiplies by is affected by the load on its output.   Circuits automatically ensure that the load is correct when the computer is in the POT SET mode.   Should any patching changes be made at the potentiometer output it must be reset.

(v)   Analogue computers do not normally contain units to differentiate (with respect to time).   This is because they are 'noisy', i. e. they amplify any 'high' frequency random noise or spurious (mains hum) signals contained in the input variables.   Integrators on the other hand attenuate such 'noise'.   [Cf. the way in which numerical integration smooths out irregularities in data points whereas differentiation accentu-

18

ates these irregularities.]

2.3 Simple parallel logic hybrid computer

The range of problems that can be simulated can be greatly increased if parallel logic and interface units are added to the basic analogue units (Fig. 2.5). The table of Fig. 2.6 shows the logic and inter-

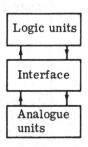

Fig. 2.5

face units normally to be found in a simple computer of this type.

LOGIC units comprise GATES and BISTABLES. They are normally provided with both normal and inverse outputs so that logic inverters are not needed. [†]

Two sets of units are provided to communicate between analogue and logic variables. The basic analogue → digital unit is the COMPARATOR which compares the sum of 2 (or perhaps 3) analogue variables with zero and outputs a binary logic variable the value of which depends on the sign of the sum. A comparator cannot detect whether this sum is + or - if the sum is of very small magnitude, i.e. there is a small band of uncertainty (e.g. ±0.0002 machine unit) in the point at which the device operates.

---

† In this text logic HIGH corresponds to logic 1 and logic LOW corresponds to logic 0. Readers not familiar with the behaviour of logic units are advised to read the introductory sections of ref. 8 quoted in the Further Reading list given at the end of this book.

Unit	Function	Notation	Equation
COMPARATOR	Comparison of 1, 2 (or 3) variables with zero	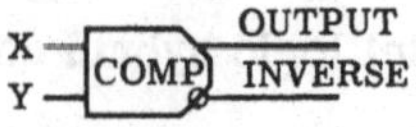 X, Y, COMP, OUTPUT, INVERSE	Logic Output = HIGH if X+Y>0. Logic Output = LOW if X+Y< 0
RELAY	Switch between analogue variables	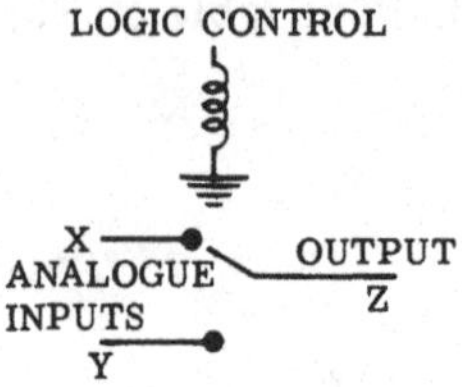 LOGIC CONTROL, X, Y, ANALOGUE INPUTS, OUTPUT Z	Z=X if Logic Control HIGH. Z=Y if Logic Control LOW
D/A SWITCH*	Acts as a switchable input to summer or integrator	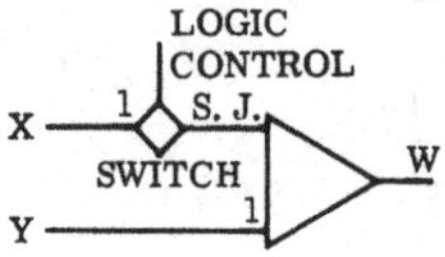 LOGIC CONTROL, X, Y, S. J., SWITCH, W	-W=X+Y if logic HIGH. -W=0+Y if logic LOW
AND(and NAND gate)	Logical AND (and NAND)	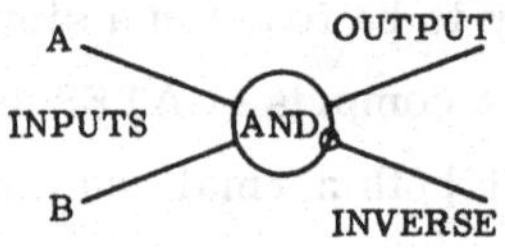 A, B, INPUTS, AND, OUTPUT, INVERSE	Output = HIGH if A AND B HIGH. Otherwise Output is LOW
BISTABLE	Divide by two and memorise state of logic variable	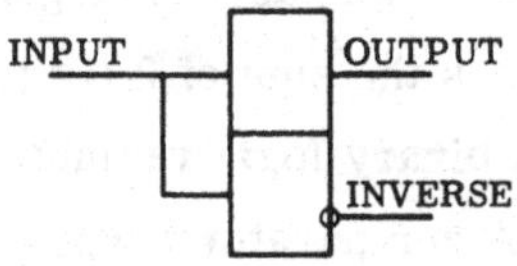 INPUT, OUTPUT, INVERSE	Changes state when INPUT goes from HIGH to LOW

Note. S. J. (Summing Junction) is a special input to a summer or integrator to which the output of the D/A switch must be connected. The meaning of the term 'summing junction' is explained in Appendix 1 which describes in detail the operation of analogue and hybrid units.

Fig. 2.6 Simple interface and logic units

SWITCHES are used to enable logic variables to control the state of the analogue model (e. g. switching different units in and out of a model). These switches are of two types; slow relay and fast electronic.

Slow RELAY switches are generally used to change conditions between successive compute periods of a repetitively operating machine. Their time of operation is typically about one thousandth of a second.

Fast electronic D/A switches, which operate in about 1 μs, i. e. one millionth of a second, are normally used to make changes within the compute period (without having to freeze the solution momentarily). These fast switches are essentially switchable inputs which must be used in conjunction with inverter, summer or integrator units. Such D/A switches (when closed) provide inputs of gain 1, 10 or even 2 depending on the type of machine. In all the following notes it will be assumed they are gain 1 switches.

2.4 Characteristics of analogue computation

(i) Limited accuracy and precision

Analogue computers are relatively low precision devices. In the best machines available variables are read with a precision of 4 significant figures, linear operations are carried out with an accuracy of 3-4 figures and non-linear operations with an accuracy of about 3 figures. Reasonably sized problems (20-100 amplifier problems) are likely to be solved with errors of 1% or more. (As already pointed out in §1, such errors are often of little importance in dynamic simulation problems.) Total error analysis is very complex and is not usually attempted even with small problems. To examine errors arising in the solution of a simple 2nd order differential equation model could involve the need to solve a 4th or 5th order equation! Validity checks on particular analogue solutions are best made using digital simulation or, if possible, relating the solutions to actual observations made on the system under study.

Analogue errors can be minimised by use of careful scaling and choice of solution speed. Scaling, a tedious but not difficult process, is regarded by many as the bane of analogue computation. In digital simulation scaling is not needed as floating point numbers and arithmetic are used though this disguises some notorious sources of numerical error. The following brief notes outline some of the sources of error in analogue machines and ways of minimising their effect.

(a) Static errors. The digital voltmeter or D. V. M. which forms an important part of the set up and monitoring system normally has a resolution of 0. 0001 machine unit, i. e. 0. 01% of 1 machine unit. Potentiometers can normally be set to this resolution. Thus a pot to be set to 0. 5 will usually set to within ±0. 0001 of 0. 5, i. e. an error of 0. 02%. A pot to be set to 0. 05 will also be set with the same absolute magnitude of error producing, therefore, a percentage error of 0. 2. If it be required to multiply accurately by a very small constant coefficient two pots connected in series should be used. (Compare the likely errors involved in multiplying a variable by 0. 0025 using a single pot or by means of two pots, each set to 0. 05, in series.)

The gains of linear amplifier units (summers, integrators) are usually correct to within 0. 01 or 0. 02%. Thus for example if the input of an inverter is -X the output should be within 0. 02% of X if only the effect of gain error is included. This type of error is independent (as a percentage) of the amplitude of the variable concerned.

All amplifier units have 'offset' errors which are constant in absolute value irrespective of the magnitude of the variables. The effect of these errors (typically 10^{-5} of a machine unit) is minimised if the magnitude of the variables is made as large as possible (on average) throughout the computation. When a variable is read using the D. V. M. an additional error of magnitude 0. 0001 machine unit is likely to be introduced. Again the effect of this is minimised by good scaling.

Errors in non linear units are rather larger than in linear units. Typically multipliers and function generators are likely to introduce errors of the order of 1 part in 1000 of a machine unit.

(b) Dynamic errors. These errors are introduced in the compute phase due to limitations in the frequency and phase response of the amplifiers, stray capacity across components, inductance in leads, etc. These dynamic errors may be much larger than the static errors, e. g. a quality inverter, having a static gain error of 0. 01%, may introduce a total dynamic gain error of 1% when the input is a sinewave of frequency 1000 cycles per second. Thus the high-speed mode of operation should only be used for initial investigation of problems or when accuracy is of little importance.

In the slow (normal seconds) time scale dynamic errors are usually so small that total errors approximate to the static errors.

(c) Switching errors. Each time the computer is switched from one mode into another small errors (0.0001 machine unit) may be introduced into the variables at the amplifier outputs. This type of error is of little consequence except if the computer is made to go through very many COMPUTE – HOLD cycles in succession, e.g. if the mode sequence is

I.C. → COMP → HOLD → COMP → HOLD → etc.

Such a sequence might be used if analogue variables are to be sampled at many instances in the solution period (e.g. perhaps by a data logger or digital computer). Switching errors in this situation may well accumulate to produce a considerable error at the end of the total computing time.

(d) Time drift errors. The analogue integrator integrates by 'accumulating' a charge in a capacitor, a process described in more detail in Appendix 1. However, even when the integrator input is zero, the charge in the capacitor may change slowly and so produce a slow change in magnitude of the integrator output variable. This is caused by current 'leaking' into or out of the capacitor and leads to the effect called DRIFT. In early analogue machines drift was a major source of error and the maximum length of the COMPUTE (and also HOLD) period had to be severely restricted to avoid error build up due to this cause. In modern machines drift is much less of a problem and COMPUTE periods in excess of 100 seconds can generally be used without introducing any noticeable drift errors. (< 0.0001 of 1 machine unit.)

(ii) **Fast interactive nature**

The analogue computer is able to solve differential equations at high speed, so fast in fact that generally a user is able to observe 'immediately' the effect of changing a parameter (initial value, input, coefficient) in the equations. Thus the user, by 'feeling' how a model

responds to changing conditions, is able to gain understanding of the behaviour of the physical system simulated. The user is best able to interact with the model by making adjustments to manually set potentiometers.
A good analogue simulation is a 'model with knobs on', i.e. a model in
which all sorts of adjustments can be made and the effects observed.

The highly interactive nature of analogue computing is, perhaps,
its most important and best feature.

However, for many problems the analogue machine is too interactive (everything has to be set up by hand) and not sufficiently automatic.
This non-automatic nature is largely overcome in the full hybrid computer
discussed later.

2.5 Discussion concerning the role of parallel logic facilities

Great uncertainty exists, both by manufacturers and some users,
as to what logic units should be provided on parallel logic hybrid computers. Certain makes contain very extensive logic facilities (e.g. shift
registers, counters, monostable pulse generators, etc.) so complex in
fact that they enable sequential programming to be implemented. Even
multidimensional optimisation by steepest descent can be programmed
with such facilities.

However, it is very difficult to de-bug parallel logic (even if shift
registers are used for programming) and such applications are considered
by the authors to be largely of academic interest but otherwise a waste of
effort. The time spent in getting a complex program to operate may well
exceed the time needed to get answers from the problem by simple manual
interaction. Parallel logic should be used to extend the range of problems
capable of being studied by analogue simulation, e.g. the continuous
generation of certain non-linear functions (e.g. hysteresis). Automatic
sequencing is both better and more simply carried out using the digital
part of a full hybrid computer to control the inputs and read data from
an analogue computer model. Consequently no applications of programming using parallel logic are given in these notes. Applications are restricted to function generation (by direct use of logic and interface and by
high-speed subroutines). Such applications can be implemented using
very few logic units and provide real advantages for relatively little effort.

24

3 · Study of Differential Equation Problems by Analogue Simulation

3.1 An illustrative example involving radio-active decay

The basic units to be found in analogue computers have already been introduced in §2 together with the relationships obeyed by their input-output variables. In this section we wish to examine how a small problem is studied and how the various static and dynamic modes of operation of an analogue computer are used. The problem considered, one of radio-active decay, has been chosen so that scaling is not needed. The equations relating to this problem appear also in simple chemical reactions.

Problem specification. An atom of radio-active material A decays completely to form material B, also radio-active, which in turn decays to form stable material C. Assuming that initially only A is present, find the maximum mass of B, the time when max B occurs and the time when 90% of original A is converted to C. Assume half-life of A is 2 seconds and half-life of B is 4 seconds.

Discussion. A radio-active material decays at a rate proportional to the amount of material present. If y = amount at time t then

$$\frac{dy}{dt} = -\alpha y,$$

where α = <u>decay constant.</u> Thus

$$y = y_0 \cdot e^{-\alpha t},$$

where y_0 = initial amount of y. Half-life τ is time y takes to decay from any value to half that value. Thus when $t = \tau$, $y = y_0/2$. Therefore

$$\frac{y_0}{2} = y_0 e^{-\alpha \tau}$$

giving $\alpha \tau = \log_e 2$ as the basic relationship between decay constant and half-life.

Mathematical model

A   B   C (Stable)

     2 seconds   4 seconds

Let α = decay constant A = $\frac{1}{2}\log_e 2$ = 0. 347

    β = decay constant B = $\frac{1}{4}\log_e 2$ = 0. 174

Equations:

$$\frac{dA}{dt} = -\alpha A \qquad\qquad \text{given } A = A_0 \text{ at time } t = 0$$

$$\frac{dB}{dt} = +\alpha . A - \beta . B \qquad \text{given } B_0 = 0 \text{ at time } t = 0$$

$$\frac{dC}{dt} = \beta . B \qquad\qquad \text{given } C_0 = 0 \text{ at time } t = 0$$

Computer model. The equations are already reduced into a form where each can be simulated using a single computer amplifier unit. Therefore, they only need to be rewritten with a negative sign on their L. H. S. to take account of the sign reversal introduced by analogue integrators. If we assume the initial, time $t = 0$, amount A_0 of A is 1 machine unit, no scaling is required.

Machine or computer equations:

$$-\frac{dA}{dt} = 0. 347A \qquad\qquad \text{INT1}$$

$$-\frac{dB}{dt} = -0. 347A + 0. 174B \qquad \text{INT2}$$

$$-\frac{dC}{dt} = -0. 174B \qquad\qquad \text{INT3}$$

Each equation is in the form

$$-\frac{d}{dt} \text{ output} = \text{sum of the inputs}$$

The computer diagram is deduced directly from these equations. For example, the second equation shows that two inputs are required into the integrator producing B. One input '-0. 347A' must be derived from the integrator producing A by means of a sign reverser (inverter) and potentiometer. The other input '+0. 174B' must be derived from the integrator producing B by means of a potentiometer set at 0. 174. The final

26

computer diagram, showing the one initial condition needed, is drawn below (Fig. 3.1). It shows clearly the patching interconnections needed to link the various units and also the reference numbers of the units used. Note that to produce +1 machine unit initial output of integrator 1, -1 must be connected into the I. C. input.

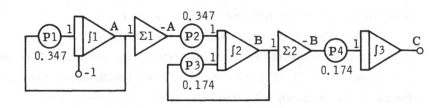

Fig. 3.1   Computer diagram for radio-active decay problem

From the equations and the diagram a POT list showing the required potentiometer settings is drawn up:

POT	COEFF
P1	0.347
P2	0.347
P3	0.174
P4	0.174

In addition, an initial 'time t = 0' condition list is produced showing the initial values of all the amplifier unit outputs:

AMP	VARIABLE	I. C. VALUE
∫1	A	+1
∫2	B	0
∫3	C	0
Σ1	-A	-1
Σ2	-B	0

These lists are used during set-up and check-out of the problem before entering the dynamic phase of solution.

Sequence of solution on the computer:

(i)   The problem is patched.

(ii)   The computer is switched into a special mode called POT SET and all potentiometer coefficients are set. (It should be noted that a

27

potentiometer must only be set when its output is properly connected. Changing the 'load' changes the setting of the pot.)

(iii)   The computer is switched into its INITIAL CONDITION mode. All units, except integrators, are fully operational in this mode. Integrator outputs are determined by the values input to the I.C. inputs. This mode is used in setting the initial state of the problem. It is also used in checking, a process discussed more fully later.

(iv)   The computer is switched into the COMPUTE or OPERATE mode and the solution of the equations begins. The variation of the integrator outputs A, B, C can be observed using the metering system of the computer, or recorded graphically using a chart recorder.

Solutions obtained for this problem are shown in Fig. 3.2.

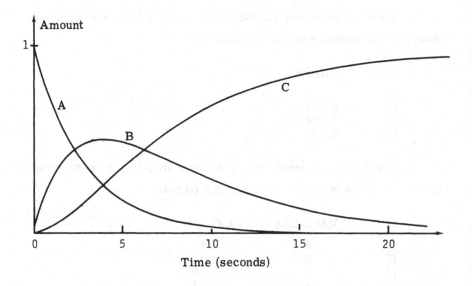

Fig. 3.2   Solutions to radio-active decay problem

(v)   The computer solution may be halted at any time by switching the computer to the HOLD mode. In this mode the integrator inputs are automatically disconnected so that the outputs remain constant. The integrators store the current state of the solution. The solution may be continued by switching to compute or operate.

(vi)   Most computers have a high-speed **REPETITIVE** mode of operation. In this mode the simulation is cycled between the initial condition and operate modes and the equations are solved at high speed (10-1000 solutions per second). This enables the solutions to be observed in graphical form using simple oscilloscope displays.

3. 2   Generation of a timebase reference

When using oscilloscopes or X-Y recorders to observe or record equation solutions it is best to use the computer to produce a linearly sweeping voltage to act as a timebase reference input to the **X** (horizontal) control of the oscilloscope or recorder. This ensures that the timebase is in synchronism with the computer solution even if the computer is switched to HOLD. The linearly sweeping voltage is produced using an integrator with a constant input:

Fig. 3. 3

Thus with $k = 0.1$ the output $0.1t$ will vary from 0 to 1 machine unit (e. g. 10 volts) in 10 seconds.

If required, a voltage sweeping from -1 machine unit to +1 machine unit may be generated, viz.

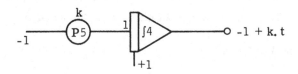

Fig. 3. 4

The output $-1 + kt$ will sweep from -1 to +1 machine unit in a time of $\frac{2}{k}$ seconds.

It is recommended that an integrator is assigned to act as time-base with all simulations and the constant 'k' and integrator initial output added to the POT and I. C. lists. This comment does not apply when using an analogue machine which has a timebase reference generator, based on an integrator, as a built-in feature.

3. 3   Examples for practical study

(1) Radio-active decay

Set up the problem as described in the text and generally investigate the various computer modes and operation of the recording equipment. Record the solutions A, B and C using a timebase of 20 seconds duration.

(2) Damped harmonic motion

Problem description.   An equation which occurs in many studies of vibration is:

$$\frac{d^2Y}{dt^2} + 2.\ \zeta.\ w\ \frac{dY}{dt} + w^2Y = 0.$$

If $\zeta = 0$ it reduces to the well-known S. H. M. equation $\dfrac{d^2Y}{dt^2} + w^2.\ Y = 0$ the solution of which is in the form $Y = A \cos wt + B \sin wt$, where A and B are determined by the initial conditions.

The term $2\zeta w\dfrac{dY}{dt}$ is a damping term proportional to velocity which causes the amplitude of any oscillation in the solution to decrease with time. ζ is called the damping coefficient and w the (undamped) natural angular frequency of oscillation. It is required to find the way 'ζ' effects the decay of the oscillations.

Simulation.   It is convenient to consider the case $w = 1$ radian/ second, $\dfrac{dY}{dt} = 0$ and $Y = 0.5$ at $t = 0$ in which case the equation becomes

$$\frac{d^2Y}{dt^2} + 2\zeta\frac{dY}{dt} + Y = 0.$$

If V is substituted for $\dfrac{dY}{dt}$ the equation can be written in reduced form as:

$$-\frac{dV}{dt} = 2.\ \zeta V + Y$$

and

30

$$-\frac{dY}{dt} = -V.$$

Each of these first order differential equations can be implemented by an integrator and a suitable patching diagram is shown in Fig. 3.5.

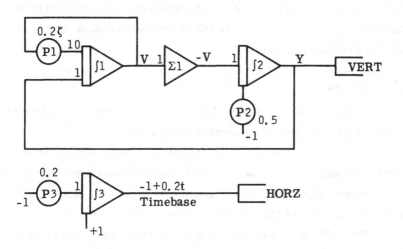

Fig. 3.5 Simulation diagram for damped harmonic motion

A 10 second timebase is included and connections are shown to recording and/or display equipment.

Practical work

(i)   Simulate the above system and observe or record the solution Y (and also V) for each value of ζ between 0 and 1 in steps of 0.2, i.e. $\zeta = 0[0.2]1$ or $0.2\zeta = 0[0.04]0.2$.

Note the oscillatory nature of the solution until the critical damping value $\zeta = 1$ is reached. The effect of the variation of parameter ζ can best be observed using the high-speed repetitive mode of operation.

(ii)   In the repetitive mode note the effect of variation of the initial value of Y.

(iii)   Reset Yo to 0.5. Make $\zeta = 0$ so that the equation is S.H.M. and note that $Y = 0.5 \cos t$ and $-V = 0.5 \sin t$. Disconnect the timebase and using a long operate time display Y against V and note the generation of a circular display of radius 0.5 machine unit.

Observe the effect of increasing the damping ζ. (This type of display, called an X-Y display or phase plane plot, is a useful way of showing the solution of d. e. s.)

(iv)   Set $\zeta = 0$. Leave $-V$ joined to the horizontal input of the display and route Y via a potentiometer set at k so that $(-V, Y)$ becomes 0. 5 (sin t, k cos t), i. e. the parametric representation of an ellipse. Observe elliptic display for various values of k and finally note the effect of increasing ζ.

3. 4   Scaling

Scaling is the process by which physical problem equations are converted into machine (computer) equations so that:

(1)   The amplitudes of all the machine variables are as large as possible throughout the computation but do not exceed one machine unit. This process, which ensures maximum accuracy being attained without overloads, is called AMPLITUDE scaling.

(2)   The equations are scaled in a 'reasonable' time to match the computer and its peripheral recording devices. This process, which is achieved by choosing the relationship between problem independent variable and computer time, is called TIME scaling.

Various methods, some very elaborate and confusing, have been derived to perform scaling. Amplitude and time scaling can be performed in either order or together. The method for amplitude scaling, now widely used, described below and also the technique for time scaling, are considered by the authors of these notes to be the simplest for general use.

3. 5   Normalised variable method for amplitude scaling

The method briefly described below follows very closely the technique explained by Charlesworth and Fletcher in 'Systematic Analogue Computer Programming' and is also very similar to the method suggested by manufacturers of analogue equipment, e. g. E. A. L. In the following section the method is discussed and then illustrated by means of a fully worked example.

(i)   **Maximum values**

The first requirement before commencing any method of scaling is to obtain estimates of the maximum modulus values the dependent problem variables are likely to reach during the computer solution of the equations. Once these maximum values are obtained it is easy to derive scaled computer variables from the problem variables by dividing each problem variable by its estimated maximum modulus value or a convenient larger value. For example, if it is estimated that the temperature, T, of a liquid is always less than about 85°C then $(\frac{T}{100})$ [or $(\frac{T}{90})$ or $(\frac{T}{85})$] could be chosen as the normalised computer variable. Clearly it should never exceed 1 m. u. amplitude during the simulation.

After having chosen normalised variables the problem equations are rewritten in terms of these variables and amplitude scaled computer equations are obtained. Before considering how this is done it is worth discussing the many methods by which maximum modulus values may be derived.

(a) Reference to the actual physical problem to be simulated (common sense guesses). This is by far the best and simplest method. In many years of programming advice the authors have never yet had a problem to simulate where it has not been possible to obtain at least rough estimates of these maximum values from the person supplying the problem. Indeed, if that person cannot supply such estimates it is not likely that he has reached a point of understanding where he ought to be simulating the problem as clearly he will not be able to judge whether or not the results obtained are correct.

(b) Mathematical methods using knowledge of differential equation solution. Although such methods are favoured by some, not necessarily mathematicians, the authors believe that use of such techniques is generally, but not always, not needed and is of little value. In some cases more effort will be needed to 'solve' analytically the equations in order to determine these estimates than will be needed to determine complete computer solutions by simulation using common sense guesses for maximum values. Mathematical methods can be of use, for example, when solving non-linear equations. Sometimes by deleting the non-linear terms in an equation it reduces to a form the solution of which is well known. First estimates of maximum values can then be found from the solution of the simplified equation. (The analytical solutions for the simplified equations can be of value in checking validity of simulations.)

(c) Rule of thumb methods found to have worked in other problems. Such methods are clearly of value to the experienced programmer rather than to the novice.

(d) Trial and error on the computer. In this method the problem is simulated using very rough guesses of the maximum values. From the solutions obtained more accurate estimates are obtained and the problem is re-scaled. Clearly a method to be avoided if possible as it is wasteful of computer and programmer's time. Often simulations do become trial and error efforts due to lack of adequate preparation and understanding of the problem!

(e) By trial runs on a digital computer using a Continuous System Simulation Language. Before studying the problem on the analogue computer a typical case is solved using digital simulation. The solution obtained is not only used to provide estimates of maximum values but provides very valuable dynamic check information.

Any combination of the above methods can be used; (a) combined with (e) and a little mathematics is probably ideal.

(ii) **Scaled equations**

The scaled equations can be very simply obtained from the problem equations once normalised variables have been chosen. It is best, but not absolutely necessary, that the problem equations are in reduced form before carrying out this process.

If, for example, a problem equation is

$$-\frac{d}{dt} V = 2V - 4.7 + 0.001.x$$

and maximum modulus values of V and x cause normalised variables $(\frac{V}{5})$ and $(\frac{x}{1000})$ to be chosen, the equation becomes

$$-\frac{d}{dt}(\frac{V}{5})5 = 2(\frac{V}{5})5 - 4.7 + 0.001(\frac{x}{1000})1000,$$

or

$$-\frac{d}{dt}(\frac{V}{5}) = 2(\frac{V}{5}) - \frac{4.7}{5} + \frac{1}{5}(\frac{x}{1000}),$$

or finally

34

$$-\frac{d}{dt}\left(\frac{V}{5}\right) = [0.2]10\left(\frac{V}{5}\right) - [0.94]1 + [0.2]1\left(\frac{x}{1000}\right),$$

where the square bracket values refer to potentiometer coefficients and the 1s and 10 refer to integrator gains. Note scaled variables and not multiples or submultiples of them must appear directly at the outputs of the units. Thus equations are always manipulated into the form

- scaled output = sum of inputs   (Summer)

or

$-\frac{d}{dt}$ (scaled output) = sum of inputs   (Integrator)

Scaling of inverters (sign reversers) is not needed and equations for such units are not normally written. Multipliers, when used for simple direct multiplication, also do not need to be scaled but it is sensible to derive equations for such units to be used in checking. The total process leading up to production of scaled computer diagrams and check lists can be understood from the following simple example.

3.6   Example illustrating use of amplitude scaling

Determine by computer simulation the maximum height reached by a body projected vertically upwards in a medium producing a frictional drag force proportional to the square of the speed.

Model equations:

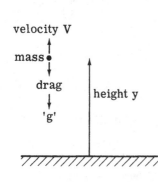

Acceleration $\frac{dV}{dt} = -g - \lambda V^2$.

Speed $\frac{dy}{dt} = V$,

where g = acceleration due to gravity, and λ is the frictional constant. Equations valid for upward motion $(V \geq 0)$ only.

Fig. 3.6

35

Case to be studied:

$$g = 9.8, \; \lambda = 0.01,$$
$$y_0 = 0 \; \text{and} \; V_0 = 50 \; \text{metre-sec units}$$

Object:

To obtain solutions for $y(t)$ and $V(t)$ including the maximum height reached, H.

Step 1. Unscaled diagram

This step is not absolutely necessary but it does show what units are needed and their interconnections.

Potentiometers for scaling and other purposes are drawn at integrator and summer inputs. Inverters and multipliers normally should not have potentiometers at their input as they do not require scaling. The model equations should be reduced so that there is one equation per (amplifier) unit used.

i.e. Equation (3.1) becomes $-\dfrac{dV}{dt} = 9.8 + 0.01.W$ (Integrator)   (3.3)

where $W = V^2$ (Multiplier or Squarer)   (3.4)

Equation (3.2) becomes $-\dfrac{dy}{dt} = -V$ (Integrator)   (3.5)

Thus a suitable simulation is shown in Fig. 3.7. Note values '9.8',

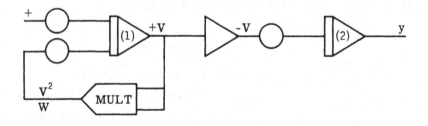

Fig. 3.7 Unscaled simulation for projectile problem

'0.01' or 'g' and 'λ' are not written next to the potentiometers as the actual values needed to be set will be affected by the scaling.

The simulation could be simplified if $-V$ were produced at integrator (1) output, thus avoiding the need for the inverter. If this were done equation (3.3) would need to be written as

36

$$-\frac{d}{dt}(-V) = -9.8 - 0.01.W$$

and the computer diagram would become:

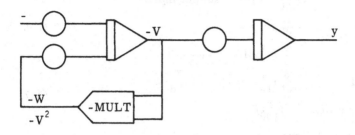

Fig. 3.8   Simplified version of Fig. 3.7

However, if a recording of +V was required an inverter to produce +V from -V would be needed and thus there would be no saving of units.

Step 2.   Estimation of maximum values and choice of normalised variables

Obviously as $V_0 = 50$ metres/sec then $|V| \leq 50$. Therefore, choose $(\frac{V}{50})$ which has an initial value $(\frac{V}{50})_0 = +1$. The maximum value of W is obvious and the normalised variable chosen is $(\frac{W}{2500})$.

The maximum value for y can be guessed by commonsense experience of ball throwing. (50 metres/sec $\simeq$ 110 m.p.h., rather faster than a very fast bowler bowls, hence 100 metres or 5 cricket pitch lengths upwards will probably be suitable!) It can also be obtained by use of the very well known formula '$V^2 = 2gH$' applicable to the case of no friction. If this is done, $H = \max y \simeq \frac{50^2}{2 \times 10} = 125$ metres. This gives an overestimate and thus allowing for friction a value of 100 metres should be suitable. Hence choose $(\frac{y}{100})$.

Step 3.   Scaled equations and diagram

Integrator (1)

$$-\frac{d}{dt} \text{ output} = \text{sum of inputs}$$

Unscaled

$$-\frac{d}{dt} V = 9.8 + 0.01.W \qquad \text{(i.e. 3.3)}$$

$\therefore$

$$-\frac{d}{dt}(\frac{V}{50})50 = 9.8 + 0.01(\frac{W}{2500})2500$$

37

or Scaled $\quad -\dfrac{d}{dt}\left(\dfrac{V}{50}\right) = [0.196]1 + [0.5]1\left(\dfrac{W}{2500}\right)$ $\qquad$ (3.6)

Initial Condition $\quad \left(\dfrac{V}{50}\right)_0 = 1.$

Integrator (2)

$$-\dfrac{d}{dt}\text{ output } = \text{ sum of inputs}$$

Unscaled $\qquad -\dfrac{d}{dt}y = -V$ $\qquad\qquad\qquad$ (i.e. 3.5)

$\therefore \qquad\qquad -\dfrac{d}{dt}\left(\dfrac{y}{100}\right)100 = -\left(\dfrac{V}{50}\right)50$

or Scaled $\qquad -\dfrac{d}{dt}\left(\dfrac{y}{100}\right) = -[0.5]1\left(\dfrac{V}{50}\right)$ $\qquad$ (3.7)

Initial Condition $\quad \left(\dfrac{y}{100}\right)_0 = 0.$

Multiplier (or Squarer):

Unscaled $\qquad W = V \times V$ $\qquad\qquad\qquad$ (i.e. 3.4)

Scaled $\qquad \left(\dfrac{W}{2500}\right) = \left(\dfrac{V}{50}\right) \times \left(\dfrac{V}{50}\right)$ $\qquad$ (3.8)

The amplitude scaled diagram follows immediately from equations (3.6), (3.7) and (3.8)

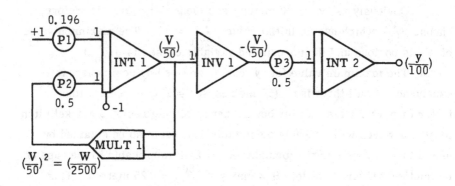

Fig. 3.9 Amplitude scaled simulation for projectile problem

Step 4. Assignment and static test values

Actual computer units are assigned to the units indicated on the scaled diagram (this has been done on the above diagram). Initial values of the outputs of all units, and the value of the derivative input to each integrator, are calculated to form a static test which is made prior to the dynamic phase of the simulation. These values are calculated from the

38

original problem equations and then checked from the final scaled equations (or from the scaled diagram) to eliminate working errors. As $V_0 = 50$ the initial values of each term in equations (3.3) to (3.5) are:

from (3.4), i.e. $W = V^2$

$$W_0 = 50^2 = 2500$$

from (3.3), i.e. $-\dfrac{dV}{dt} = 9.8 + 0.01.W$

the initial values on the R.H.S. are 9.8, 25 and that on the L.H.S. (i.e. $-\dfrac{dV}{dt}$) is 34.8.

from (3.5), i.e. $-\dfrac{dy}{dt} = -V$

the initial value of $-\dfrac{dy}{dt}$ is -50.

Scaling these three equations, i.e. (3.3), (3.4) and (3.5) again independently therefore, initially:

$$(\frac{W}{2500}) = 1$$

$$-\frac{d}{dt}(\frac{V}{50}) = \frac{9.8}{50} + \frac{25}{50}$$

$$= 0.196 + 0.5$$

$$= 0.696$$

and

$$-\frac{d}{dt}(\frac{y}{100}) = -0.5.$$

These values can be directly checked with those derived from the scaled diagram. For example, as the initial output of INT 1 is +1, the multiplier output is also +1, and the output of P2 should be 0.5. The derivative input into INT 1 consists of two terms 0.196 and 0.5 giving 0.696 which agrees with the values calculated from the original equations. Proceeding in this way a final table is drawn up showing the units used and their initial output values.

POTS	COEFFICIENT	STATIC TEST OUTPUT
P1	0.196	+0.196
P2	0.5	+0.5
P3	0.5	-0.5

AMPS	OUTPUT	DERIVATIVE
INT 1	+1	+0. 696
INT 2	0	- 0. 5
INV 1	-1	
MULT 1	+1	

This table is used when setting up potentiometer coefficients and checking out the initial static state of the simulation.

The above, for reasons discussed later, does not provide a particularly good static check but it is sufficient for small problems. This check can be shortened a little without losing its value by omitting the check on potentiometer output values, i. e. assuming that these must be correct if all the rest is correct. It is a good idea to mark initial outputs on the computer diagram, using a different colour to the rest of the diagram. This is of value when debugging problems after a systematic tabular check has failed.

Alternative solution. In the simulation above, although the acceleration $\frac{dV}{dt}$ is used 'inside' integrator 1 nowhere does this variable appear where it can be measured or recorded. If it is required that the highest derivative is to appear at the output of a unit so that its variation can be observed, the problem preparation is slightly different. An explicit symbol is introduced for the highest derivative, acceleration A in this case, and the model equations (3. 1) and (3. 2) are reduced to:

$$-A = g + \lambda W$$
$$W = V \times V$$

Algebraic equations

$$-\frac{dV}{dt} = -A$$
$$-\frac{dy}{dt} = -V$$

Differential equations

The scaling process is as before except that the highest derivative A has to be scaled. In this case A is obviously a maximum when $t = 0$, i. e. $|A| = 9. 8 + 0. 01 \times 50 \times 50 = 34. 8 < 50$. A normalised variable $(\frac{A}{50})$ is introduced and the equation $-A = g + \lambda W$ becomes

$$-(\frac{A}{50}) = [0. 196]1 + [0. 5]1(\frac{W}{2500}).$$

This equation is implemented using a summer and the total new diagram is as shown in Fig. 3.10. This simulation, producing +acceleration,

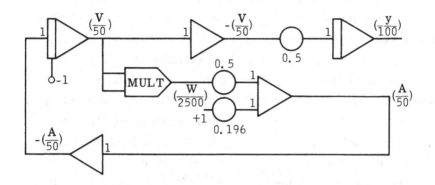

Fig. 3.10 Simulation to generate acceleration

+speed and +position, could clearly be simplified to remove both inverters if it is acceptable to produce +acceleration, -speed and +position (Fig. 3.11).

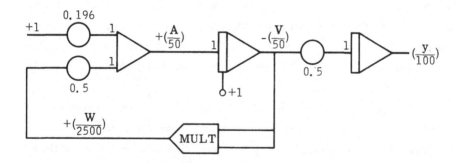

Fig. 3.11 Simplified diagram of simulation producing acceleration, velocity and height

Although this juggling can be done on the diagram it is better to modify the signs in the equations themselves in order to avoid making sign errors. This is essentially the value of producing an unscaled diagram and simplifying it if necessary before starting the scaling process.

3.7   Time scaling

The object of time scaling is to control the rate of solution of the computer equations depending on the speed at which the computer can operate and the type of recording or display equipment to be used. Time scaling is essentially the way in which the computer independent variable time is related to the problem independent variable (which is generally time). Although it can be performed before, after or at the same time as amplitude scaling, it is usually best to do it after amplitude scaling by the normalised variable method. The rate at which the equations are solved can be changed by changing the gains of all the integrators used in the simulation. To $\begin{Bmatrix} \text{slow down} \\ \text{speed up} \end{Bmatrix}$ rate of solution by a factor n the gains of the integrators used must be $\begin{Bmatrix} \text{decreased} \\ \text{increased} \end{Bmatrix}$ by a factor n. Providing all integrator gains are changed by the same factor the amplitude scaling is entirely unaffected.

The usual technique is to try to choose the time scaling factor so that the problem is solved at normal (slow) speed. The integrator time constants are 1 second and solution times are likely to be from a few seconds to perhaps 50 seconds. This enables slow speed graph or X-Y recorders to be used to record the solution. Should a high rate of solution be required, e.g. in order to use oscilloscope displays, the whole solution may be speeded up automatically using the master computer time scale control. Most machines provide at least one high-speed mode of operation. Some allow solution rates to be increased automatically by factors of 10, 100, 1000 or 10,000.

The choice of time scale factor needed to make the solution period be 5-50 seconds can normally be made from knowledge of the original problem. It is interesting to note, however, that an appropriate scaling factor can be determined by examining the effective integrator gains on the amplitude scaled diagram. If a factor is chosen so that all or most of these gains lie in the range 0.05 to 2 the solution time is likely to be of the order of 10 seconds. The technique of time scaling is illustrated below using this method to estimate the scaling factor.

Example

Determine by computer simulation the solution of

$$\frac{d^2y}{dt^2} + 0.04 \frac{dy}{dt} + 0.0004y = 0 \tag{3.9}$$

given $\dot{y}_0 = 0$, $y_0 = 100$ cm, $|\dot{y}| \leq 10$ cm/sec and $|y| \leq 100$ cm, where $\dot{y}$ is used to denote $\frac{dy}{dt}$.

The small coefficients in the equation imply that its solution is slow and it can be predicted that some speed up will be required.

Amplitude scaling:

write $V = \frac{dy}{dt}$ so that the equation reduces to

$$-\frac{dV}{dt} = 0.04V + 0.0004y$$

                                    Unscaled

and $-\frac{dy}{dt} = -V$

or $-\frac{d}{dt}\left(\frac{V}{10}\right) = +[0.04]\left(\frac{V}{10}\right) + [0.004]\left(\frac{y}{100}\right)$

                                         Scaled

and $-\frac{d}{dt}\left(\frac{y}{100}\right) = -[0.1]\left(\frac{V}{10}\right)$

The appropriate amplitude scaled diagram is shown in Fig. 3.12.

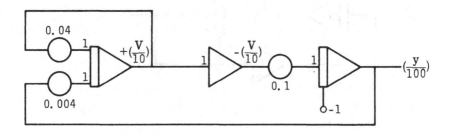

Fig. 3.12   Amplitude scaled simulation diagram

Time scaling.   From this diagram (Fig. 3.12) it can be seen that the equation will be solved rather slowly. It should also be noted that the value 0.004 is so small that it could not be set up accurately on a single potentiometer. By increasing the gains at the integrator inputs by a factor of about 10 the effective gains will nearly be in the recommended range of 0.05 to 2. Thus a time scale speed-up factor of 10 is applied and the final fully scaled diagram becomes as shown in Fig. 3.13. The simplicity of the technique of time scaling is well illustrated in Fig. 3.13.

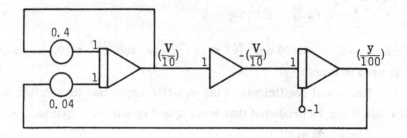

Fig. 3.13 Scaled simulation diagram including speed-up factor
of 10

In the following two sections justification is given for the method.

(i)   **Effect of integrator gains upon the speed of solution**

Consider the 2 integrator plus inverter loop

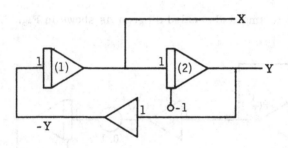

Fig. 3.14

As $-\dfrac{d}{dt} X = -Y$ Integrator (1)

and $-\dfrac{d}{dt} Y = X$ Integrator (2)

therefore $\dfrac{d^2 Y}{dt^2} + Y = 0$ with $Y_0 = +1$ and $\dot{Y}_0 = 0$.

This is the equation for S. H. M. having solution

$$Y = \cos t \quad \text{and} \quad X = -\frac{dY}{dt} = \sin t.$$

Thus the loop will generate both $\cos t$ and $\sin t$ with equal unit amplitudes.

Suppose the gains of the integrators are increased by a factor of
10:

44

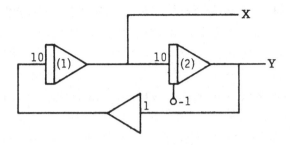

Fig. 3.15

The equations now satisfied by X and Y are

$$-\frac{d}{dt}X = -10Y \qquad\qquad \text{Integrator (1)}$$

and $\quad -\dfrac{d}{dt}Y = 10X \qquad\qquad$ Integrator (2)

so that $\dfrac{d^2Y}{dt^2} + 100Y = 0 \qquad\qquad$ with $Y = 1$ and $\dot{Y} = 0$ at $t = 0$.

This is the S. H. M. equation with $\omega^2 = 100$ and solution $Y = \cos 10t$.

Also $X = -\dfrac{1}{10} \cdot \dfrac{dY}{dt} = \sin 10t$.

Thus the loop will now produce $\sin 10t$ and $\cos 10t$ instead of $\sin t$ and $\cos t$. The oscillations have increased in speed by a factor of 10 - the amount by which the integrators gains have been increased. The amplitudes of the variables at the outputs of the units have not been affected.

(ii)   **Time scale factor** β

Suppose the problem independent variable is time t and an amplitude scaled diagram has been obtained. Consider an integrator of the system which has an effective gain of 'k':

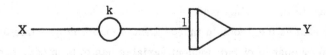

Fig. 3.16

where **X** and **Y** are the amplitude scaled input and output variables. The equation for this integration process (i. e. potentiometer plus integrator) is:

$$-\frac{d}{dt} Y = kX.$$

Let τ = computer time and make $\tau = \beta t$, where β is a constant. Then

$$-\frac{d}{d\tau} Y = \frac{k}{\beta} \cdot X$$

and the new gain of the integration process is $\frac{k}{\beta}$, i. e. to <u>change</u> time scaling by a factor of β means the gain of the integrator must be <u>changed</u> by a factor of β. This obviously applies to all the integrators used in the simulation.

If $\beta > 1$ then one unit of problem time corresponds to more than one unit of machine time and so the problem has been slowed by a factor of β.

If $\beta < 1$ then one unit of problem time corresponds to less than one unit of machine time and so the problem has been speeded up by a factor of $\frac{1}{\beta}$.

<u>Notes</u>:

(a) β can be negative. The particular case when $\beta = -1$, i. e. $\tau = -t$, is called reverse time scaling.

(b) β can be made a function of time, in which case the problem is said to have variable time scaling.

3. 8 General discussion

(1) When making final recordings for publication or to be given to the supplier of the problem, all the axes of the graphs should be calibrated in terms of the original problem variables. The programmer may in addition wish to mark his recordings in machine units and computer time to give reference to the scaling used.

(2) Sometimes the problem independent variable is not time and so a conversion or change of independent variable has to be made, e. g. distance x ≡ computer time t. In such problems the <u>exact</u> relationship needed can be determined in advance (e. g. 100 cm length of beam ≡ 10

seconds of machine time) and it is possible to include this when converting the problem equations prior to amplitude scaling (e.g. computer
time $t = 0.1x$, where x = distance in cm). Thus time scaling can be
performed before amplitude scaling. The method, although still simple,
is no better than that suggested earlier, as care is needed to allow for
the change of independent variable when determining estimates of maximum values, particularly of derivatives, needed for amplitude scaling.

3.9   Further examples for practical study

(3) **Projectile problem 1.**   Set up the simulation of the projectile
problem discussed in the text and record the variation of y, V and V^2
against time using a 10 second timebase. If the computer is equipped with
an automatic HOLD logic control, terminate the COMPUTE period by
switching to HOLD when V becomes zero, i.e. at the top of the flight
path:

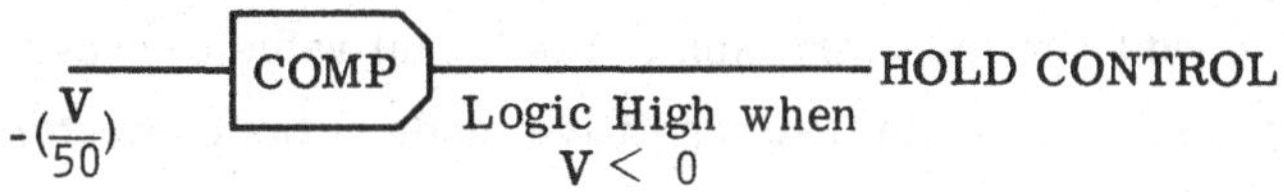

$$-\left(\frac{V}{50}\right) \quad \boxed{\text{COMP}} \quad \xrightarrow{\text{HOLD CONTROL}}$$

Logic High when
$V < 0$

Fig. 3.17

The value of the maximum height H and the time to reach this maximum
can be read off on the computer's metering system. (This type of technique is a good way of determining special values in solution without using
graph recording equipment. It is also a more accurate technique as
recording errors are not introduced.)

(4) **Projectile problem 2.**   A particle is projected in a vertical
plane in a medium giving frictional force proportional to the speed. Assuming the angle of launch is 45°, determine the speed of launch so that
the horizontal range of the particle is 100 metres.

Equations: $\ddot{x} = -\lambda\dot{x}$ where $\lambda = 0.2 \text{ sec}^{-1}$

$\ddot{y} = -\lambda\dot{y} - g$ $g = 9.8 \text{ metres/sec}^2$

$x_0 = 0$, $y_0 = 0$, $\dot{x}_0 = \dot{y}_0$ (unknown)

47

Simulation:

(i)   Reduce the equations to first order form using

U for $\frac{dx}{dt}$ and V for $\frac{dy}{dt}$.

(ii)   Estimate the maximum values of the variables (ignore the friction terms when doing this). Select normalised variables (using the same dividing factor for U and V) and amplitude scale the equations.

(iii)   Draw an amplitude scaled computer diagram and prepare set up and check lists.

(iv)   Set up the system on the computer. Display height against horizontal range. Adjust initial values of U and V (both equal so that particle is projected at 45°) until, on computing, the particle is seen to achieve a range of 100 metres. Measure the speed of launch.

Experimental hints

(1)   Drive the initial condition of the integrators producing the U and V terms from one potentiometer so that the initial values of U and V may be varied together by a single potentiometer control.

(2)   A good first approximation to the initial value of speed can be obtained very easily using the fast repetitive mode of the computer and an oscilloscope. As it is more accurate to aim for a zero than a non-zero value, make $x_0 = -100$ metres, $y_0 = 0$ and aim for (0, 0).

(3)   Final adjustment of U and V can be made if necessary when using the computer in the normal (slow) speed of operation.

(4)   An X, Y pen recording can be made for reference.

Note. The above example shows how an analogue computer, essentially an initial value machine, can be used to solve split boundary value problems. It also shows the usefulness of the analogue computer as a design tool, i. e. as a means of selecting a special value of a parameter to give a desired result.

(5) Coupled Tank Problem

In Fig. 3.18 water is shown flowing into a rectangular tank of cross-sectional area A_1 at a rate F_1 and leaving the tank via a hole in the base at a rate F_2 into another tank of area A_2. The water is then shown leaving this second tank via a long pipe at a rate F_0. The equations determining the heights of the water in the tanks are:

48

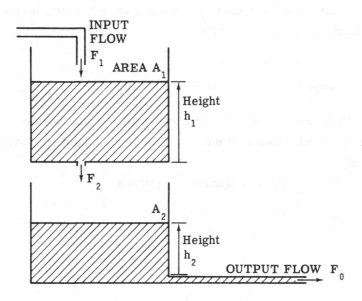

INPUT FLOW F_1 AREA A_1

Height h_1

F_2

A_2

Height h_2

OUTPUT FLOW F_0

Fig. 3.18

Tank 1 $\quad A_1 \dfrac{dh_1}{dt} = F_1 - F_2,$ where $F_2 = K_1 \sqrt{h_1}$ (flow via orifice) and K_1 is a constant.

Tank 2 $\quad A_2 \dfrac{dh_2}{dt} = F_2 - F_0,$ where $F_0 = K_2 h_2$ (viscous flow) and K_2 is a constant.

Determine solutions to this problem showing how the water level builds up to steady state values H_1 and H_2 assuming F_1 is constant. Consider the case when the tanks are initially empty and

$$F_1 = 0.01, \quad A_1 = 1, \quad A_2 = 2, \quad K_1 = 0.01 \text{ and } K_2 = 0.02 \text{ metre second units.}$$

Also investigate the effect of starting from various initial levels, including levels above the final steady state values.

Hints. Estimate maximum values for h_1 and h_2 from the steady state solutions of the equations. Include time scaling to speed up rate of solution.

49

(6) An x-y plotter, for which the independent drives to the x and y axes have flat frequency responses up to 0. 75 Hz, is to be used to display x against time when

$$50\ddot{x} + 8\dot{x} + 900x = 425$$
subject to $x(0) = 3.75$ and $\dot{x}(0) = 0$.

Both 'time' and x are to be generated explicitly and the fully scaled circuit, based upon a 10 V machine, should use amplifier gains of 1 and 10 only.

Produce the scaled machine equations.

4 · Generation of Functions of the Independent Variable

4.1   Introduction to Chapters 4 and 5

There are two types of functions which need to be generated in the computer.

A.   Functions explicitly expressible in terms of the <u>independent</u> computer variable 'time'. The exact way in which these functions vary with 'time' is known prior to the actual simulation.

B.   Functions of one or more <u>dependent</u> computer variables. These functions do, of course, vary with time but their exact form is not known prior to simulation.

Explicit functions (A) of the independent variable appear as forcing functions or as variable coefficients in linear differential equations.   For example, the small-scale deflection θ of a pendulum of variable length and subject to a varying disturbing force may be written as

$$\frac{d^2\theta}{dt^2} + f(t)\theta = g(t),$$

where $f(t)$ is a variable coefficient dependent on the length of the pendulum at any time t and $g(t)$ is a forcing function produced by the disturbing force.

Functions of dependent variables (B) are required in order to simulate and solve non-linear differential equations. A simple example of such an equation occurs in the study of the large-scale motion of a pendulum of fixed length, i. e.

$$\frac{d^2\theta}{dt^2} + K \sin \theta = 0,$$

where K is a constant. In this example the function $\sin \theta$ must be derived from θ in the simulation. Clearly, $\sin \theta$ will vary with time but the actual variation is not known prior to equation solution.

The methods used to generate these two types of functions are very different and should not be confused. The former type (A) need extensive use of integrators and other linear units with occasional use of non-linear analogue units, such as multipliers, whereas the latter type (B) need extensive use of non-linear equipment. The generation of both types of functions may involve use of simple hybrid and logic elements. In this chapter many methods used to generate functions of the independent variable are described while discussion of the simulation of functions of type (B) is considered in detail in the next chapter and again in §7 and §11.

4.2 Generation of explicit functions of the independent computer variable 'time'

These functions may be grouped into three main types which are considered in detail in the following sections.

4.3 Functions which can be made the solutions of linear constant coefficient differential equations

The general method used to generate a function of this type is to simulate on the computer the simplest differential equation whose solution is the required function. Continuous functions which may be generated this way include polynomials in t, $\exp(\pm kt)$, $\sin wt$, $\cos wt$ and products (e.g. $e^{-kt}\cos wt$) of these functions. The generation of one function of this type has already been considered, i.e. the production of a time base reference variable 'x = kt'. This is generated using an integrator set up to solve the equation

$$\frac{dx}{dt} = k \quad \text{with} \quad x_0 = 0.$$

These functions can and should be generated using <u>linear</u> computer units and not less accurate, more expensive and generally less available non-linear units. For example, the function te^{-t} could be generated by producing t and e^{-t} separately and multiplying them together. However, te^{-t} is the solution of the simple 2nd order differential equation

$$\frac{d^2y}{dt^2} + \frac{dy}{dt} + y = 0$$

52

with $y = 0$ and $\frac{dy}{dt} = 1$ at time $t = 0$ and is best generated by simulating this equation on the computer.

Scaling of the equations used to generate these functions is normally straightforward as the functions are completely known prior to the simulation and maximum values of the variables can be determined exactly.

Examples

(i) **Negative exponential function** $y(t) = e^{-kt}$, where k is a positive constant and $t \geq 0$.

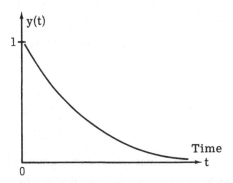

1

0

y(t)

Time
t

Fig. 4.1 Graph of e^{-kt}

As $y(t) = e^{-kt}$ $\therefore$ $\frac{dy}{dt} = -ke^{-t} = -ky$. Thus the simplest differential equation whose solution is e^{-kt} is the equation

$$\frac{dy}{dt} = -ky$$

with initial condition $y = 1$ at $t = 0$. No amplitude scaling is needed as $|e^{-kt}| \leq 1$ for $t \geq 0$. The computer set-up needed to simulate this equation expressed in the form $-\frac{dy}{dt} = ky$ is therefore:

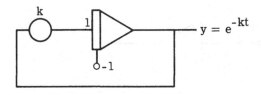

k

1

-1

$y = e^{-kt}$

Fig. 4.2

53

(ii)   **Polynomial function** $y(t) = 1 + 4t - 0.5t^2$ for $0 \le t \le 8$. Clearly this function could be generated in a number of ways the most obvious, perhaps, being to generate 't' using an integrator, square it to give t^2 and combine 1, 4t and $-0.5t^2$ together (suitably scaled) in a summer.

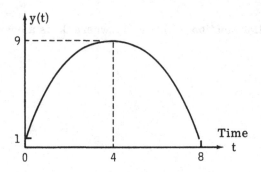

Fig. 4.3

However, this method is poor as it makes unnecessary use of a non-linear multiplier or squaring unit. The best way is to observe that the function $y(t)$ can be made the solution of the simple 2nd order linear differential equation ' $\dfrac{d^2y}{dt^2} = -1$ ' which can be simulated using two integrators for, as

$$y = 1 + 4t - 0.5t^2$$

$\therefore$ $\dfrac{dy}{dt} = \dot{y} = 4 - t$

and $\dfrac{d^2y}{dt^2} = -1.$

This function can, therefore, be generated using a scaled version of:

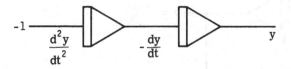

Fig. 4.4

In fact, any quadratic can be generated using two integrators, i.e. by simulating the equation

$$' \frac{d^2y}{dt^2} = \text{constant}'$$

the actual quadratic generated being dependent on the constant used and the initial values of y and $\frac{dy}{dt}$.

A systematic way to determine the scaled computer set-up is presented below:

Function	Max|Value|	Scaled variable	Initial value of scaled variable
$y=1+4t-0.5t^2$	9	$(\frac{y}{10})$	$(\frac{y}{10})_0 = 0.1$
$\dot{y}=4-t$	4	$(\frac{\dot{y}}{5})$	$(\frac{\dot{y}}{5})_0 = 0.8$

From the diagram above it can be seen that the equations to be simulated by the two integrators are:

$$-\frac{dy}{dt} = -\dot{y}$$

and $\quad -\frac{d}{dt}(-\dot{y}) = -1$ $\qquad$ Unscaled

or $\quad -\frac{d}{dt}(\frac{y}{10}) = [0.5](-\frac{\dot{y}}{5})$

and $\quad -\frac{d}{dt}(-\frac{\dot{y}}{5}) = -[0.2]$ $\qquad$ Scaled

The resulting computer simulation is

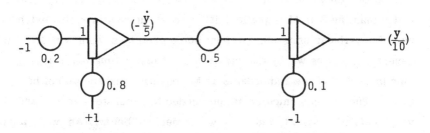

Fig. 4.5

Normalised variables $(\frac{y}{9})$ and $(\frac{\dot{y}}{4})$ could have been chosen instead of $(\frac{y}{10})$ and $(\frac{\dot{y}}{5})$ and this would have resulted in a slightly simpler simulation which uses one less potentiometer. Slight changes in scaling can often be made in these types of simulation to economise on use of potentiometers.

The technique shown above for the generation of a quadratic can, of course, be generalised for all polynomials of t. A polynomial of degree n can be generated using n integrators plus, at most, 2n potentiometers.

(iii)   **Trigonometrical function** $y = \cos wt$, where w is a constant in the range $0.1 \leq w \leq 10$. By direct differentiation of y it is seen that this function is a solution of the standard 2nd order linear S. H. M. equation $\ddot{y} + w^2 y = 0$ or $-\frac{d}{dt}(-\dot{y}) = -w^2 y$ and consequently it can be generated using a scaled version of the 2 integrator plus inverter loop (Fig. 4.6).

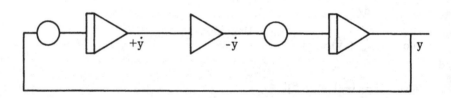

Fig. 4.6

However, it is interesting to note that it could also be produced by solving a 1st order differential equation $\frac{dy}{dt} = -w\sqrt{(1 - y^2)}$. Although of lower order than the S. H. M. equation, its simulation would require extensive use of non-linear units (and present some problems when $y \to 1$). Clearly, generation of $\cos wt$ by the use of this 1st order equation is less simple than by means of the 2nd order S. H. M. equation and should not be used.

The scaled computer set up needed to generate $\cos wt$ (and also very usefully $+\sin wt$ and $-\sin wt$) is derived below. As w is a parameter ≤ 10 it is scaled $\frac{w}{10}$.

Function	Max|Value|	Scaled variable	Initial value of scaled variable
$y = \cos wt$	1	$\left(\frac{y}{1}\right)$	$\left(\frac{y}{1}\right)_0 = 1$
$\frac{dy}{dt} = \dot{y} = -w\sin wt$	w	$\left(\frac{\dot{y}}{w}\right)$	$\left(\frac{\dot{y}}{w}\right)_0 = 0$

The equations to be set up are

$$\frac{dy}{dt} = \dot{y}$$

and $\quad\dfrac{d\dot{y}}{dt} = -w^2\cos wt = -w^2 y$ Unscaled

or $\quad -\dfrac{d}{dt}\left(\dfrac{y}{1}\right) = -\left[\dfrac{w}{10}\right]10\left(\dfrac{\dot{y}}{w}\right)$ Scaled

and $\quad -\dfrac{d}{dt}\left(\dfrac{\dot{y}}{w}\right) = +\left[\dfrac{w}{10}\right]10\left(\dfrac{y}{1}\right)$

The appropriate simulation is:

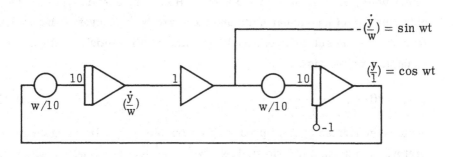

Fig. 4.7

In this simulation two potentiometers are used to control the value of the frequency w. If $\dot{y}$ is scaled $\left(\frac{\dot{y}}{10}\right)$ instead of $\left(\frac{\dot{y}}{w}\right)$ the setting of w could be controlled by one potentiometer as shown in Fig. 4.8.

Although the frequency is controlled by means of one potentiometer, using this method, the technique has two obvious defects:

(a) the frequency of the oscillation cannot be set accurately when w is small (e.g. 0.1) as it is impossible to set the potentiometer $\frac{w^2}{100}$, (e.g. 0.0001) accurately to very low values.

57

(b) the amplitude of the variable at the output of the 1st integrator,
i. e. $(\frac{y}{10}) = -\frac{w}{10} \sin wt$ varies with the value of w used. Thus the loop
cannot be used to generate both variables $\sin wt$ and $\cos wt$ with equal
amplitude independent of frequency.

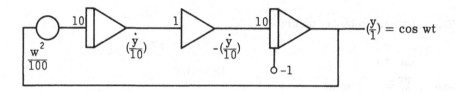

Fig. 4. 8

4. 4 Continuous functions of time generated using both linear and non-linear units

Many functions required in simulations can be generated using
linear units, as described in 4. 3 above. However, certain types do require the use of non-linear units and these are best generated, if possible,
by making them solutions of simple non-linear differential equations. For
example, the function

$$y(t) = \frac{1}{(1 + 0.1t)^2} \tag{4.1}$$

could be generated by first producing a variable $1 + 0.1t$ using an integrator, then using a division unit to give $\frac{1}{1 + 0.1t}$ and finally a squaring
unit to give $(\frac{1}{1 + 0.1t})^2$. (The order of these last two operations could,
of course, be reversed.) However, it is much better to try to find an
equation whose solution is the direct function required. In this case as

$$y = \frac{1}{(1 + 0.1t)^2}$$

$$\therefore \quad \frac{dy}{dt} = -\frac{0.2}{(1 + 0.1t)^3}$$

and $\quad \frac{d^2y}{dt^2} = +\frac{0.06}{(1 + 0.1t)^4} = + 0.06. y^2. \tag{4.2}$

58

This equation can be simulated using two integrators and a squaring unit. As it uses less non-linear elements than the first method described, it is obviously to be preferred. It also does not involve the need to scale a division process, something that generally causes difficulties, and is overall much easier to scale. A scaled computer simulation of equation (4.2) used to generate the function of equation (4.1) is:

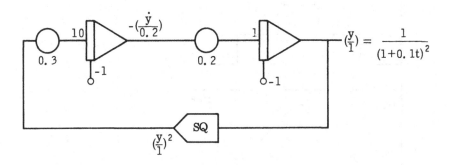

Fig. 4.9

Although some functions can be generated by making them solutions of non-linear differential equations, there are many others which need to be, or are best, generated by using the methods described for functions of dependent variables. For example, the function $\sqrt{t}$ can be generated most simply by using an integrator to generate a variable t followed by a square rooting unit. No general rules can be laid down for the best method to use. In practice it is best to consider a variety of ways of generating any particular function and select the method which uses least units, matches the units available or offers advantages in simplicity or accuracy. If possible it is best to avoid having to generate functions the amplitude of which increase with time as initial condition errors become greatly amplified. Sometimes it is possible to avoid such trouble by reversing the relationship between problem independent variable and computer time, as in Example 6 at the end of this chapter.

4. 5 Functions of time containing discontinuities or other abrupt changes

The functions in this group include those which are discontinuous themselves (e. g. step changes) or contain discontinuities in their derivatives, (e. g. triangular functions).

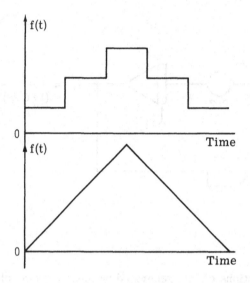

Fig. 4.10

They are normally generated using methods 1 or 2 already discussed combined with use of simple hybrid elements, particularly comparators and switches. They are generally required to simulate forcing functions, e. g. as test inputs to control systems or loading distributions in beam problems. The range of functions to be simulated is very large and the techniques used are best illustrated by means of examples. Some very clever simulations have been produced for certain functions and it is recommended for any complicated function that considerable effort is made to try to derive an efficient simulation which uses the minimum of units.

The functions are frequently made up of various sections. Often each section is easy to produce, e. g. constants, ramps, quadratics, etc.

The problem is then to determine how

(a) to produce logic signals to indicate the time at which it is necessary to switch from one section to another,

(b) to perform the necessary switching operations in the analogue units, and

(c) to link (a) and (b) using logic elements.

Examples

(i) **Delayed pulse**

$f(t) = 0$ for $t < a$

$ = 1$ for $a < t < b$

$ = 0$ for $b < t < 10$

Step (a) The times at which the function has abrupt changes are $t = a$ and $t = b$ seconds. Clearly some kind of timing circuit is needed

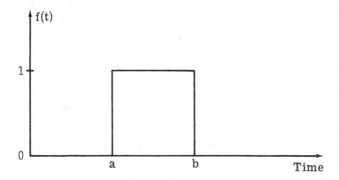

Fig. 4.11

to detect these instances. In sophisticated machines counters, etc. are available and these could be used. However, it is generally simpler to use a time base generator and comparators:

61

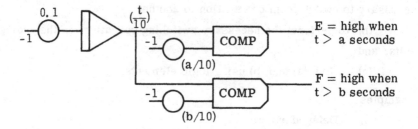

Fig. 4.12

Step (b) The production of the analogue signal 0, 1 or 0 can be most easily achieved using a simple D/A switch controlled by a logic signal G:

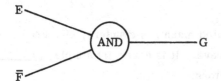

Output = +1 if G is high
= 0 otherwise

Fig. 4.13

Step (c) This is essentially the design of the linking between (a) and (b) needed to provide the correct control of the switch from the logic signals E and F. In this case it is clear that the switch must be closed when

$$t > a \quad \underline{\text{and}} \quad t < b$$

and not otherwise. Thus a simple and gate is needed.

E —
        AND — G
F —

G is high when E is high and when $\overline{\text{F}}$ is high
i.e. when time > a and time < b

The complete set-up needed, using the inverse logic output of comparator 2 is, therefore:

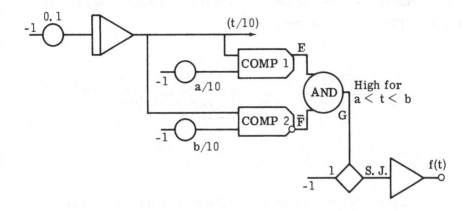

Fig. 4.14

Using the method illustrated above it is clear that one is working from both ends of the problem towards the middle. Although this might appear illogical at first sight, it is often the simplest technique leading to efficient simulations.

(ii)   **Triangular function**

$f(t) = 0.2t$ for $0 \le t < 5$

$\quad\;\; = 2 - 0.2t$ for $5 < t \le 10$

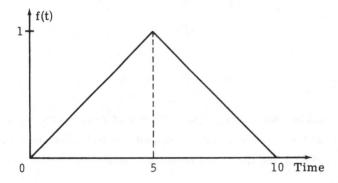

Fig. 4.15

If we assume that the compute period is limited to 10 seconds then no special control is needed to switch f(t) to zero at 10 seconds. The problem is therefore simplified.

Step (a) detection of time t = 5 when the abrupt change in f(t) occurs. This is easily produced by:

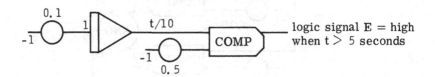

Fig. 4.16

Step (b) This is the part of the problem which presents most scope for the programmer. Clearly it is possible to generate (scaled versions of) both 0.2t and 2 - 0.2t and select them in some way using switches:

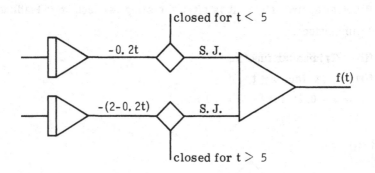

Fig. 4.17

This method is rather inefficient in the use of integrators. The functions -0.2t and -(2 - 0.2t), suitable scaled, could be derived from the integrator producing the time base reference but the simulation would still be inefficient.

A far better method to produce the increasing and then decreasing function required is to switch an integrator input between -0.2 and +0.2

64

and make its output change by ±0.2 machine unit per second:

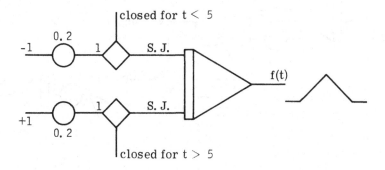

Fig. 4.18

If this technique is used, step (c) is obvious and the final simulation is:

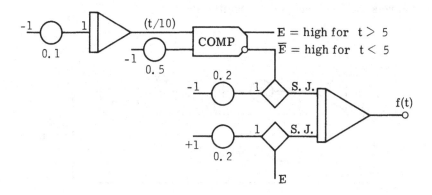

Fig. 4.19

An alternative to the above which uses one less D/A switch is shown in Fig. 4.20.

In this simulation the D/A switch is open when t < 5 so that the summer output is -0.5. When t > 5, the switch closes and the summer output becomes +0.5. This simulation could be simplified further by combining the operation of summation and integration in a multi input integrator.

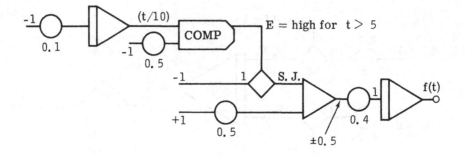

Fig. 4.20

(iii)   Continuous generation of triangular and square waves

A particularly efficient circuit which generates a triangular waveform, of amplitude ±0.5, an analogue square wave function, of amplitude
±0.5, and a logic square wave function, is shown below.   The potentiometer
controls the frequency of the oscillation.

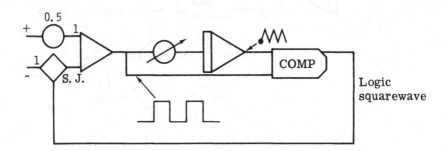

Fig. 4.21   Generator for triangular and square waves

4.6   Miscellaneous examples

Generate the functions of Examples 1-3 on a computer and check
the validity of the simulations by use of graphical recordings.

1.   (i) $e^{0.1t}$ for $0 < t < 10.$

       (ii)   sinh 0.5t and cosh 0.5t for $0 < t < 4$ (use 2 integrators
               and no other amplifier units).

(iii) $1 - (\frac{t}{10})^3$.

(iv) $0.2 + k \sin t$, where $0 < k < 0.2$ (use three amplifier units only).

2.   In the following examples, in addition to linear units, you may need to use squarers or multipliers.

(i) $\frac{1}{1+t}$ for $0 < t < 10$ (iv) $\frac{1}{1 + 0.1t^2}$ for $0 < t < 10$

(ii) $\sqrt{(1 + t)}$ for $0 < t < 10$

(iii) $\frac{1}{\sqrt{(1 + 0.5t)}}$ for $0 < t < 40$ (v) $\frac{1}{(1 + 0.2t)^3}$ for $0 < t < 5$

3.   (i)   The function

   $f(t) = -1$ for $0 < t < 2$
   $= 0$ for $2 < t < 4$
   $= +1$ for $4 < t < 6$

   (ii)   Trapezium function

   $f(t) = 0.5t$ for $0 < t < 2$
   $= 1$ for $2 < t < 4$
   $= 3 - 0.5t$ for $4 < t < 6$

   (iii) $f(t) = 1 - \frac{t}{8}$ for $0 < t < 2$
   $= 0.5 - \frac{t}{8}$ for $2 < t < 4$
   $= 0$ for $t > 4$

   (iv) $f(t) = 0.4t - 0.04t^2$ for $0 < t < 5$
   $= 2 - 0.2t$ for $5 < t < 10$

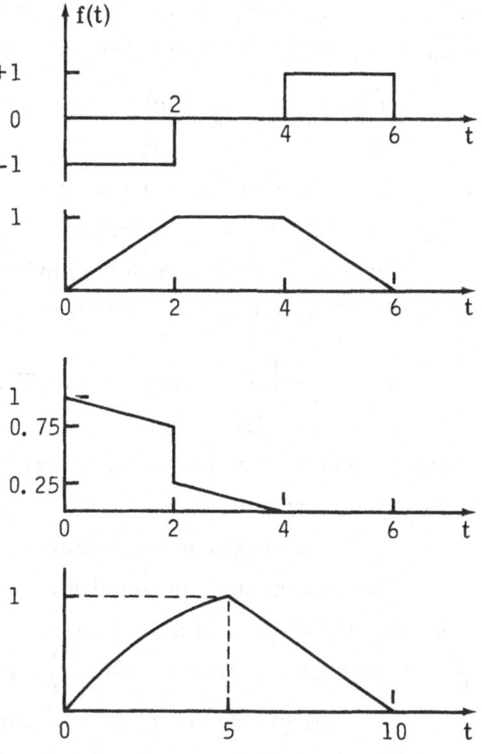

Fig. 4.22

4.   Obtain graphs of $e^{+0.2t}$ for $0 \le t \le 10$ by

(i)   generating $e^{+0.2t}$ as a positive exponential

(ii)   generating the function 'backwards' as a negative exponential.

Consider theoretically the effect of computing errors in each case and compare with the graphs obtained.

5.   Show how to obtain the first four positive roots of the algebraic equation $\cos t + 1 - 1.5e^{-0.2t} = 0$ by means of an analogue computer.

(a)   Generate $-\cos t$ and record it against time t. Generate $1 - 1.5e^{-0.2t}$ (using 1 integrator) and record it against t. Read off the intersections of the two graphs to give the roots of the equation.

(b)   Generate $-\cos t$ and $1.5e^{-0.2t} - 1$ separately, combine them in a summer, suitably scaled, and record the L. H. S. of the equation against time. Read off the roots of the equation.

Determine the negative root of the equation.

6.   The equations for a certain horizontal tapering beam of length L subject to a variable loading density $w(x)$ are

$$\frac{d^2M}{dx^2} = w(x) \quad \text{and} \quad \frac{d^2y}{dx^2} = f(x). M ,$$

where M is the bending moment, y is the deflection and $f(x)$ is the reciprocal of the flexural rigidity at a point a distance x from one end.

Draw a general computer simulation to be used to solve these equations. Ignore boundary conditions. Assume

$$f(x) = \frac{K}{(1 - \frac{3x}{4L})^2} \quad \text{and} \quad w(x) = W. \sin\frac{x\pi}{L},$$

where K and W are constants. Consider carefully the effect on errors in the generation of $f(x)$ of

(i)   choosing computer time $t \propto x$

(ii)   choosing computer time $t \propto L - x$.

N. B. Scaling of $f(x)$ is simplified if computer time t is made equal to $\frac{10x}{L}$ in case (i) and equal to $10(1 - \frac{x}{L})$ in case (ii).

7.   An analogue computer may be used to determine the Fourier coefficients of a function provided that the function can be generated within the computer or input to the computer.

Generate the function $f(t) = e^{-0.2t} (0 < t < 2\pi)$ and, by a series of computer runs, determine the integrals

$$\int_0^{2\pi} f(t)\cos(nt)dt, \quad \int_0^{2\pi} f(t)\sin(nt)dt \quad \text{for } n = 0, 1, 2, 3, 4, 5.$$

Hence deduce a Fourier representation of the function over the specified range. Check the accuracy by calculating the coefficients using any method (analytical or numerical). Comment on the experimental technique.

5 · Generation of Functions of a Dependent Variable

In this chapter the simpler methods for generating functions of one dependent variable are considered. More advanced techniques for one or more variables are considered in §7 and §11.

5.1   Continuous functions of one dependent variable

(i)   Diode function generators

The basic unit for generating continuous single valued functions of one dependent computer variable is the diode function generator or D. F. G. This unit contains a large number of diode-resistor networks plus one or two amplifiers. The unit has a non-linear input-output characteristic and the actual shape of this characteristic is determined by the values of the resistors used. Any particular function to be simulated is approximated to in a series (10-20) of straight line segments; variable resistors are used to control the starting or break point and slope of each section.

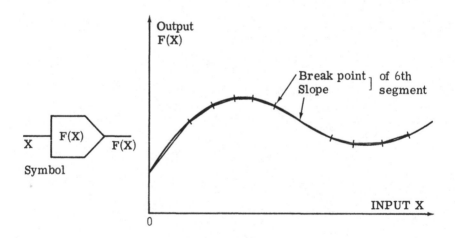

Fig. 5.1   Diode function generator

The actual procedure needed to set up a diode function generator varies a little from one make of unit to another. Basically the method is to determine the best positions for the break points and the best values for the slopes of each segment. Where the function is changing 'slowly' with X the break points can be spaced far apart but at 'corners' in the function they are spaced closely together. Makers' handbooks normally advise on a method for both determining the break points and slopes and also on how systematically to set up and check the D. F. G.'s characteristic. Because of the nature of a diode's current-voltage turn on characteristic the transition from one segment to another is generally fairly smooth and if a plot is obtained of the final overall characteristic there is often little evidence of the segmented nature of the function approximation.

Variable diode function generators

These units are provided on computers for users to set up themselves in order to simulate particular functions needed in a simulation. Their chief merit is that they generally provide the most efficient method of generating sometimes quite difficult functions using as few computer amplifier units as possible. Their main disadvantage is the time needed to set them up. This is typically 30 minutes even with an experienced user. Automatic D. F. G. units, set using a digital computer, have been manufactured but these are only available in some very large hybrid installations. D. F. G. units are best used in permanent simulations; their use is to be avoided if possible where the computer is available only for relatively short periods at a time.

Fixed diode function generators

These units are preset by manufacturers to simulate certain standard mathematical functions, e. g. X^2, $\sqrt{X}$, log X, exp X, sin θ, cos θ, arcsin X, etc. which are likely to be required in a large range of applications. Normally they are very easy to use having a single input and a single output. It should, however, be noted that these units differ in detail from one manufacturer to another; particularly different is the scaling characteristic of trigonometrical function generators. Some of these units are scaled so that 1 M. U. at the input represents $\pi/2$ or 90°. Others are scaled for 180° and others for 200°. The outputs require no scaling as they are already scaled over 1, i. e. $(\frac{\sin \theta}{1})$, $(\frac{\cos \theta}{1})$. Thus with a 200° type the variable input to the unit must be scaled $(\frac{\theta}{200})$ if θ appears in the equation in degrees or as $(\frac{\theta}{3.47})$ if θ is in radians (3. 47 radians = 200 degrees).

The log X, exp X function generators can also be used to generate integer or non-integer powers of X by implementing the relationship $X^n = \exp(n \log X)$.

(ii)   Multipliers and their uses

Although very many techniques have been developed for multiplying variables together the one most used in modern computers is the so-called quarter square method. The quarter square multiplier consists of two squaring function generator networks and one or more amplifier units. Multiplication is achieved by implementing the relationship

$$XY = \frac{1}{4}[(X + Y)^2 - (X - Y)^2] .$$

The multiplier is made up of two squaring networks and, by appropriate patching or switching, it can be used to produce two separate squares or square roots, i. e. it can be used as two (fixed) function generators. The multiplier can also be arranged to divide (and hence of course to generate the reciprocal $\frac{1}{X}$ of a variable X) and even to produce $X|X|$ from X. Circuits involving two multipliers and a summer can also be used to generate cube roots. Thus the multiplier unit directly plays an important role in function generation.

Multipliers can also be used in function generation by polynomial approximation. In this method the function required is represented approximately as a low degree polynomial in X, i. e. $F(X) = a + bX + cX^2 + dX^3$ and multipliers are used to implement this relationship. Clearly the method is very inefficient in the use of hardware but if the hardware is available it is certainly to be preferred to the use of variable diode function generators providing sufficient accuracy for the function is obtained. Polynomials can be simulated in direct or nested form, i. e. as $a + bX + cX^2 + dX^3$ or as $a + X(b + X(c + dX))$. In analogue computers the direct form is the more efficient in terms of hardware, particularly if more than one function of a certain variable is to be produced. The reason for this is that potentiometers are used to multiply by constants and non-linear units are needed only to generate the X^2 and X^3 terms.

Multipliers can also be used in a parametric method of function generation described in §7. 2.

5. 2   Application to the problem of the large-scale motion of a pendulum

The large-scale motion of a pendulum moving in a vertical plane is governed by the equation $\dfrac{d^2\theta}{dt^2} + K \sin \theta = 0$ (friction ignored), where K is a constant dependent on the length, etc. of the pendulum and θ is the angle made by the pendulum with the vertical direction.

If the angular movement is small ($|\theta|$ less than about 10°) $\sin \theta$ may be replaced by θ and the equation becomes that for S. H. M. , i. e. $\dfrac{d^2\theta}{dt^2} + K. \theta = 0$, which can be easily solved analytically or simulated using linear computing units. If θ is large the correct equation needs to be considered. This presents considerable difficulties if solved analytically. In simulations $\sin \theta$ must be produced from θ using a D. F. G. or otherwise. $\sin \theta$ can also be approximated to by $\theta - \dfrac{\theta^3}{3!}$ providing $|\theta|$ is not too large. This approximation can be generated from θ using multipliers. The general unscaled simulation diagram for the original equation written in the form $-\dfrac{d}{dt}(-\dfrac{d\theta}{dt}) = -K \sin \theta$ is:

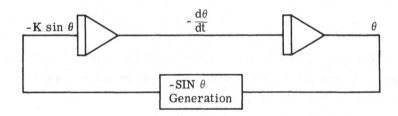

Fig. 5. 2

Practical work

Set up a simulation of the pendulum problem for the case when

73

$\theta_0 = 1$ radian and $\left(\frac{d\theta}{dt}\right)_0 = 0$. Record the solution of the equation and carefully compare the results (particularly the period of the oscillation) for the three cases

      (i)   When $\sin\theta$ is simply replaced by θ and the motion is approximated to by S. H. M.

      (ii)   When $\sin\theta$ is replaced by $\theta - \frac{\theta^3}{6}$ and generated approximately by multipliers.

      (iii)   When a D. F. G. is used to simulate $\sin\theta$ directly.

Choose the scaling of θ (for all three cases) to match the characteristic of the D. F. G. used in case (iii).

5.3   Discontinuous functions and functions with discontinuous derivatives

This group comprises those functions which contain abrupt changes. A few examples are illustrated below.

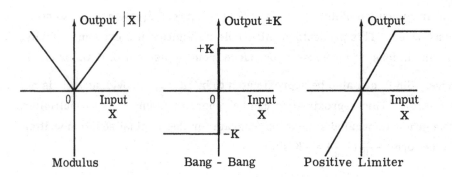

Fig. 5.3

These functions appear in the equations describing many physical systems: a particular example is considered in detail at the end of this section. There are two basic techniques

      (i)   an analogue method using diodes

and   (ii)   a hybrid method using simple hybrid elements, i. e. comparators and switches.

(i)   Diodes and their use

Diodes have been used to simulate non-linear functions

74

since the early days of electronic analogue computers and until relatively recent times the programmer has needed some basic knowledge of electronics to make best use of them. Fortunately the use of these elements in modern machines is disguised in such units as zero limiters and the programmer may not even be aware that diodes are being used. Therefore, in this section only one simple direct example is shown of the use of diodes; the reader interested in other applications, and preferably knowledgeable in electronics, is recommended to consult some of the very good texts on the subject (e. g. ref. 3).

The diode. The diode is an electronic valve or semiconductor device which allows current to pass through it in one direction only. It is helpful to consider it as a self-operating switch, the state of which depending on the polarity of the voltage across the device. This is illustrated in the diagram below:

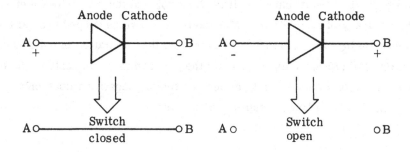

Fig. 5.4

Thus if the anode is made more positive (in voltage) than the cathode, current is allowed to pass through the diode, i. e. it 'turns on'. However, if the anode is negative with respect to the cathode, current cannot pass and the diode is 'cut off'. This represents the ideal situation. In practice a certain amount of forward voltage is needed before the device switches on and the diode never appears as a perfect short circuit. The reverse characteristic is very nearly ideal with the silicon diodes normally used in analogue computers. Ideal and practical characteristics are illustrated in Fig. 5.5:

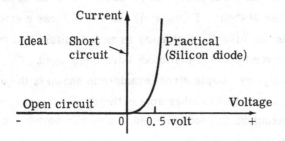

Fig. 5.5   Diode characteristics

The 0.5 volt turn on voltage of a silicon diode limits its direct use in function simulation as this voltage pedestal appears as an error in the characteristic.   In 100 volt reference machines the turn on voltage is about 0.5% of 1 machine unit and is generally of little consequence. However, in 10 volt machines it is about 5% and thus it seriously effects the accuracy of simulations.   Manufacturers have developed special techniques, using pairs of diodes, to overcome this limitation in units like ZERO LIMITERS.   With these units the programmer can restrict the output voltage of an amplifier to either positive or negative values only. Fig. 5.6 shows a limiter applied to an inverter.

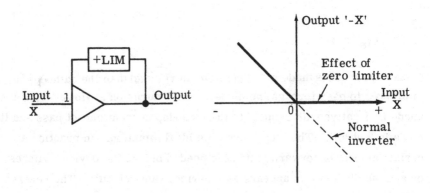

Fig. 5.6   Zero limiter and characteristic

Considerable ingenuity is needed in using these units to simulate any but the simplest of functions. One use is considered below in detail and others appear in the examples at the end of this chapter.

Example

Generation of modulus $+|X|$

A graph of the modulus function is given on page 74.

(a) Direct use of diodes

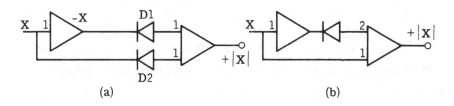

(a)   (b)

Fig. 5.7

Two arrangements are shown to produce $+|X|$ from X. The operation of the first (a) is described below and the reader is left to deduce the operation of (b) which only uses one diode.

In (a) when X is positive, $-X$ is negative so that D2 is reverse biased and cut off, whereas D1 is forward biased and turned on. When X is negative the inverse is true. This is illustrated in Fig. 5.8. In

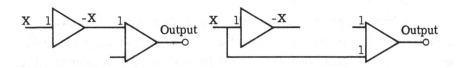

Input X positive D1 turned on   Input X negative D1 off
              D2 switched off   D2 on

Fig. 5.8

both cases the input to the summer is negative and, as the gains in both cases are 1, the output is always $+|X|$, i.e. whether X is positive or negative.

(b) Use of zero limiter

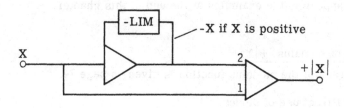

Fig. 5.9

Although there is a direct equivalent to (a) above using two zero limiters, only the more efficient set-up using a single zero limiter is shown.

If **X** is positive the output of the limited inverter is -**X** so that the total effective input to the summer is -2**X** + **X** = -**X**. Hence the resulting output is +**X**.

If **X** is negative the output of the inverter is limited to zero, i. e. it is not allowed to go positive and hence the total input to the summer is 2 times zero +**X** = +**X**. The output from the summer is therefore -**X** but as **X** is negative the actual value is positive. Thus whether **X** is positive or negative the output is always positive and equal in amplitude to **X**, i. e. the output is +|**X**|.

(ii) Hybrid methods

In hybrid methods the self-operating diode switch is replaced, effectively, by a comparator (to detect the polarity of the applied voltage) and an electronic D/A switch (to switch from short to open circuit). The overall characteristic does of course not show any evidence of the diode turn on characteristic! Circuits of particular simulations are in general much easier to design using hybrid units than using zero limiters or diodes. One use is considered in detail below; others appear in examples at the end of this chapter.

Example

Production of modulus +|**X**| from **X**

Simple arrangements for producing |**X**| (or 0.5|**X**|) from **X** are shown below.

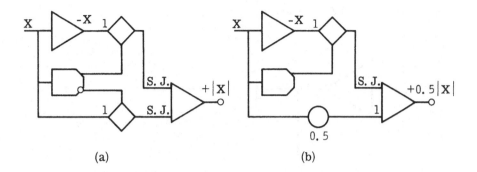

(a)   (b)

Fig. 5.10

X is compared with zero and the output of the comparator is used to control the states of the D/A switches. The operation is directly similar to that of the diode circuits already considered.

5.4   Application involving use of modulus in projectile problem

The equation derived already $\frac{dV}{dt} = \ddot{y} = -g - kV^2$ for a projectile moving vertically in a medium producing drag (friction) proportional to the square of the speed is valid only when the projectile is moving upwards. As the direction of motion changes the direction of the frictional force also changes:

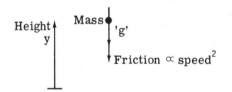   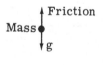

Upward motion   Downward motion

$$\ddot{y} = \frac{dV}{dt} = -g - kV^2$$ $$\ddot{y} = \frac{dV}{dt} = -g + kV^2$$

Fig. 5.11

79

In any simulation of this problem some means must be provided to account for this change in the direction of the frictional force. One way this can be done with hybrid elements is simply to arrange to switch the sign of the term $'kV^2'$ depending on the sign of V:

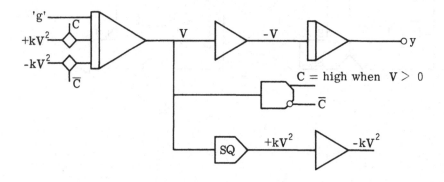

Fig. 5.12

However, the two equations can be combined together in one equation, viz. $\ddot{y} = \dfrac{dV}{dt} = -g - kV|V|$, where the use of $|V|$ takes account of the sign. The simulation (unscaled) becomes:

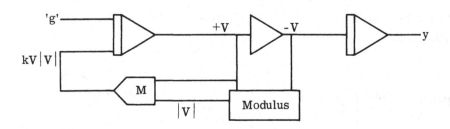

Fig. 5.13

The modulus term may be produced using any of the three circuits already considered, i.e. by means of diodes directly, zero limiters or hybrid elements. Note that as both +V and -V are produced in the simulation drawn in Fig. 5.13, the modulus circuit will not require an extra inverter.

Practical work

Simulate the projectile problem, with the initial conditions and scaling already considered in §3.6, using various methods to generate the modulus. In each case record the variation of y, V, $|V|$ and $V|V|$ against time.

5.5   Note on checking and displaying function generator characteristics

Whenever a function is simulated some check must be made on its characteristic prior to commencement of the main simulation. This is often best done by running the computer repetitively at high speed and displaying the characteristic on an oscilloscope. Two methods are possible, (a) in which the actual characteristic is displayed, and (b) in which the effect of the characteristic on some test waveform is displayed against time. They should not be confused!

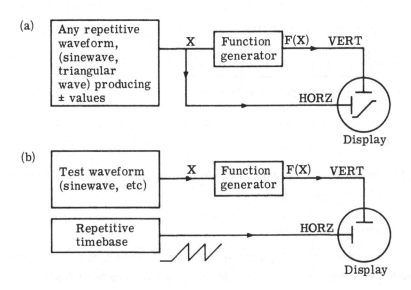

Fig. 5.14

If, for example, a set-up has been built to simulate a non-symmetrical ± limiter (e.g. to simulate saturation in an electronic amplifier) which has a characteristic:

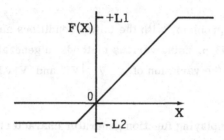

Fig. 5.15

then if method (a) is used the characteristic displayed should appear as above (providing the waveform input is of sufficient amplitude) but if it is checked as in (b) with a triangular test waveform the result should appear on the display as:

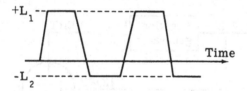

Fig. 5.16

Method (a) essentially gives the characteristic of the function; method (b) shows its effect on some input.

5.6   **Miscellaneous examples**

The correct solutions of all the following examples are best checked by simulation. Problems 4(a) and 5(b) are considered to be of particular general interest value and should be attempted practically. Further examples of function generation including applications to control appear in later chapters.

(1)   Work out the characteristics of the following four circuits using zero limiters

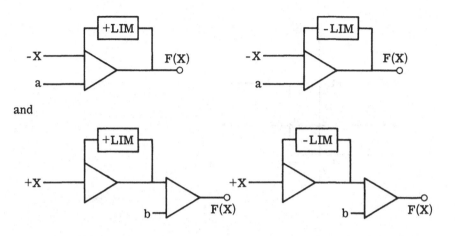

and

Fig. 5.17

Deduce simulations for the following characteristics using the above or combinations of the above. Try to use as few units as possible.

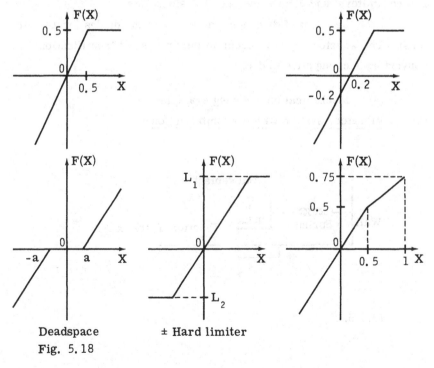

Deadspace   ± Hard limiter

Fig. 5.18

(2)   Derive simulations for the examples in (1) above using hybrid units.   Also derive a simulation for the characteristic:

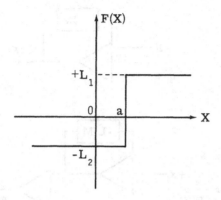

Fig. 5.19

(3)   Generate $+\sin t$ and $-\sin t$ using a 2 integrator plus inverter   loop.   Input these into a modulus circuit which uses 2 diodes (or 2 zero limiters) and display the output against time.

Note the effect of disconnecting either of the diodes (or zero limiters).   The waveforms above occur in the process of 'rectification' or converting a.c. supplies to d.c.

(4)   **Mechanical engineering examples**

(a)   Vibratory system with Coulomb friction

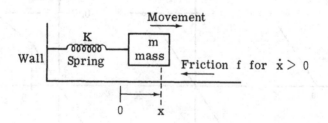

Fig. 5.20

In this vibratory system the frictional force is assumed to be only dependent on the normal force between the mass and the ground. Frictional force is therefore a constant force acting in the opposite direction to the motion. The mass can be at rest over a range of positions i. e. whenever the frictional force is greater than the force exerted by the spring.

Equation

If $x =$ distance of the mass from the zero friction equilibrium position '0'

then $\quad m\ddot{x} \pm f + kx = 0 \qquad$ $+f$ if $\dot{x} > 0$

$$\text{and} \quad -f \text{ if } \dot{x} < 0$$

Simulation

To avoid scaling simulate as

$$\ddot{X} \pm F + X = 0 \qquad +F \text{ when } \dot{X} > 0$$

$$-F \text{ when } \dot{X} < 0$$

In the simulation make the acceleration appear at the output of a summer (so that it can be recorded)

i. e. $\quad$ set up $\quad -A = \pm F + X$

$$-\frac{d}{dt}(-V) = A$$

$$-\frac{d}{dt}(X) = -V,$$

where $A =$ acceleration and $V =$ velocity.

From $-V$ produce, using hybrid elements, a constant ± 0.5 the sign of which being determined by the sign of V. Make $V = 0$ at time $t = 0$ and allow X_0 and the value of F to be variable. Initially set X_0 to 0.5, make $F = 0$ and observe that the system produces 0.5 sin t, 0.5 cos t and a square wave ± 0.5.

Observe the effect of varying F and X_0 on the solutions position X, speed V and acceleration A.

In particular note:

(i) $\quad$ The system comes to rest within a range about $X = 0$, the size of the range being dependent on the magnitude of F.

(ii)   The amplitude of the oscillations decays <u>linearly</u> with time. This is best seen if a slow timebase is used and F is made small.

Theoretically it can be shown that the system will come to rest anywhere where $|x| < \frac{f}{k}$ (or $|X| < F$) and the amplitude of the oscillations decrease $4\frac{f}{k}$ (or $4F$) per cycle.

(b)   <u>Movement of a truck between two separated spring buffers. Use of a deadspace simulator</u>

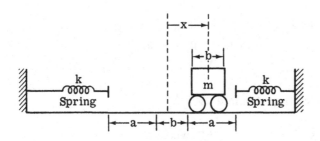

Fig. 5.21

Equation

Assuming no friction then $m\ddot{x} = -f(x)$ where

$$f(x) = 0 \quad \text{for} \quad -a < x < a$$
$$= k(x - a) \quad \text{for} \quad x > a$$
$$= k(x + a) \quad \text{for} \quad x < -a$$

Simulation

Set up $\ddot{X} = -f(X)$, where

$$f(X) = 0 \quad \text{for} \quad -0.5 < X < 0.5$$
$$= X - 0.5 \quad X > 0.5$$
$$= X + 0.5 \quad X < -0.5$$

Make $X_0 = 0$ and $\dot{X}_0 = 0.2$ and use zero limiters or hybrid elements to simulate the deadspace function. As in (a) above make the acceleration appear at the output of a summer.

Observe the variation of position X, velocity $\dot{X}$ and acceleration $\ddot{X}$ against time.

Effectively increase the stiffness k of the springs by a factor of 10 (by increasing the gain of the integrator converting acceleration to velocity) and observe the effect.

86

(5)   **Civil engineering problems**

(a)   Deflection of a long thin cantilever

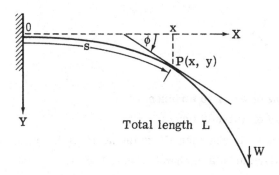

Fig. 5.22

In the above figure a long thin cantilever of length L is shown supported horizontally at one end and carrying a weight W at the other. The equations for a point P of the cantilever are

$$\frac{d^2\phi}{ds^2} = -\frac{W}{EI} \cdot \cos\phi$$

$$x = \int_0^S \cos\phi. ds$$

$$y = \int_0^S \sin\phi. ds ,$$

where ϕ, x, y are defined in the diagram and EI is the flexural rigidity of the cantilever. Boundary conditions are $\phi = 0$ at s = 0 and $\frac{d\phi}{ds} = 0$ at s = L.

Set up a simulation for the case when L = 100 inches, EI = 1000 lb-in^2 and W = 1 lb. Use 1 second of compute time to represent 10 inches of arc length, s. Solve the equations repetitively and manually adjust the value of $\frac{d\phi}{ds}$ at s = 0 until $\frac{d\phi}{ds} = 0$ at s = L. Record the solution and note the deflection of the free end.

(b)   Reservoir surge chamber problem

A reservoir is connected to an electric turbine generator via a tunnel in which there is a surge chamber. When sudden changes are made in the demand for water by the generators, valves are opened or closed and oscillations occur in the level of water in the surge chamber.

Equations

$$q = A \frac{dz}{dt} + Q$$

$$-\frac{L}{ag} \cdot \frac{dq}{dt} = z + \frac{F}{a^2} q|q|$$

where

Q = rate of flow of water to turbines

q = rate of flow of water in tunnel

z = height of water in chamber above the height in the reservoir

A = area of water surface in chamber = 250 sq. ft.

$$\frac{L}{ag} = 0.2, \quad \frac{F}{a^2} = 0.2 \times 10^{-4}.$$

Set up a simulation of the system with Q = 500 and check that the system reaches a steady state condition (i. e. $\frac{dz}{dt} = 0$ and $\frac{dq}{dt} = 0$) with q = 500 and z = -5.

When the system is operating in steady state, suddenly switch Q to zero to simulate the effect of the turbines being switched off suddenly. Record the variation of z with time and determine the maximum height of the oscillation and the time at which this maximum occurs.

Hint: Assume $|z| < 20$ ft and speed up solution rate by a factor of 10.

(6)　Derive a fully scaled analogue computer circuit for the trajectory under gravity of a rubber ball, having a mass of 0.1 kilograms, which is thrown with a horizontal velocity of 4 metres per second from a height of 70 metres on to a horizontal surface. Take the coefficient of restitution as 0.6, and the air resistance proportional to the square of the velocity with a value of 0.2 newtons at 1 metre per second.

(BCS 1971)

6 · Analogue Memory and its Applications

6.1   Introduction

Two units, integrators and track-stores, are available in analogue computers to enable a special value of a variable to be memorised or stored.

The behaviour of an integrator in various modes of operation has already been described (page 16).

The output of an INTEGRATOR, operating in the COMPUTE mode, will remain constant if the normal inputs are made zero, i.e. the integrator can be used to 'hold' or store a value. The same effect can be produced by switching the integrator mode to HOLD. The example below shows how an integrator may be used to obtain and store the maximum value of a continuous variable $y(t)$ (assumed to have only one stationary and maximum value in the COMPUTE period):

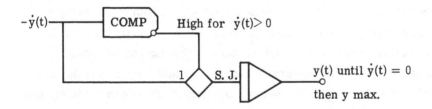

$-\dot{y}(t)$ —— COMP   High for $\dot{y}(t) > 0$

1 S.J. $y(t)$ until $\dot{y}(t) = 0$
then y max.

Fig. 6.1

The switch is closed, and hence the integrator produces $y(t)$ from $-\dot{y}(t)$, when $\dot{y}(t)$ is positive, i.e. as $y(t)$ is increasing towards its maximum value. When the maximum is reached at $\dot{y}(t) = 0$ the comparator changes state, the D/A switch turns off and the integrator stores the value of $y(t)$ at this time, i.e. y max.

Although this technique is of value it has rather limited application. A more versatile technique is to use an integrator in such a way that it is switched between its IC and COMPUTE modes, using local logic control. The analogue variable is connected to the IC input and the normal inputs are not used:

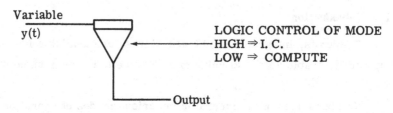

Variable
y(t)

LOGIC CONTROL OF MODE
HIGH ⇒ I. C.
LOW ⇒ COMPUTE

Output

Fig. 6.2

When the integrator is in the I. C. mode it operates as an inverter and the output 'equals', i. e. follows or tracks, the I. C. input y(t), i. e. - output = y(t). If at a time τ the integrator is switched to the COMPUTE mode the output remains constant at the last value tracked, i. e. - output = y(τ). This value will be memorised until the integrator is switched again into the I. C. mode to track a new value. Thus, by logic control, the integrator can be made to track an analogue variable and store any specific value. This represents the ideal situation. Unfortunately there is a lag or time constant associated with the tracking process (i. e. when the integrator is operating as an 'inverter' in the I. C. mode) and the output lags behind the input. This lag can introduce considerable error if y(t) is varying rapidly. In addition, during the time the integrator is storing, the output may drift slowly due to the integrator capacitor discharging. To use an integrator in this way to the best advantage the user must know the precise tracking/storing characteristics of the unit as a function of the integrator timescale. A small (fast) timescale is required for good tracking and a large timescale for good storing. Thus the use of this device is rather complex and is not recommended for the general user. For this reason no applications of the device will be considered.

The limitations and difficulties in use, mentioned above, have largely been overcome by the introduction of general-purpose TRACK-

STORE or TRACK-HOLD devices.   These units are able to track to within 0. 01% of an analogue variable in a few microseconds and store with
a drift rate of less than 0. 01% of a machine unit over a period of 10
seconds.   They combine summation (with the usual choice of gains) with
tracking and are represented:

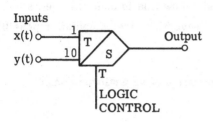

If T is HIGH

-Output = Sum of inputs

= x + 10y

If T is LOW

-Output = last value (of
sum of inputs) tracked.

Fig. 6. 3

Thus if only a single continuous input y(t) is applied and the logic control
is switched from HIGH to LOW when $t = \tau$, the output will equal -y(t)
until t becomes τ and then the output will remain constant at a value
-y(τ).

Track-store units can be and occasionally are used to store (e. g.
until the end of a compute period) a special value (e. g. maximum) which
has occurred sometime during the compute period.   For example, if
y(t) has a single maximum and no other stationary values in the compute
period, the following arrangement would enable this maximum to be
measured and stored:

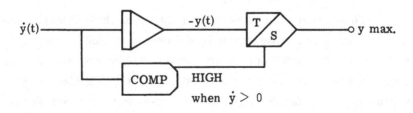

Fig. 6. 4

However, track-store units play a much more important role than suggested by the above example as they are the essential tool used to memorise (perhaps with modification) analogue values from one compute run to the next in a repetitively operating computer. They thus enable iterative rather than purely repetitive computation to take place and allow great use to be made of the high-speed capabilities of a modern analogue/hybrid computer. Before discussing how this is done it is necessary to examine some of the types of repetitive/iterative computation possible in an analogue machine.

6.2 Repetitive and iterative operation of an analogue computer

(i) Repetitive operation

In this mode of operation the equations are solved over and over again generally so that the solutions can be displayed on an oscilloscope. Changes to parameters can be made manually and the effect observed on the displayed solutions. The computer is normally cycled:

I. C. →RESET (to initial conditions)→COMPUTE→RESET→COMPUTE→ RESET→ etc.

but occasionally more complex sequences are used, e. g.

I. C. →HOLD→RESET→HOLD→COMPUTE→HOLD→RESET→HOLD→ COMPUTE→ etc.

depending on the problem studied and the mode control characteristics of the particular computer used.

(ii) Iterative operation

This is essentially repetitive operation in which changes are automatically made to certain parameters between successive compute periods so that families of solutions are produced either for display purposes or more often in order that a special (optimum) solution is obtained by a converging process. As with repetitive operation there are various mode sequences possible: the only sequence to be considered in these notes is the basic repetitive sequence

I. C. → RESET → COMPUTE → RESET → COMPUTE →

and all applications will assume this sequence.

6.3   Memory pair

In iterative computation track-store units are used in pairs, the basic configuration being:

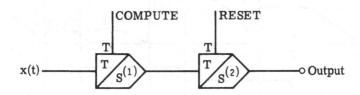

Fig. 6.5

The 1st track-store unit tracks the value of $x(t)$ during the nth compute period (as COMPUTE is HIGH) so that at the end of this period and throughout the following reset period the output is minus the last value of $x(t)$ tracked, i.e. $-L_n$. During the next reset period (when RESET is HIGH) the 2nd T/S unit tracks the constant output $-L_n$ of the 1st T/S unit and stores this value during the following $(n+1)$th compute period. Thus during the $(n+1)$th compute period (and in the reset period before it) the output is the <u>last value of</u> $x(t)$ <u>computed in the</u> n^{th} <u>period</u>, i.e. L_n.

This pair of units enables a value to be available in the $(n+1)$th period of an event which occurred in the nth period. Thus comparisons can be made and actions taken accordingly.

The operation of this memory pair can be understood by reference to the following diagram in which successive solutions $x_n(t)$, $x_{n+1}(t)$, ... are shown to differ (Fig. 6.6).

The value stored during the $(n+1)$th compute period is the <u>last</u> or <u>end</u> value of the input $x(t)$ during the nth compute period. $x(t)$ may be a function like an error criterion which needs to be evaluated each compute period in order to be compared with a previous value or $x(t)$ may be a special value, such as the root of an equation, to which the iterative

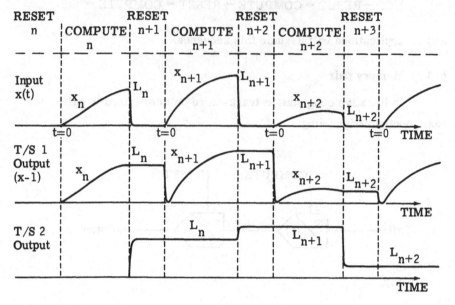

Fig. 6.6

process is converging. Such functions are called RUN FUNCTIONS.

The memory pair is also called 'bucket brigade' because of its action of 'scooping' up a value using one T/S unit and passing it on to the other.

Initialisation of track-stores

Frequently it is necessary to make the output of a memory pair have a prescribed initial value at the commencement of the simulation. This can be achieved using certain makes of units which are provided with I.C. inputs and appropriate logic control:

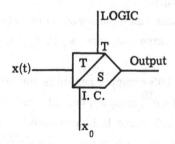

Fig. 6.7

During the time when the computer is in the I. C., mode prior to the iterative phase, the output of each T/S unit is made equal to the I. C. input (times -1). Unlike integrators, track-store units do not switch back to the I. C. mode during the RESET period. The reason for this is partly explained in the discussion on page 99.

When an initial output from a memory pair is required during the I. C. period and during the first reset period before the first compute period the following arrangement is required:

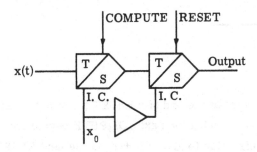

Fig. 6. 8

This basic configuration, with or without an I. C. input but including the logic control inputs, will be called a LAST VALUE circuit in subsequent notes and will be drawn, viz.

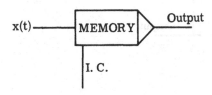

Fig. 6. 9

Modify and circulate circuit

If the output of a memory pair is connected to the input, the circuit should store a value continuously (neglecting errors due to drift in hold,

95

etc.), when the computer is operating repetitively. The value 'circulates'.

If an additional input Δ (assumed constant at present) is applied, the circulated value will be modified by Δ each complete reset-compute cycle:

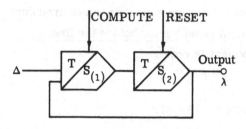

Fig. 6.10

Thus if the output is λ at the end of a RESET period, the 1st T/S unit will track $-(\lambda + \Delta)$ during the next COMPUTE period and the 2nd T/S unit will track this value to give $+\lambda + \Delta$ in the next RESET and subsequent COMPUTE period. This basic configuration enables stored values to be modified (perhaps as a result of some other computation) and is the key to iterative computation. Note the output value is updated at the start of the RESET period. This configuration, including initialisation circuits if needed, will be drawn as:

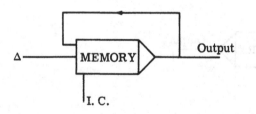

Fig. 6.11

in subsequent notes and will be referred to as a MODIFY and CIRCULATE circuit.

6.4   Applications of memory pairs in parameter sweeps

The modify and circulate circuit, with Δ constant, may be used to produce a parameter λ which increases by a constant amount Δ each repetitive cycle. If this parameter is used in a simulation, e. g. as a coefficient, input or I. C. value, families of solutions can be generated and certain properties (e. g. maximum value) of solutions may then be extracted and automatically plotted as a function of the parameter. It must be arranged that the property to be measured is generated at the end of each compute period and memorised using a last value circuit.

As an example, suppose there is a simulation set up of the 45° projectile problem (§3. 4) and it is required to know:

(i)   the variation of range,

(ii)   the variation of time of flight,

(iii) the variation of the maximum height reached,

as functions of the speed of launch V_0.

The computer model is arranged so that the compute period terminates when y becomes 0 with $\dot{y}$ negative, i. e. when the projectile 'hits the ground'. The value of x(t) at that time will give the horizontal range R and the value of the timebase reference will give the time of flight. Both of these functions are in the correct form for memorising by a last value circuit. The maximum height reached H can be memorised until the end of the compute period using a T/S or integrator (cf. pages 89-92) in which y(t) = height at time t.

Parameter sweeps may then be obtained using the arrangement below shown producing the Range versus Speed characteristic:

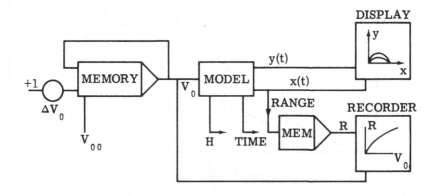

Fig. 6. 12

The speed of launch starts at V_{00} and is increased by a small amount ΔV_0 each cycle. The projectile's orbit is displayed each cycle to give a family of solutions. The variation of RANGE with V_0 is obtained in graphical form.

The parameter sweep curve is in the form of a step stair approximation to the required characteristic as the parameter V_0 is incremented in small steps each cycle. However, if the step is made very small (~0.1% of total variation in the parameter) the curve recorded will contain such a large number of very small steps that it will appear as a smooth curve. The time taken to obtain the parameter sweep need only be a few (e.g. 5) seconds (with fairly simple problems) if the model equations are solved repetitively at high speed (e.g. $\simeq 200$ solutions per second). Some results obtained for this problem are shown below:

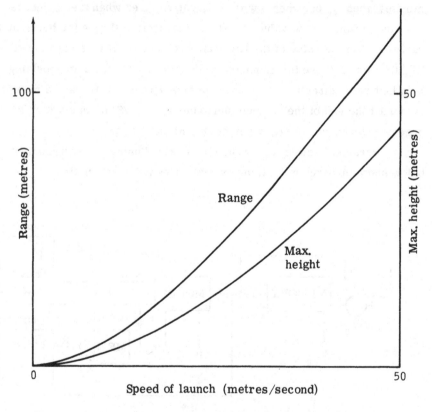

Fig. 6.13 Variation of range and maximum height with speed of launch

As mentioned earlier, the parameter could be an input to a model, an initial condition (as in the example considered) or a coefficient in an equation. In this last case the implementation will involve use of a multiplier. For example, if a family of solutions of $\frac{dy}{dt} + \lambda y = 0$ with $y_0 = 1$ are required for $\lambda_0 < \lambda < \lambda_{max}$ the following set-up could be used:

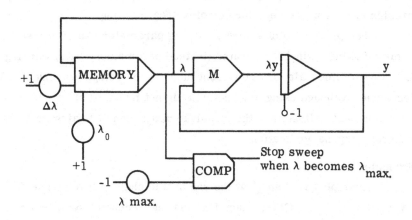

Fig. 6.14

Discussion

Parameter sweeps provide an excellent way of making use of the high-speed capabilities of an analogue computer. They are useful in simple optimisation problems where some cost or error function is to be minimised as a function of a parameter (or a number of parameters). In these situations not only are the optimum conditions able to be deduced from the graphs but also the variation about the optimum. This vital information, showing the sensitivity to a parameter near the optimum, is often not obtained (for reasons of cost) with digital search techniques.

With high-speed analogue computers it is possible to generate double parameter sweeps at a sufficiently high repetitive rate to be able to display the sweeps on an oscilloscope. For example, in the projectile problem ΔV_0 could be made about 10% of the range of V_0 needed, 5 values of the friction coefficient could be used and the whole problem involving 50 or so solutions each lasting a few milliseconds could be repeated perhaps 5 times every second. To achieve this repetitive operation the T/S units have to be re-initialised at the end of each sweep. Although not described in the notes, T/S units are provided with an extra local logic control to switch them into the I. C. mode. The user could then interact manually further with the simulation (e. g. by varying the angle of launch) and observe the effect. This provides a fairly easy way of studying 3 parameter problems (e. g. optimisation problems) without the need for complex programming.

The production of a slowly varying parameter can of course be achieved using a single integrator (instead of a memory pair) working in a slower timescale and a different mode to the computer model. This technique, although using one less unit, is not favoured simply because it is more specialised than the technique using memory pairs which have general-purpose application.

Examples

Examples 1, 2 and 5 at the end of this chapter involve use of parameter sweeps. Other examples relating to control systems are to be found in §12.

6. 5 Application of memory pairs in the study of split boundary value problems

Analogue computers are essentially initial value machines. Their natural role is to solve differential equations in which the complete state of all variables is specified at a particular value, corresponding to computer time $t = 0$, of the problem independent variable. Fortunately very many problems are of the initial value type, e. g. dynamic physical systems which are started or 'switched on' at a particular time. Digital computer simulation languages are also written to solve equations, by forward integration, which are completely specified at one value of the independent variable. However, there are many situations where boundary conditions are specified at a number of values or points of the independent variable. Many of these are classed as two-point boundary value problems as the conditions are specified at two points. For dynamic systems these instances are the times of the initial and final (or terminal)

100

states of the system. Most examples of static systems, e.g. beams, are multipoint boundary value problems. These notes describe the study of split boundary value problems by analogue computer simulation. Study by digital and hybrid computer simulation is considered later.

It should be noted that the techniques described are also applicable to Eigenvalue differential equation problems.

Boundary value problems can be studied by parameter sweeping techniques. The computer is operated repetitively and the magnitudes of the variables not known at time $t = 0$, i.e. initially, are changed in slow linear sweeps so that families of solutions are generated and recorded. The special solution needed to satisfy all the boundary conditions is selected from the recorded (graphed) results using interpolation if necessary. Although this technique is of value (particularly when there are only one or two unknown initial values) the more usual method used, known as the SHOOTING method, is to solve the equations repetitively and adjust the unknown initial values manually until boundary conditions specified at other times are satisfied. This manual iteration technique is most easily applied if the computer is operated at high speed and the solutions displayed on an oscilloscope. The whole process, one of trial and error, can be understood from the following simple example:

Problem 1

Single unknown initial value

Find the value of the speed of launch of a projectile, so that a given horizontal range, R_F, is achieved for a specified angle of launch:

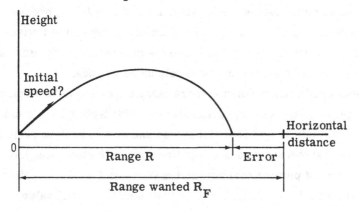

Fig. 6.15

A simulation is set up and the equations solved for a guessed value of the launch speed V_{01} to give a range R_1. The sign and magnitude of the miss distance or error $R_F - R_1$ is noted and a suitable new initial value of launch speed V_{02} for the next run is deduced and set up. Proceeding in this for many runs the error is systematically reduced to 'zero' (i. e. an acceptable small value) and the required speed of launch V_{0F} to give range R_F obtained. With even a slow analogue computer (5 solutions per second) the process of matching the boundary condition '$R_n = R_F$' should be achieved in a few seconds.

The last value of $x(t)$ in the compute period, i. e. the range R can be very conveniently monitored on the digital voltmeter (D. V. M.) of the computer using a last value circuit:

Fig. 6.16

It is then a simple matter to operate the computer repetitively and adjust the speed of launch manually until the correct range is displayed on the D. V. M.

This method of manual iteration is very effective when there are 1 or 2 unknowns to adjust particularly if a composite error function $(E = \Sigma |Ei|)$ is output on the D. V. M. Even problems involving 3, 4 or more unknown initial values can be studied but the matching process can become tedious if the errors depend in a complex way on the initial values set. The transition from 2 to 3 unknowns is surprisingly difficult; only 2 adjustments can be made simultaneously using 2 hands.

With production problems where many cases are to be studied it is best if possible to use some automatic iteration technique to avoid the tedious manual adjustment of initial values and also to achieve rapid convergence thus avoiding waste of computing time. The technique most easy to apply is that of proportional correction shown in Fig. 6.17 applied to a problem in which there is one error and one unknown initial value:

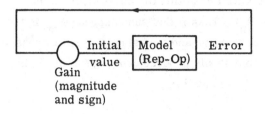

Fig. 6.17

The error in the boundary condition on one computer run (or solution) is used to adjust the initial condition ready for the next run. The actual change made is proportional to the error. If convergence is to be achieved it is necessary, though not always possible, to choose correctly both the sign and magnitude of the gain. The storing and updating of the initial value can be simply implemented using a circulate and modify memory pair circuit. The technique is shown below applied to the projectile problem discussed earlier.

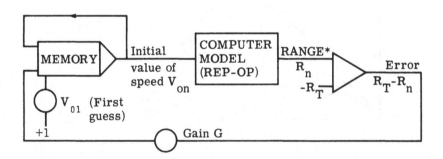

Fig. 6.18

*This is simply $x(t)$ at the end of the compute period if the model recycles when y becomes zero.

During the reset period before the nth compute period the initial value of the speed V_{on} is set, the computer solves the equation to produce the horizontal range R_n which is compared with the required range

103

R_T to give an error $E_n = R_T - R_n$. A fraction GE_n of this error is added to V_{on} so that the initial condition for the (n+1)th run is $V_{on+1} = V_{on} + G.(R_T - R_n)$. Thus if the launch speed V_{on} is too low, the error $R_T - R_n$ will be positive and the value of speed increased for the next run. Such a scheme should produce convergence if G is positive and not too large (Figs. 6.19(a) and (b)).

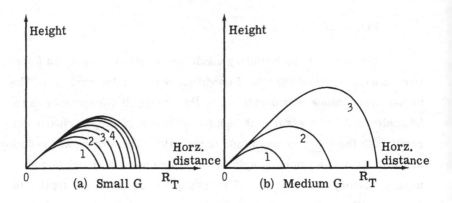

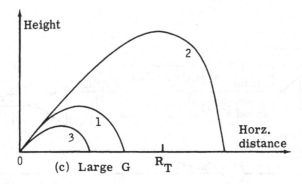

Fig. 6.19

If G is large the correction applied to V_{on} may be so large that an even larger error is produced on the following run, Fig. 6.19(c), and the process diverges. There is no guarantee that the technique will work for all problems. However, if convergence to a single result is achieved then the result must be correct as the error is zero. The essential re-

104

quirement is that the error-initial condition characteristic must have a
single sign near to the final desired result, e. g. Fig. 6. 20(a). 'Quadratic' characteristics, as in Fig. 6. 20(b), either produce divergence

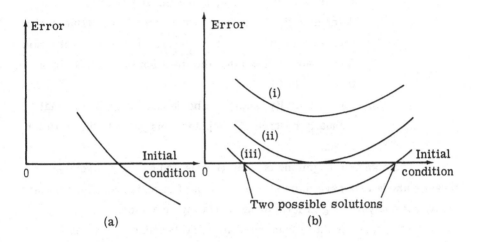

Fig. 6. 20

(i) and (ii) or possible ambiguity in the solution (iii). Ambiguities of this
kind were one of the bugbears of early wartime navigational radar systems. A problem of type (iii) is discussed in Example 3 at the end of
this chapter.

When studying split B. V. problems, it is best to choose the correct sign and also an estimate of a suitable magnitude for G prior to
the actual simulation. The sign can usually be chosen by (i) commonsense
deductions from the problem, or (ii) ensuring negative loop feedback,
i. e. that the total number of sign inversions around the iteration loop is
odd.

Although the exact magnitude of gain is not critical, its value does
need to be chosen with some care if reasonably rapid convergence is to
be achieved. This may be done by:

(i)   Commonsense knowledge of the problem.

(ii)   Selecting the value of total gain round the iteration loop
        (using the scaled computer diagram) to be 0. 1 to 0. 5 (and

certainly less than 1) so that the error should decrease in
magnitude in successive compute periods.

(iii)   Sensitivity analysis:

   (a) the problem can be analysed theoretically near the re-
       required solution value, using linear perturbation, to
       determine the sensitivity of the error to the value of the
       initial condition, i. e. $S = \dfrac{\Delta E}{\Delta I.\,C.}$. The value of the gain
       G is made $< \dfrac{1}{S}$ so that the iteration loop gain is less
       than 1 as in (ii) above.

   (b) The sensitivity factor can be deduced from a few trial
       manually controlled computer runs prior to the iteration
       phase.

The sign and magnitude of gain G selected by one or more of
these methods may have to be altered in light of experience. Unnecessary
analytical analysis (e. g. iii(a)) should certainly be avoided.

When there is more than one non-initial boundary condition to
satisfy the design of the iteration process can become very difficult due
to the complex interaction between initial values and boundary condition
errors. Ideally if each initial value affects each error then each error
should be used to control each initial value. Such a scheme can become
unwieldy even with two unknowns and two errors as is shown in the simplified diagram of Fig. 6. 21.

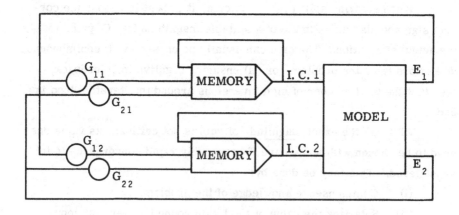

Fig. 6. 21

106

The gains can be chosen by extension of the methods explained for the one loop case. Generally it is simplest to try to make each initial value be controlled by one error only. The choice of which error to use to control which initial value can be determined by:

(i)   Commonsense (but it is easy to get the wires crossed).

(ii) Selecting simple negative feedback loops from the scaled computer diagram (i. e. choosing iteration loops so that the total number of sign reversals around each loop is odd).

(iii) Performing a few trial computer runs to determine which initial value effects which error the most.

(iv) Sensitivity analysis.

When there are 3, 4 or more non-initial boundary conditions to meet it is often tedious (or impossible) to design a scheme which will give convergence automatically. In such cases it is best to arrange to fit all but 1 or 2 of the conditions automatically and use manual adjustment for the remainder. This technique has been found to be very effective. The design of the iteration scheme for a two unknown initial value problem is explained below. This problem is of special interest as it is a 3-point boundary value problem and because the duration of the compute period varies from run to run.

Problem 2

Two unknown initial values

Determine the speed and angle of launch for a projectile to just clear a wall and achieve a given range:

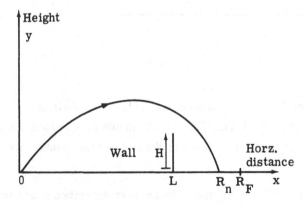

Fig. 6.22

The simulation can be set up so that the speed and angle of launch are controlled by the magnitude of the horizontal and vertical components of velocity at launch, i. e. $\dot{x}_0$ and $\dot{y}_0$. One error could be defined (but not necessarily) as the range miss distance $R_F - R_n$. The other must indicate the amount by which the projectile misses the top of the wall. This could be the shortest distance from the flight path to the wall top - very hard to compute - or more simply the vertical or horizontal miss distance. Although both $\dot{x}_0$ and $\dot{y}_0$ will effect both errors, common-sense investigation of the problem suggests that it is reasonable to use the range error $R_F - R_n$ to adjust $\dot{x}_0$ and the vertical miss distance from the wall, y(when $x = L$) - H, to control the value of $\dot{y}_0$.

Assuming the compute period is terminated when y goes positive to negative (i. e. when the projectile hits the ground) then a simplified scheme is:

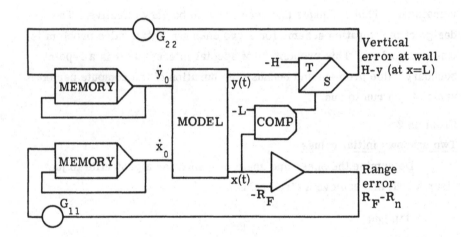

Fig. 6.23

The single T/S unit is used to track $H - y(t)$ until $x = L$ and memorise $H - y$(at $x = L$) until the end of the compute period. A numerical case of this example is given at the end of this chapter (Ex. 5).

Discussion

Both the manual and automatic techniques described above provide

108

simple but powerful tools for solution of split boundary value problems. The techniques described are equally applicable to both linear and non-linear equations. Although the proportional correction scheme may seem very unsophisticated to a specialist in numerical methods, it is as complicated a scheme as is worth implementing on an analogue computer equipped with T/S and parallel logic units.

6.6 Miscellaneous examples

(1) Set up a simulation of the projectile problem, page 79, and obtain sweeps of
  (a) maximum height,
  (b) time to reach maximum height,
  (c) total time of flight,
as functions of the speed of launch $V_0[5, 50]$ metres/sec.

(2) Newton's Law of Cooling states that under certain conditions a body loses heat at a rate proportional to the difference in temperature between it and its surroundings. If this temperature difference is y then $\frac{dy}{dt} = -\lambda y$, where λ is a constant. A simple Eigenvalue problem is: given $y = A$ at time $t = 0$ and $y = B$ at time $t = T$ determine the value of the constant λ. Prepare an analogue computer simulation for this equation (when $A = 1$, $B = 0.2$ and $T = 5$) using a multiplier to implement the production of λy from y.
  (i) Generate a parameter sweep giving the variation of y at $t = 5$ as a function of λ. Select the value of λ required.
  (ii) Determine the solution of the problem using an automatic boundary value fitting technique.
  (iii) Compare the results obtained with the theoretical solution.

(3) A body is projected with speed V_0 at an angle α_0 with the horizontal. For a given fixed value of V_0 it is required to find the angle α_0 such that the body achieves a certain fixed range R. Consider this problem carefully and note that the 'error in range' versus 'angle of launch α_0' characteristic can assume any of the forms shown in the diagram of Fig. 6.20(b). Thus this problem only has a unique solution

for very special values of V_0 and R. For other values of V_0 and R the problem may have two solutions or no solutions at all. Prepare an iteration scheme for finding the lower value of the angle of launch to solve this problem assuming conditions are such that solutions exist. How could the technique be changed to produce the larger value of α_0? In both cases consider what will happen if V_0 is too small for there to be a solution to the problem.

(4)   A vehicle, starting and finishing at rest, is to travel a distance of 2000 metres in as short a time as possible. It is to be subject to a constant accelerating force for the first L metres of its journey and to a constant retarding force for the remainder. The equations determining its position x in terms of time t (in metre second units) for both sections of the journey are:

$$\ddot{x} + 0.5.10^{-4}\dot{x}^2 = 0.4 \qquad \text{Acceleration phase}$$

and $\quad \ddot{x} + 0.5.10^{-4}.\dot{x}^2 = -1.3 \qquad \text{Retardation phase}$

Determine, by computer simulation, the required value of L and the total time for the journey.

(5)   Set up the 'projectile over the wall' problem (Problem 2, page 107) for the case $L = 50$, $H = 30$, $R_F = 80$ using the simple equations:

$$\ddot{x} = -0.2\dot{x}$$
$$\ddot{y} = 0.2\dot{y} - 9.8$$

for the model. Assume $|x| < 100$, $|\dot{x}| < 50$, $|y| < 50$ and $|\dot{y}| < 50$ metre sec units.

When values of the iteration gains are obtained giving rapid convergence then add on a parameter sweep to the system so that the values of $\dot{x}_0$ and $\dot{y}_0$ needed to satisfy the boundary conditions are plotted as functions of (a) the position (L) of the wall, (b) the height (H) of the wall, (c) the range R_F. Also plot the maximum height reached by the projectile for these cases. In all cases ensure that the boundary values are correctly fitted (for a certain combination of L, H and R_F) before the slow sweep starts. <u>Note.</u> With this problem it is worthwhile introducing a scheme to show the ground and the wall on the display as well as the flight path of the projectile.

(6)   Set up Example 5(a) of §5 using automatic iteration to match the boundary conditions.

(7)   The equation determining the deflection at a distance x from one end of a beam of length L, i.e. $EI\dfrac{d^4y}{dx^4} = w(x)$ can be reduced to the following set of equations:

$$\frac{dy}{dx} = \text{slope}, \quad \frac{d(\text{slope})}{dx} = \frac{\text{bending moment } M}{EI}$$

$$\frac{dM}{dx} = \text{shear force } S, \quad \frac{dS}{dx} = \text{loading distribution } w(x),$$

where EI is the flexural rigidity of the beam. The boundary conditions depend on the way in which the beam is supported or held at each end, e. g.

(a) Beam clamped at one end and free at the other: $y = 0$, slope $= 0$ at $x = 0$; bending moment and shear $= 0$ at $x = L$.

(b) Beam supported at both ends: $y = 0$ and bending moment $= 0$ at both $x = 0$ and $x = L$.

(c) Beam clamped at one end and supported at the other: $y = 0$, slope $= 0$ at $x = 0$; $y = 0$ and bending moment $= 0$ at $x = L$.

Set up a general simulation for these equations using computer time $t[0, 10]$ to represent x and assuming $EI = 1$ for the case $w = 0.005$ (i. e. uniform beam with constant load) [suitable scaling $(\frac{y}{1})$, $(\frac{\text{slope}}{0.5})$ $(\frac{M}{0.25})$ and $(\frac{S}{0.05})$].

Design and test iteration schemes to fit the bounding values for cases (a), (b) and (c). Study case (b) for various loading distributions, e. g.   (i)   Sinusoidal Load $w(x) = 0.005 \sin\frac{\pi x}{10}$

(ii)   Uniform + Triangular Load $w(x)$, where $1000\, w(x)$ is shown in Fig. 6.24

(iii) Uniform + Point Load $w(x)$, where the point load is at the centre of the beam. This point load cannot be directly

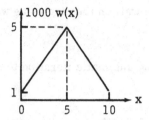

Fig. 6. 24

generated but, as it causes a step change to occur in the shear force, it can be introduced, viz:

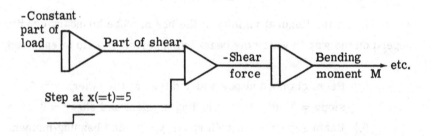

Fig. 6. 25

Finally, for case (iii) above, slowly sweep the position of the point load in the simulation from one end of the beam to the other and obtain relevant parameter sweeps (e. g. max M versus position of load).

7 · Miscellaneous Advanced Techniques

7.1   Introduction

In this chapter we wish to examine three uses of analogue and parallel logic hybrid units which are of special interest.   Each application has been chosen so as to illustrate important techniques, i. e. integration with respect to a variable other than time, variable timescaling and multi-speed computing.   These techniques are applicable to a wide range of problems; the special cases chosen just illustrate the techniques.

The techniques are not difficult to understand but their use will generally be restricted to the larger more sophisticated type of analogue/ parallel logic hybrid computer.   Worthwhile implementations of the first and second techniques require the use of high-quality multipliers.   The third technique, involving multi-speed computation, requires use of electronic mode controlled integrators whose mode and timescale can be controlled by logic signals.   In addition a high degree of 'feel' for the hardware by the user is likely to be required for successful implementations.

7.2   Function generation by use of multipliers and integrators

Common functions such as $e^{\pm ax}$, cos x, sin x, cosh x, sinh x, of a dependent variable, x, are most simply generated by means of fixed function generators (reference §5).   They may also be generated using multipliers and integrators.   This method provides an alternative technique useful if fixed function generators are not available.   It is inefficient in the use of computer units and does not offer any significant improvement in accuracy compared with fixed function generators.   However, it is certainly to be preferred to the use of variable function generators which have to be set by the user.

The technique can be most simply illustrated by consideration of the function $y = e^{-kx}$, where k is a positive constant and x a <u>dependent</u>

computer variable, i.e. $x = x(t)$.

As $y = e^{-kx}$,

∴ $\frac{dy}{dx} = -ke^{-kx} = -ky,$

or $\quad y = -\int ky \cdot dx.$ $\hspace{3cm}$ (7.1)

Thus, if it were possible to integrate with respect to dependent variable x, the function y could be generated very simply:

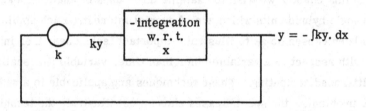

Fig. 7.1

Unfortunately such units do not exist in commonly available analogue computers[†] and the integration w.r.t. x has to be achieved artificially using normal integrators, i.e. those which integrate with respect to the independent computer variable time, t.

As $y = e^{-kx}$,

∴ $\frac{dy}{dt} = \frac{d}{dx}(e^{-kx}) \cdot \frac{dx}{dt}$ using the function of a function rule of calculus,

i.e. $\frac{dy}{dt} = -ke^{-kx} \cdot \frac{dx}{dt},$

or $\quad -\frac{dy}{dt} = ky \cdot \frac{dx}{dt},$ $\hspace{3cm}$ (7.2)

i.e. $\quad -y = \int ky \cdot \frac{dx}{dt} \cdot dt.$ $\hspace{3cm}$ (7.3)

This equation (7.3) can obviously be deduced directly from (7.1). It can be set up (in the form (7.2)) as:

---

† One make of 'analogue' computer, which use digital integrators, contains such units.

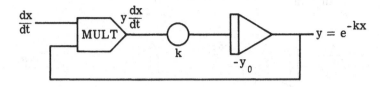

Fig. 7.2

Thus integration with respect to a dependent variable is achieved using a multiplier and a normal integrator. Any variation in x is accompanied by a change in dx/dt; this change produces an input to the integrator and hence a change in the output 'y'.

Note

    (i)   The method requires the existence of the variable $\frac{dx}{dt}$ in order to generate a function of x.

    (ii)   The initial condition of the integrator cannot be ignored. Thus if $x = x_0$ at $t = 0$ then the initial condition $y_0 = e^{-kx_0}$ must be set at the integrator output.

    (iii)   To achieve high accuracy multiplier offset errors must be small or the integrator output will 'drift' even when $\frac{dx}{dt} = 0$.

    In the next example the technique is shown applied to the generation of the function $\sin \theta$ needed to solve the exact equation for the motion of a pendulum, i. e.

$$\frac{d^2\theta}{dt^2} + K.\sin\theta = 0 \qquad (7.4)$$

a problem already considered earlier in §5.2.

    To generate $\sin \theta$ we need to implement the relationships

$$+\frac{d(\sin\theta)}{dt} = +\cos\theta \cdot \frac{d\theta}{dt} \quad \text{or} \quad +\sin\theta = +\int\cos\theta \cdot \frac{d\theta}{dt} \cdot dt \qquad (7.5)$$

and

$$+\frac{d(\cos\theta)}{dt} = -\sin\theta \cdot \frac{d\theta}{dt} \quad \text{or} \quad +\cos\theta = -\int\sin\theta \cdot \frac{d\theta}{dt} \cdot dt. \qquad (7.6)$$

115

The total unscaled computer set-up needed to solve the equation (7. 4) written as $-\dfrac{d}{dt}(-\dfrac{d\theta}{dt}) = -K\sin\theta$ is then:

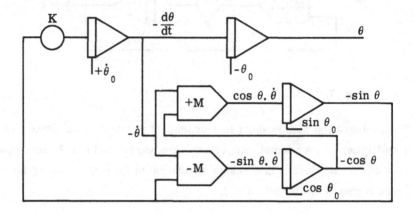

Fig. 7. 3

It is interesting to note that θ is not used to generate $\sin\theta$ (cf. the previous example where $\dot{x}$ rather than x was required to generate e^{-kx}). If only the information $\dot{\theta}$ is required, the integrator producing θ can be excluded.

The technique applied to this problem is inefficient in use of hardware, 2 multipliers and 2 integrators are used instead of one D. F. G. to produce $\sin\theta$, but the simulation is easier to set up than by use of a variable D. F. G. If both $\sin\theta$ and $\cos\theta$ are needed then the method is rather more efficient.

Practical work

Set up the simulation to solve the pendulum equation using this method and compare the results with those obtained by the methods discussed in §5. 2.

Examples

(1)   Derive computer simulations to generate the following functions using the technique described above:

(a) $\cosh x$ and $\sinh x$

(b) e^{x^2} and xe^{x^2}.

(2)   If x is a function of the independent variable time, show
how to generate
        (a) sin(x + 0.4); and
        (b) $\sqrt{x}$
without using diode function generators. (Assume that $\dot{x}$ is available).

                                 (BCS 1969)

(3)   The variable x is a function of time only. Its derivative
$\dot{x}$ is also available on an analogue computer with the usual complement
of computing devices. Produce unscaled computer diagrams to generate
the following functions:
        (a) cosec(x - 0.7)
        (b) $(x + t)^{1/3}$.

                                 (BCS 1970)

7.3   Avoidance of division by the parametric use of computer time

Division of analogue variables is usually achieved by a special
unit incorporating a multiplier and an operational amplifier. The process
can be difficult to scale and is very prone to error in operation. If a
division unit is to be used to produce $W = \dfrac{U}{V}$ from U and V then in
estimating the maximum value of W account must be taken of the maximum value of the modulus of numerator U and the <u>minimum</u> modulus
value of the denominator V. If allowance is made in the scaling of the
quotient W for the minimum value of V to occur at the same time as
the maximum of U then the scaled process is

$$\left(\frac{W}{W\ max}\right) = \left[\frac{V\ min}{V\ max}\right] \cdot \left(\frac{U}{U\ max}\right) / \left(\frac{V}{V\ max}\right),$$

where $W\ max = \dfrac{U\ max}{V\ min}$.

This is implemented as:

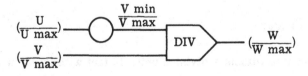

Fig. 7.4

If V min/V max is small then the numerator input to the division unit will be small and, for values of the variable V about V min, the denominator will also be small. In these conditions it can be shown that the errors in the quotient W will be very much greater than the error inherent in the multiplier used in the division unit.   The generation of this type of error, and other aspects of division units, is discussed fully in chapter 12 of Charlesworth and Fletcher's book Systematic Analogue Computer Programming.

In problems involving a number of division operations little can be done to avoid errors introduced by division even if careful scaling has been carried out and the advanced technique 'Variable Amplitude Scaling' sometimes has to be applied. However, in problems involving a single division operation, it is frequently possible to avoid the use of division units by carefully choosing the relationship between the independent computer variable time, τ, and the problem independent variable which is, of course, generally time t. The technique used can enable solutions to problems to be found near singular points, e.g. where $V \to 0$ in the ratio $\frac{U}{V}$. Although division errors are removed, errors due to drift may appear near singularities.

A very simple and obvious situation where division can be avoided is in the solution of the equation

$$\frac{dy}{dx} = \frac{ax + by}{a'x + b'y} .$$ (7. 7)

If computer time τ is used to represent x then

$$\frac{dy}{d\tau} = \frac{a\tau + by}{a'\tau + b'y} .$$ (7. 8)

Simulation of this equation clearly involves use of a division unit. .However, the equation (7. 7) can be replaced by two equations

$$\frac{dy}{d\tau} = k(ax + by)$$

and $$\frac{dx}{d\tau} = k(a'x + b'y)$$ (7. 9)

which can be simulated without a division unit; in fact with linear units only. When solving these equations y is recorded against x. 'τ' is only used as a parameter and the constant k is chosen in order to produce a suitable speed of solution. It is interesting to note that two integrators are needed to solve this 1st order differential equation by this method.

The advantages of the technique are very well illustrated by studying the problem of simulating the equations controlling the motion of a projectile moving in a medium where frictional drag is proportional to the square of speed. This problem presents certain difficulties of formulation if cartesian coordinates are used due to the adjustment in sign needed in the vertical component of friction as the projectile passes through the highest point. An excellent way to avoid this difficulty is to choose as dependent variables the velocity V along the flight path and the angle θ the flight path makes with the horizontal.

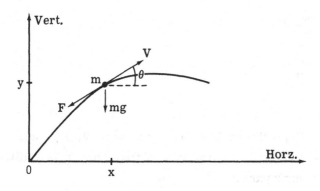

Fig. 7.5

The equations of motion are then:

Acceleration along flight path $\frac{dV}{dt} = -g \sin \theta - kV^2$,
where k is constant

Acceleration perpendicular to
flight path $\qquad\qquad\qquad V\frac{d\theta}{dt} = -g \cos \theta$ (7.10)

Horizontal component of speed $\frac{dx}{dt} = V \cos \theta$

Vertical component of speed $\quad\frac{dy}{dt} = V \sin \theta$

The simulation of the second of these equations involves the use of a

119

division unit as $\frac{d\theta}{dt} = -\frac{g \cos \theta}{V}$. Knowledge of the variation of $\frac{\cos \theta}{V}$ is needed to scale this equation. Unfortunately $\cos \theta \rightarrow$ maximum and $V \rightarrow$ minimum at the top of the flight path so that, if the angle of launch θ_0 is large (~80°) and the particle goes nearly vertically, the ratio $\frac{\cos \theta}{V}$ will become very large. The division process is therefore difficult to scale and error prone. It is impossible to scale as $V \rightarrow 0$ when $\theta_0 = 90°$.

The division operation can be eliminated from this equation if computer time τ is introduced as a parameter, i. e. $\frac{d\theta}{d\tau} = \frac{g \cos \theta}{V} \cdot \frac{dt}{d\tau}$ (7.11) and τ is chosen to satisfy the relationship $\frac{dt}{d\tau} = kV$, where k is a constant. (7.11) then becomes $\frac{d\theta}{d\tau} = -kg \cos \theta$ (7.12) and thus does not include a division operation.

Introducing this substitution makes the other equations only a little more difficult to solve. The complete set are now:

$$\frac{dV}{d\tau} = -(g \sin \theta + V^2)kV$$

$$\frac{d\theta}{d\tau} = -kg \cos \theta$$

$$\frac{dx}{d\tau} = kV^2 \cos \theta \qquad\qquad (7.13)$$

$$\frac{dy}{d\tau} = kV^2 \sin \theta$$

and $\qquad \frac{dt}{d\tau} = kV$

When simulating this problem the variation of V, θ, x and y with t should be recorded. The variation of these with τ is of little interest as τ is only a parameter.

This technique may be regarded as an example of <u>variable time-scaling</u>. Instead of the simple relationship $\tau = \beta t$ (or $d\tau = \beta. dt$) being used to link the computer and problem independent variables, where β is a constant, the relationship used, in the above example, is $d\tau = \frac{dt}{kV}$.

Thus computer time varies both with problem time and velocity. The more slowly the projectile moves ($V \rightarrow 0$) the greater is the amount of computer time needed to simulate one unit of problem time.

The technique should ideally enable the solution of the equations to be determined except for the case when $\theta_0 = 90°$ and V becomes zero at the top of the flight path. In fact, in this case, the solution approaches the singularity increasing slowly and never reaches it. In practice, however, paths very near to the vertical cannot be studied due to drift errors present in the very long computing times involved as V becomes small. Otherwise the technique works very well.

Notes

(1)   In order to spot the substitution needed to remove the division operation it is best to reduce any given set of problem equations to a simple set of first order equations.

(2)   The method does not work if the solution has to start at a singularity. This point is not entirely obvious and the reader is left to consider the 'solution' of Bessel's equation of order zero, i. e.

$x\dfrac{d^2y}{dx^2} + \dfrac{dy}{dx} + xy = 0$, by this technique using $\dfrac{dx}{d\tau} = x$. Everything appears to go well until one tries to get the solution under way; why?

Practical work

Set up the projectile problem for the case $g = 9.8$, $\lambda = 0.01$, and $V_0 = 25$ (all m-sec units) using both methods. Compare the results obtained and, in each case, note carefully the effect of making $\theta_0 \to 90°$.

Examples

(1)   Legendre's polynomial P_n of degree n is defined as the solution of the equation

$$(1 - x^2)\frac{d^2y}{dx^2} - 2x.\frac{dy}{dx} + n(n+1)y = 0 \quad \text{for } 0 \le x \le 1$$

subject to certain boundary conditions:

Degree n	y_0	$(\frac{dy}{dx})_0$
1	0	-1
2	-0.5	0
3	0	+1.5
4	+0.375	0
5	0	-1.875
6	-0.3125	0

(a) Observe the scaling difficulty when $x \to 1$ of simulating the equation as $\dfrac{d^2y}{dx^2} = [2x\dfrac{dy}{dx} - n(n + 1)y]/(1 - x^2)$ with computer time $t = x$.

(b) Derive a simulation in the form $\dfrac{d^2y}{dx^2} = 2x\dfrac{dy}{dx} - n(n+1)y + x^2\dfrac{d^2y}{dx^2}$ again using computer time to represent x. Note carefully the appearance of the highest derivative on both sides of the equation. Consider the effect of $x \to 1$.

(c) Reduce the original equation to a pair of first order equations and using computer time as a parameter derive a simulation for the equation which does not involve use of a division unit. Consider the effect of $x \to 1$.

(d) Obtain solutions in graphical form using each of the above methods for $n = 1$ to 6. Compare accuracy as $x \to 1$. Hints: use 10 seconds of computer time to represent 1 unit of x for methods (a) and (b). Scale $(y/1)$ as $|P_n| \le 1$ for all n. Choose the scaling for $\dfrac{dy}{dx}$ depending on the value of n using the fact that $\dfrac{dy}{dx} \to \dfrac{n(n+1)}{2}$ as x (and hence $y) \to 1$.

(2) The differential equation relating the slope ϕ to the distance x from the centre of a loaded circular plate of radius $r = 10$ cm supported at its rim is

$$\frac{d^2\phi}{dx^2} + \frac{1}{x} \cdot \frac{d\phi}{dx} - \frac{\phi}{x^2} = 0.05x \quad \text{with } \phi = 0 \text{ at } x = 0 \text{ and } x = r.$$

Using computer time t as a parameter show how the equation may be solved on an analogue computer without using any division units. (Try using both $\dfrac{d\tau}{dx} = x$ and $\dfrac{d\tau}{dx} = x^2$.)

Prepare fully scaled computer diagrams for determining the solution of the equation and also for calculating the deflection $w = \int_r^x \phi dx$ at any point on the plate. Assume that $\max|\phi| \le 0.05$, $\max|\dfrac{d\phi}{dx}| \le 0.25$ cm^{-1} and $\max|w| \le 0.25$ cm.

(3) The length of path followed by a satellite moving in an elliptic orbit with the earth at one of the focal points is given by

$$s = \frac{1}{c} \int_{\theta_1}^{\theta_2} \frac{\sqrt{(1 + 2e\cos\theta + e^2)}}{(1 + e\cos\theta)^2} \cdot d\theta ,$$

where c is a constant, $e \le 1$ is the eccentricity of the ellipse and θ_1 and θ_2 are angular points on the orbit. Derive a fully scaled computer simulation, not involving any division circuits, which will enable the value of s to be calculated for the case when $c = 1$, $\theta_1 = 0$ and θ_2 is any value between 0 and π. Explain what will happen if $e = 1$ and $\theta = \pi$.

7.4   Function generation by high-speed subroutine

The provision of individually controlled integrators, mode and timescale, in modern high-speed computers enables separate parts of the machine to be operated at different speeds. This multi-speed facility is useful in a range of problems, e.g. simulation of predictive control systems, evaluation of double integrals and function generation.

When used to generate functions by high-speed subroutines, the technique enables non-linear functions to be generated by high precision commonly available linear units. In many cases functions can be generated using less equipment than by use of more conventional D. F. G. units and with similar accuracy. The functions are generated as step stair approximations to the required function and the function value is updated at irregular intervals. The basic technique is illustrated below, applied to generating a function of three dependent computer variables:

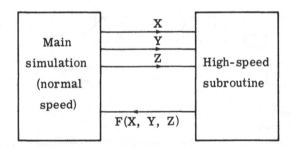

Fig. 7.6

Variables X, Y, Z are sampled from the main simulation and $F(X, Y, Z)$ evaluated rapidly in the subroutine by solving (linear) differential equations. The new function value is applied to the main simulation and new values of X, Y, Z are sampled, etc. The frequency of the sampling depends on the time taken to evaluate the function. This in turn depends on the magnitudes of the input variables. To provide an accuracy equivalent to that obtained by D. F. G. s it is arranged that about 100 evaluations are made in 'one cycle' of the input variables. This is normally achieved if the integrator gains (and hence the rate of integration) in the subroutine are made 100-1000 times as large as those in the main simulation.

Example 1

The general technique for one variable can be most simply illustrated with reference to the function $y = e^{-kx}$, where x is a dependent variable and k a positive constant. The function $e^{-k\tau}$ is generated repeatedly at high speed using a single integrator, the period of integration continuing until a variable proportional to time τ in the subroutine reaches the value x input from the main simulation. When this occurs the value of $e^{-k\tau}$, which is now e^{-kx}, is sampled and applied back to the main simulation. The integrator is reset to its initial value and the generation of $e^{-k\tau}$ recommenced. The diagram below shows the essential components:

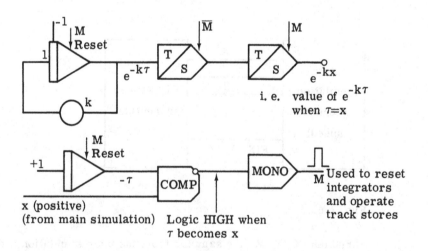

Fig. 7. 7

124

The integrators are operated in high-speed mode (time constant
~1 millisec) and the integration period is terminated when τ becomes
x by means of a comparator and monostable, i.e. when τ becomes x
the comparator output goes HIGH which causes the monostable to produce
a narrow pulse (~.05 msec) sufficiently long to enable the integrators to
be reset to their initial conditions. A bucket brigade circuit is used to
sample the last value of $e^{-k\tau}$, i.e. e^{-kx} in the integration period. The
operation can also be understood by reference to the following timing
diagrams.

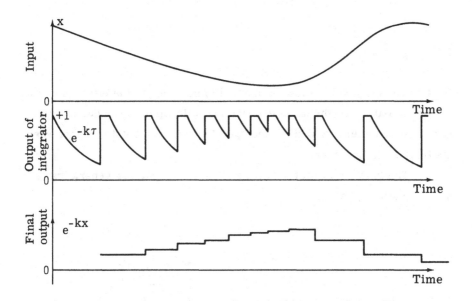

Fig. 7.8

An important feature of the method applied to this function is that
the larger the value of x, the smaller is the value of e^{-kx} and the larger
is the integration time to evaluate e^{-kx}. Thus when the function is small
(i.e. x large) it is evaluated less frequently than when it is large. This
minimises the effect of sampling error, for when the function is small it
will have a relatively minor effect in the total simulation and consequently
it does not need to be updated frequently.

Example 2

Although it would appear that the function $y = Ae^{kx}$, $k > 0$, should be generated using an integrator-inverter loop

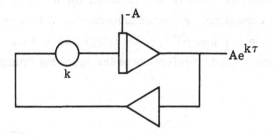

Fig. 7.9

in the high-speed subroutine the method is poor due to the effect of errors for two reasons: (i) the usual exponential build-up of error due to any initial condition error, and (ii) the updating would be least frequent when the function is maximum.

The function is best produced using the circuit for generating e^{-kx} modified slightly, viz.

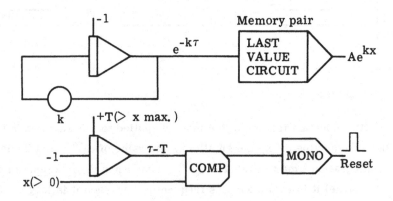

Fig. 7.10

The integration period is terminated when

$\tau - T + x$ becomes 0,

i. e. when τ becomes $T - x$.
The last value of $e^{-k\tau}$ is, therefore,

$$e^{-k(T-x)} = e^{-kT} \cdot e^{kx}$$
$$= \text{Constant.} \, e^{kx}.$$

The examples considered above appear to provide an alternative
method for generating functions, which is rather inefficient in the use of
hardware (even if easier than setting up a variable D. F. G.). The usefulness of the technique becomes apparent when it is realised that the
I. C. s of the integrators may also be variables derived from the main
simulation. For example, if $-y$ instead of -1 is input to the integrator
producing $e^{-k\tau}$ (in the circuit for e^{-kx}), the output from this integrator
would be $ye^{-k\tau}$ and the last value ye^{-kx}. Thus multiplication with respect to a further variable could be combined with the function generation
at no increase in complexity. One of the most efficient circuits in terms
of use of units is:

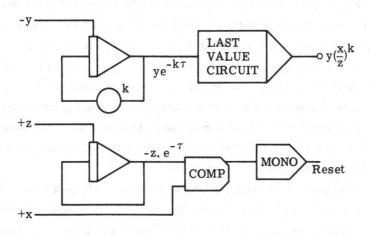

Fig. 7.11

The integration period is terminated when $-ze^{-\tau} + x$ becomes 0, i. e. when $e^{-\tau} = \frac{x}{z}$. The last value is, therefore, the value of $ye^{-k\tau} = y(e^{-\tau})^k$ when $e^{-\tau} = \frac{x}{z}$. This value is, therefore, $y \cdot (\frac{x}{z})^k$.

Thus x can be divided by z, the quotient raised to any power and multiplied by y using only 4 amplifier units.

The range of functions that may be generated in this way by high-speed subroutines using linear units include $\sin\theta$, $\cos\theta$, $e^{-k\theta}$, $\sin\theta$, $\arcsin x$, $R\cos\theta$, $\sqrt{(1-x^2)}$ and the functions needed for axes rotation and polar to cartesian conversion. Some ingenuity is often needed to determine how (if possible) to generate any given function. Clearly if a function $f(t)$ can be made the solution of a constant coefficient linear differential equation in the independent variable time t then the corresponding function $f(x)$ of a dependent variable may be generated by subroutine. Thus functions as complex as $x^2 e^{-kx} \cos wx$ can be generated this way using linear units only. In addition, if a graph of a function can be obtained using linear units only, then it can also be generated by high-speed subroutine. For example, as a graph of arccos x can be produced by generating t and $\cos t$ and recording t <u>against</u> $\cos t$ then arccos x may be generated by this subroutine method. This is achieved by generating $\cos\tau$ and τ repetitively at high speed, terminating the integration period when $\cos\tau$ equals x and sampling the value of τ.

In practice simulations are not generally difficult to scale but in use they may be prone to failure if the value of an input variable is such that the integration period required is zero. This is caused by the slight uncertainty in the value at which the comparator used to terminate the compute period operates. For example, when generating e^{-kx} if $x = 0$ the comparator can be in either of its states in the reset period when $\tau = 0$. Thus repetitive control can be lost. This defect can be overcome by introducing a very small bias into the comparator or perhaps more simply by selecting another comparator.

When generating functions by this technique it is best to arrange that the subroutines are operating in the initial condition mode as well as in the compute mode in order that their accuracy can be checked prior to the computation proper.

Practical work.   Rotation of an elliptic trace.

Analyse fully the sine-cosine loop:

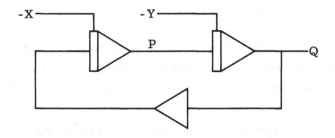

Fig. 7.12

Include the above loop in a high-speed subroutine to perform the axes rotations

$$x^1 = x \cos \theta - y \sin \theta$$
$$y^1 = x \sin \theta + y \cos \theta$$

from variables x, y and θ.   This should involve use of 3 integrators, 1 inverter, 1 comparator, 2 memory pairs plus logic units.   Note the efficiency of this technique when compared to use of D. F. G. s and multipliers.

Generate, at normal speed, an elliptic trace by producing $x = \sin t$ and $y = 0.5 \cos t$ (parametric form for an ellipse) using two integrators and an inverter.   Input x, y together with a value of θ set by a potentiometer to the subroutine and observe its operation by displaying P, Q etc. against (high-speed) time τ.

Display y^1 against x^1 and note the elliptic trace in sampled form.   Vary θ.   Increase the frequency of the ellipse (x, y) by increasing the integrator gains by a factor of 10 and note the resulting display (x^1, y^1).

Examples

(1)   Using linear equipment only derive simulations which will enable graphs of the following functions to be obtained.

(a) $\arcsin x$ and $\arccos x$ for $0 \le x \le 1$

(b) $\sqrt{(1 - x^2)}$ for $0 \le x \le 1$

(c) $x^2 e^{-x}$ for $0 \le x \le 5$.

Show how to generate the above functions of a dependent variable x in a high-speed subroutine.

(2) Derive a high-speed subroutine to perform polar to cartesian coordinate transformations, i.e. to compute $x = R \cos \theta$ and $y = R \sin \theta$ from R and θ. Assume $R \le 1$ and $0 < \theta \le 4\pi$. Generate a linear spiral defined in polar coordinates as $R = c\theta$ (e.g. make $\theta \propto t$ and hence $R \propto t$) at normal speed and obtain a graph of the spiral using an X-Y plotter for various values of c in the range $[\frac{1}{4\pi}, \frac{2}{\pi}]$. Generate and record other spiral shapes (e.g. $R = ce^{\theta}$) by this method.

(3) A further application of multispeed computation is in the evaluation of double integrals. Use the idea of a subroutine to evaluate the integral $\int_0^1 \int_0^1 e^{-xy} dx.\, dy$. [Hint: Express the integral as $\int_0^1 [\int_0^1 e^{-\tau t} d\tau] dt$ where, in the implementation, τ is used as high-speed (subroutine) time and t as normal time.]

8 · Digital Simulation

8.1 Introduction

In these notes the phrase 'Digital Simulation Language' will mean a high-level digital computer language specially written to solve ordinary differential equations. Such languages are called 'Continuous Dynamic System Simulation Languages' in order to distinguish them from languages used to simulate systems involving discrete events. Continuous Dynamic System Simulation Languages are not, of course, just applicable to dynamic system problems but can be used to solve any problems involving the solution of ordinary differential equations, e. g. the static deflection characteristic of a beam.

Ever since the early days of electronic digital computers, considerable effort has been made to develop general purpose, easy to use languages to help users study problems involving the solution of differential equations. Some of the reasons for this activity are:

(i) Very many problems in engineering, etc. , require the solution of differential equations which cannot be solved easily or at all by analytical means.

(ii) Direct numerical techniques for solving such equations by processes involving a 'manageable' amount of arithmetic are complicated and normally require extensive knowledge of numerical analysis. However, it has long been realised that reduction to a sequence of much simpler processes can often be made, though, before the advent of computers, the arithmetic involved was prohibitive in magnitude. Much of the use of computers in scientific and engineering practice has been, particularly in the early days, concerned with carrying out these large calculations hitherto shelved as impracticable.

(iii) Numerical solutions of differential equations are often required to form independent checks of solutions obtained using analogue/ hybrid methods. These numerical solutions, as well as providing dynamic checks, are also sometimes used to aid scaling by providing useful information on the maximum values of variables.

It is interesting to note the circle of events which have occurred. The prime purpose of the infinitesimal calculus introduced by Newton and Leibnitz, and eagerly used by people such as the family Bernoulli, was to find shortcut analytical solutions to some of the problems of mathematics, astronomy and physics which had previously been expressed in terms of difference equations constraining finite increments. Accurate solutions in terms of sufficiently small increments were impracticable. But such analytical solution only works in a finite few of the infinitely many situations which can arise in physical problems. Now we are returning to the much more generally applicable solution of difference equations using finite increments with a powerful tool to see us through the large amount of arithmetic calculation involved. In essence, digital simulation involves these large discrete calculations using finite increments; analogue computation simulates the continuous integration of differential equations without the constraint, of course, of having to find a mathematically analytical solution.

A prime requirement of any digital simulation language is that it must be easy to use as it is likely to be used by application engineers, etc., rather than by specialised computer programmers. Preferably the instructions of the language should, wherever possible, be standard instructions from a general high level language such as FORTRAN or BASIC.

Two types of languages have been developed, block form and expression based. In both types, each program of instructions used for a simulation study consists of two major sections, one section being used to specify or to represent the model and the other to specify the solutions required, i.e. what values of constants and parameters should be used, what variables should be output, the output data format (tables/graphs), etc.

Block form languages require the user to prepare a block diagram to represent the system concerned, much as he would do for study by analogue means, and to supply to the computer a set of 'patching' instructions specifying how these blocks should be interconnected. The blocks

132

themselves play similar roles to those played by analogue units, i.e. integration, summation, function generation, etc., and the programmer inputs 'connecting' instructions such as:

INTG2 INTG1 CONS7 CONS4

which means that integrator 2 must have an initial output equal to constant 4 and one of its inputs must be joined to the output of integrator 1 and another to constant 7.

With expression based languages the user inputs the model equations themselves. These equations can be differential or algebraic, e.g.

$$DER(X) = Y - Z*EXP(X)$$
$$Y = X + 2$$

Whichever form is used to represent the computer model, the digital computer solves the equations by performing a sequence of arithmetical and logical operations on the variables, etc. of the model. In order to solve differential equations many of these operations will be associated with numerical procedures to perform integration. For example, if the simple 1st order equation

$$\frac{dy}{dt} = f(t) \quad \text{with } y = 0 \text{ at } t = 0$$

needs to be solved to give y as a function of t then this can be done by evaluating the integral

$$y(t) = \int_0^t f(t) . dt$$

for various values of t in the range required. For any given value T of t, this integral may be evaluated approximately by any of a whole range of numerical procedures for evaluating integrals by, effectively, finding the area under the curve f(t) against t from t = 0 to t = T (Fig. 8.1).

The methods essentially require that the integrand function f(t) is evaluated for very many values of t between 0 and T and some type of summation performed on the values obtained. Whichever numerical procedure is followed, the accuracy of the estimate improves as the average size of the interval or step, Δt, used between successive evaluations of the function decreases.

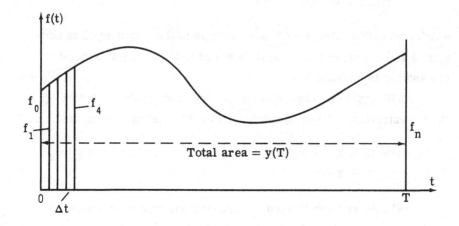

Fig. 8.1 Evaluation of integral

A powerful and accurate variation of this procedure, known as Gaussian Quadrature, applies the discrete summation to another approximating function g(t) which is chosen in such a manner that error in overestimation of area under some sections of the curve f(t) are accurately compensated by underestimation in others. Better accuracy with many fewer discrete points can often be achieved.

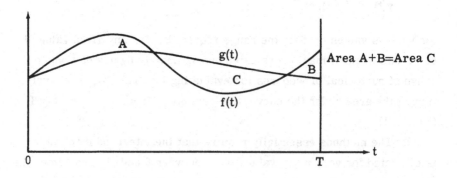

Fig. 8.2

Although digital computers can perform arithmetical and logical operations very rapidly (e. g. addition time ~1 μ sec), the enormous number of operations required to perform numerical integration makes the process relatively slow. This is particularly so if the integrand function f(t) is complicated and its evaluation involves a large number of multiplication and/or division operations. Thus solution rates for problems involving differential equations are relatively slow: sets of differential equations involving perhaps 10 integrations (e. g. 5 simultaneous equations each of order 2) may take many seconds to solve even when using modern fast digital machines.

Much effort has been devoted to producing efficient (fast) numerical procedures (like Gaussian Quadrature) for function integration and step by step integration of differential equations (such as Runge-Kutta), and also procedures which will not fail and cause excessive error if presented with certain types of 'difficult' functions. As a result there are many methods to be found in the literature (e. g. ref. 13) some relying on a fixed step or interval size and some in which this step size is automatically adjusted to meet certain error conditions at each step. One must note, however, that, with a sacrifice of speed, the accuracy can always be made to surpass the accuracy with which analogue solutions can be measured (see (ii) below). Specific methods may fail with certain types of problems and it is always wise to check simulation results using different integration formulae or, at least, using different step sizes or different error size specifications. (Some simulation languages allow the user to select which of a number of integration procedures to use.)

8. 2   Comparison of digital and analogue/hybrid simulation

(i)   The relatively slow speed of solution of differential equations compared with that achieved by analogue machines is the major, and perhaps now the only, disadvantage of using digital simulation for the solution of differential equation problems. This speed differential is at least a factor of 100 even when solving small problems. As the size of the computer model increases the difference increases even more as the digital takes longer to solve the equations, whereas the analogue solution time remains the same - the number of units used increases instead. It

135

must be emphasised at this stage that the above comparison is between the rates at which the equations are solved and not between total problem solution times.

(ii)   In principle, using digital simulation techniques, differential equation problems can be solved to any degree of accuracy by using sufficiently small step lengths. However, use of excessively short step lengths increases the time and hence the cost of computation. Thus, in practice, errors in solution are often comparable with those generated in analogue/hybrid simulation studies.

(iii)   High speed of solution combined with manual adjustment of controls to give excellent man/machine interaction has always been considered the most attractive feature of analogue computing. This interaction enables users to 'feel' the behaviour of the system modelled in the computer. In contrast, most digital simulation studies have to be carried out with the digital computing system operating in batch mode and consequently interaction between user and computer model is very poor. Users are likely to get only a few separate runs per day so that the amount of 'manual' parameter adjustment possible even in a week is likely to be very small. It is for this reason that the authors of these notes consider batch run digital simulation to be of very little value within a teaching, as opposed to research, environment. Batch mode can, for example, provide a valuable, refined and highly accurate production run of a solution when an approximation has been obtained using interactive techniques.

With the advent of fast digital machines equipped with fast alpha numeric/graphical displays, great progress has been made over the last few years in on-line/interactive digital simulation. Interactive simulation languages are available for block form (e. g. I. B. M. 1130. CSMP) and expression based (e. g. Bradford extension of BASIC) studies. Solution times for small problems are sufficiently short (a few seconds) to provide meaningful interaction between user and computer model, and even iterative techniques involving automatic adjustment of parameters between runs can be used.

(iv)   When studying problems using digital simulation, block form or expression based, scaling of variables and equations is not needed.

This cuts out a tedious, but not difficult, step in the process of getting a simulation of a problem to work and thus lessens the barrier between problem and machine. In fact, when using expression based simulation there is almost no hurdle to cross between problem equations and computer simulation - the hardest part of many simulation studies is the difficulty encountered in forming an adequate set of model equations to represent the problem. This reduction in the barrier between problem and computer set-up enables the user to concentrate more on the main purpose of using simulation (i. e. experimenting with the computer model) and less on the actual technique itself. Users are naturally more inclined to test the effect of making changes to the model - not just parameter changes - as these can be included very easily by changing or extending the instructions specifying the computer model.

The reader should be warned that, in removing from him the tedium of scaling, some difficulties such as function singularity or integration instability may be masked. At a lower level the provision of floating point hardware and the removal from the user of the hardship of fixed point scaling in most modern digital computers is a further lure to him to forget to devise checks on the meaningfulness of his results.

(v)   Complicated non-linear characteristics can be very easily included in digital computer models whereas generation of such characteristics may require special, expensive (and perhaps little used) analogue hardware.

(vi)   Digital simulations are generally much easier to debug than analogue computer simulations. This is mainly because of the inherent sequential and discrete nature of digital computer operations and the parallel and continuous nature of the analogue machine. It is very difficult to debug a problem where 'everything' is happening at once in parallel, whereas it is generally less difficult to debug a sequential problem in which the trouble can be identified down to a few instructions in a program. Often software is provided to help 'trace' a few such instructions during execution.

In addition, analogue units have a nasty habit of partially failing, i. e. they appear to work but are out of specification, perhaps only over

137

a limited range of output values. On the other hand, if a digital unit fails it is generally a total failure and the error is much easier to detect. Digital logic signals do sometimes 'blink' but generally they are either present and correct or completely absent. This again emphasises the discrete and continuous nature of the two processes.

(vii) Partly because of (iv) and (vi) above and with software compilation as well as run time diagnostics often provided, problem preparation and check out is generally much easier using digital techniques. Thus the total time of problem solution (and consequent effect on cost) may well be less using digital simulation than when using faster analogue/ hybrid computers, particularly if relatively few solutions are required, i. e. if little parameter adjustment is involved.

(viii) Digital computers are general-purpose devices. When not used for simulation studies they can be used for any of a large variety of computational tasks. In contrast analogue computers are very special purpose and can be used in relatively few applications, though an increasing use of process control and other on-line techniques is broadening the range of applications involving analogue hardware.

(ix) The size of a problem that can be simulated is not affected by the size of the digital machine in the same way as the maximum size of the analogue model is constrained by the number (and type) of units available. Size is affected by the amount of fast storage available but even fairly small digital machines (16K core) can be programmed to simulate large (e. g. 100 analogue amplifier) problems.

(x) Digital simulation batch run does not require any 'hands on' skill on behalf of users. Programs and data are prepared when convenient, programs run under operator control and results output for collection when ready. Jobs can be retained in a convenient form (punched cards, paper-tape, magnetic tape) for use again and paperwork records of work done can be very extensive. All these features of a service computing centre are good reasons for favouring use of digital simulation instead of conventional analogue computing. However, this comment is only partially true when comparing digital simulation with simulations run on a full hybrid computer containing a general-purpose digital machine.

Thus the only major advantage of analogue/hybrid techniques over digital simulation is that of speed with its consequent effect on interaction and costs when solving large problems involving many computer runs. Attempts are being made to lessen even this advantage by using digital computers containing a number of central processors operating in parallel.

There are, of course, a number of other advantages in favour of using hybrid computers instead of digital simulation both at research and teaching level. For example, a hybrid computer is a very natural medium for studies into the behaviour of hybrid systems, e. g. the digital computer control of a chemical plant. In the teaching environment an important factor is the comparatively small cost of analogue/hybrid tutors. Many such machines can be bought for the price of a digital system able only to provide single user interactive digital simulation. Analogue/hybrid tutors also provide an excellent way of introducing the use of operational amplifiers and A/D and D/A interface to students of many disciplines engaged in control and instrumentation, particularly relating to connecting instruments, etc. to digital computers.

The rest of this chapter briefly describes use of block form batch run simulation languages and, in more detail, use of a special on-line expression based language developed at Bradford for teaching purposes.

8. 3   Block form languages

With block form languages, the user must first convert the equations of the system under study into an analogue computer-like block diagram (unscaled). The major difference at this stage is that digital simulation operations do not involve sign reversals (unless specifically programmed), a feature of analogue amplifier units caused by the use of negative feedback. Thus in preparing the problem equations for digital simulation, the reduced equation for each operation (integration, summation, etc.) should be written without a negative sign being included on the L. H. S. Thus for the problem of the projectile considered at length in §3. 6 and §5. 4 the equation of motion

$$\ddot{y} = -g - k\dot{y}|\dot{y}|$$

should be expressed as

$$\frac{dV}{dt} = -g - kV|V|$$
$$\frac{dy}{dt} = V$$

for which the block diagram in Fig. 8.3 is derived.

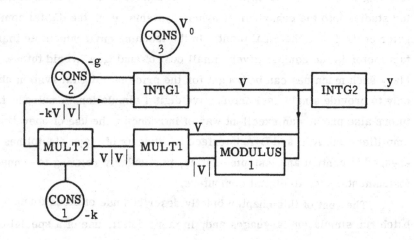

Fig. 8.3 Block diagram simulation of projectile problem

It should be noted that units for multiplying variables by constant values, i.e. 'pots', are not distinguished from units used for multiplying two variables together.

The computer instructions specifying the above model take the form of a set of patching instructions of the form:

PATCH DATA

MODS1	INTG1		
MULT1	INTG1	MODS1	
MULT2	MULT1	CONS1	
INTG1	MULT2	CONS2	CONS3
INTG2	INTG1		

where the first data element in each line is the name of the unit and the

140

other items refer to the names of units connected <u>into</u> it. CONS3 is used to specify the initial output of INTG1, i. e. the initial value of V. No I. C. constant is needed for INTG2 as the initial value of y is zero.

With some languages it is necessary to input the patch data instructions in a strict computational order because at each step the calculations are performed in the order of these instructions. Thus it is necessary to ensure that all inputs to a particular block have already been evaluated, otherwise it will not be possible to calculate the output of the block itself. Thus the order

SUMR1	MULT3	CONS5
MULT3	CONS7	INTG2

will be invalid as the value of the output of MULT3 would not have been calculated when the former of these patching instructions was reached. However, with other languages the order of the instructions is not important as the implementation sorts the instructions into a suitable order for calculation purposes.

Besides the set of model representation patching instructions, instructions are also needed to specify the values of the constants used, the results to be output, the format to be used, etc. A typical set of instructions for this problem might be:

CONSTANTS

-. 98	-0. 01	+100
RUN 5	. 1	

TABULATE

INTG1	INTG2

FINISH

These instructions will cause values of -. 01, -9. 8, +100 to be assigned to constants, -k, -g and the initial value of V and values of V and y to be tabulated against the independent variable (time) for values of the independent variable between 0 and 5 at intervals of 0. 1.

The above example illustrates how easy it is to program using this type of language. The amount of preparation needed is minimal compared

with that needed for the study by analogue means. However, languages
of this kind have limited value because of the need to form a block diagram representation. Thus their use is limited to two major groups of
people:

(a) Those who naturally use symbolic 'analogue like' diagrams
to represent the system they are studying without, necessarily, forming
model equations. This particularly applies to control engineers who often
specify systems in terms of a number of simple blocks each of which can
be represented by a single analogue or digital simulation block. Often in
languages of this type many blocks are available to simulate not only
integrators, summers, multipliers and other standard analogue units,
but also to simulate limiting, deadspace (hysteresis) and even transfer
functions.

(b) Those engaged in analogue/hybrid studies who wish to use
digital simulation to provide dynamic check information for the analogue
model. Not all simulation languages are suitable directly for this type of
check. At Bradford a modified version of the language briefly described
above has been developed to give greater correspondence between the
analogue model and the digital simulation block diagram. Sign reversal
is included in integrators, etc. , and, by use of scaled variables, results
can be directly related to analogue computer solutions.

8. 4   Expression based languages

In expression based languages the instructions used to specify the
computer model are the model equations of the system itself written in a
form acceptable as computer input. Thus, for the projectile problem
discussed earlier, the model equations

$$\ddot{y} = \frac{dV}{dt} = -g - kV|V|$$
$$\frac{dy}{dt} = V$$

will be input in the following, or a similar, form

DER(V) = -G - K*V*ABS(V)
DER(Y) = V

142

where DER represents a first order derivative.

Many languages can accept high order equations written directly, i. e. the model equations do not have to be in reduced form. Thus the equations of the example above could be input as

DER2(Y) = -G - K*V*ABS(V)

and the beam equation $EI \cdot \dfrac{d^4y}{dx^4} = W$ input as

DER4(Y) = W/(E*I)

Both algebraic and differential equations may be used to represent the model and thus the projectile problem equations could be input as

A = -G - K*V*ABS(V)
DER2(Y) = A

where A is used to represent acceleration.

A wide variety of standard functions available in high level languages, e. g. COS(X), EXP(X), etc. and special user-defined functions may be included in the equations for the model. The total set of equations used to specify the model are known as the Representation Set.

As with block form languages, some expression based languages require that the equations are input in a correct order for calculation purposes whilst others sort the equations into a suitable order.

Besides the Representation Set other instructions are needed to specify constants and initial values and to control the simulation study, i. e. what runs are made, what results output, etc.

At Bradford there are available a number of expression based batch run languages of various degrees of sophistication. There is also an on-line interactive language available, specially developed for teaching but also useful at a research level, which runs at a sufficiently high speed for manual interaction to be meaningful. This language is implemented in single user form on an 8K core, 16 bit word length, small, fast (~1 μ sec cycle time) computer. For multi-users a larger machine is required (16K core and DISC for 8 users). Communication is either via a teletype terminal if printed output is acceptable, or via a keyboard-input alpha-numeric graphic-display terminal based on a storage oscillo-scope if graphical output is also required. Solution speed is sufficiently fast for small problems (up to about 6 integrators) to be solved at a rate comparable to that obtained when using an analogue machine in normal seconds timescale. Unlike the situation in analogue computing, repetitive operation is not normally used or required as solutions are output and stored on the display terminal. Iterative operation is possible although slow if very many solutions of the equations are involved.

The language itself is called BEDSOCS (Bradford EDucational Simulation language fOr Continuous Systems) and is an extension of the widely used interpretive language BASIC and contains BASIC as a subset. [†] BASIC was chosen for the simulation language mainly because it is so widely available and is the language used at Bradford to introduce many students to computing. Its interactive nature makes it very suitable as the basis for on-line simulation studies. It is both easy to learn and use with a small set of instructions, but has many useful and powerful features. The equations defining the model are sorted by BEDSOCS into a suitable order but differential equations can only be input in their reduced form, i. e. as 1st order derivative equations. This restriction is not considered important. In fact, it is very useful in that it persuades users to prepare models as sets of simple algebraic and first order derivative equations, a form most suitable whatever type of simulation tool is used for their solution.

At present the only integration routine used is the 4th order variable step length Runge-Kutta-Merson technique.

Space does not allow a full description to be given of the language. Instead the more important features are described and applied to a variety of simple problems. Many of these problems are ones discussed else-where in this text and so a direct comparison can be made of the techniques of analogue and digital simulation.

---

† Readers not familiar with BASIC (or another high level language) are advised to study the simpler sections of BASIC as presented in a standard computer manufacturers' handbook or as in ref. 10.

8.5 BEDSOCS. An example

A BEDSOCS program to solve the vertical projectile problem discussed in §8.3 and to display the solutions for velocity V and height y against time is:

```
 10  LET G=9.8          CONSTANTS
 20  LET K=1.00000E-02
 30  LET Y=0            INITIAL VALUE OF VARIABLES
 40  LET V=50
100  DYNAMIC
150    EQUATIONS
160      DER V=-G-K*V*ABS(V)  MODEL EQUATIONS
170      DER Y=V              REPRESENTATION SET
180      DISPLAY V/100,Y/100
200    EQUEND
300  DYNEND
```

It is seen to contain standard BASIC numbered statements together with special statements used to define the model, display the solution, etc. (unlike BASIC an END statement is not required). The 'DYNAMIC' and 'DYNEND' statements enclose a region of the program called the Dynamic Region. Within this region the 'EQUATIONS' and 'EQUEND' statements enclose the Equations Section. The Equations Section contains the model equations which are written in Representation Units. 'DER' is a representation unit which represents a first order differential.

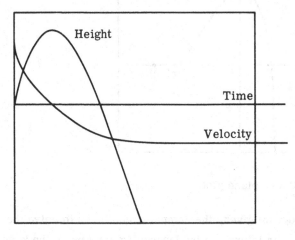

Fig. 8.4   Height and velocity against time

It should be noted that spaces do not matter when the program is input to the computer; the format is automatically 'tidied up' into the form shown when a listing of a program is requested (by typing the standard BASIC directive LIST).

The program is run by typing the standard BASIC directive RUN and the solutions obtained are shown in Fig. 8.4.

The vertical scaling of the graphical output is determined by the factors '100' and '100' introduced into the DISPLAY statement. The horizontal range corresponds to 20 units of the independent variable. Had a phase plane plot of V/100 against Y/100 been required, the display statement

      180   **DISPLAY** V/100; Y/100

should have been used instead of the statement

      180   **DISPLAY** V/100, Y/100

and the following computer output obtained:

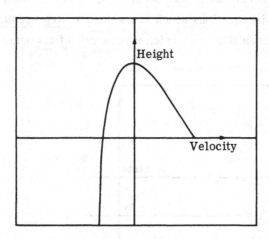

Fig. 8.5   Phase plane plot

With the program given, the computer continues to solve the equations until the user interrupts by depressing any key on the keyboard

146

terminal. When this occurs the computer outputs the statement number of the instruction being obeyed when the interrupt occurred and then outputs the usual BASIC command READY. Changes can then be made or the problem re-run.

The example illustrates the simplicity of the technique when compared with analogue computing. The number of instructions (statements and directives) needed is very small. With this example the number could be further reduced by including the constants G and K in the first model equation, i.e.

160   DER V=-9.8-0.01*V*ABS(V)

Although the number of instructions needed to perform a simulation study can often be made very small, generally users will include many more instructions than are strictly necessary in order to make the program both flexible in use and easy to understand, particularly in relation to the output data obtained. Thus the user would generally arrange that parameters (e.g. speed of launch) would be input at run time and printed results suitably headed. Thus, for this problem, the program used to produce tabulated results might be:

```
  5    REM. VERTICAL PROJECTILE PROBLEM.
 10    LET G=9.8                                    CONSTANTS
 20    LET K=1.00000E-02
 30    LET Y=0                                      INITIAL HEIGHT
 40    PRINT 'VELOCITY OF LAUNCH. METRES/SEC?'
 50    INPUT V                                      INITIAL SPEED
 60    LET T=0                                      INITIAL VALUE
 70    PRINT 'TIME', 'SPEED', 'HEIGHT'                 OF TIME
 80    PRINT 'SECS', 'METRES/SEC', 'METRES'
100    DYNAMIC
120      PRINT T, V, Y
150      EQUATIONS
155        INDVAR T
160        DER V=-G-K*V*ABS(V)
170        DER Y=V
200      EQUEND
300    DYNEND
```

The output obtained from running this program is as follows:

```
RUN
VELOCITY OF LAUNCH. METRES/SEC?
?50
```

TIME SECS	SPEED METRES/SEC	HEIGHT METRES
0	50	0
1	26. 2811	36. 6875
2	12. 6975	55. 7438
3	2. 26663	63. 0975
4	-7. 39557	60. 4869
5	-15. 7587	48. 7468
6	-21. 9074	29. 7212
7	-25. 9032	5. 65709
8	-28. 296	-21. 5503
9		

Note that in the above program the PRINT statement (120) to output the results is included within the Dynamic Region, but outside the Equations Section. Also a name T (time) is assigned to the independent variable by use of the INDVAR T statement placed in the Equation Section. Once defined in this way, the variable may be used in other parts of the program. For example, the user may want the program to run only for a specified time. Inclusion of a simple test and jump instruction involving the variable T placed after the EQUEND but before the DYNEND would enable the computation time to be restricted. Thus if in the above program an instruction

    250   IF T > 8 THEN 40

is included the equations will be solved until T > 8 and then control returned to statement 40 so that another run of the problem could be made.

The language contains many useful features to aid problem solution. However, before describing these it is valuable to consider the structure and operation of a BEDSOCS program.

8.6   Structure and operation of a BEDSOCS program

The structure of a BEDSOCS program is:

⟨BASIC Statements⟩		Part 1 of the Control Region (the Initial Region)
⟨Stmt. No.⟩DYNAMIC		
⟨BASIC Statements⟩	Procedural Part 1 of the Dynamic Region	
⟨Stmt. No.⟩EQUATIONS		
⟨Representation Set⟩	The Equations Section (contains the equations describing the system under study).	The Dynamic Region
⟨Stmt. No.⟩EQUEND		
⟨BASIC Statements⟩	Procedural Part 2 of the Dynamic Region	
⟨Stmt. No.⟩ DYNEND		
⟨ BASIC Statements⟩		Part 2 of the Control Region (the Terminal Region)

where:

⟨ BASIC Statements⟩   can be empty, or can consist of as many BASIC Statements as required, (each statement preceded by a statement number).

⟨ Stmt. No.⟩   is a statement number (an integer from 1 to 9999)

The flow chart (Fig. 8.6) outlines briefly the essential sequence of operation of a BEDSOCS program.

On typing the command RUN, the computer starts by obeying in sequence the BASIC statements in the INITIAL region of the program. The computer then enters the DYNAMIC region, obeys various BASIC statements and enters the EQUATIONS region. Once in this region, the computer solves the REPRESENTATION SET of equations by numerical integration and outputs results to the display at appropriate times throughout the integration period. Results are also communicated to the DYNAMIC region at regular COMMUNICATION points (so that they can be printed, etc.), i.e. at each COMMUNICATION point the computer leaves the EQUATIONS section and enters the DYNAMIC region where it obeys BASIC instructions (Part 2 of the DYNAMIC region) before returning to the start of the DYNAMIC region for the next stage in the solution of the equations. The computer continues to obey this loop of instructions until some statement causes it to jump out of the loop or until an interrupt is caused by

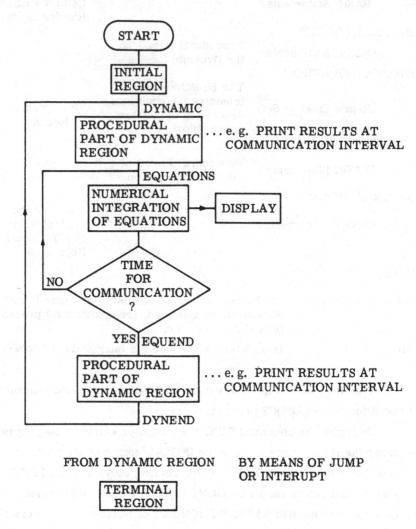

Fig. 8.6   Operation of a BEDSOCS program

depressing any key on the keyboard control. The essential point is that
the equations are solved in the EQUATIONS section and results transmitted to the DYNAMIC region for specific values of the independent
variable separated by the COMMUNICATION INTERVAL.

150

8.7 Control variables

Normal BASIC variables can be used throughout the program. However, in addition to these variables, BEDSOCS contains further variables to control the integration process, display, etc. Each of these variables, written ℂN, where N is an integer, has a prescribed default value assumed by the program unless specified otherwise. The following are two of the simpler of these control variables.

ℂ0. Communication interval

This variable enables the user to specify the interval in the independent variable at which results are transmitted from the EQUATIONS section to the DYNAMIC region. It has a default value of 1 and so results are normally updated every unit in the independent variable. Thus the program:

```
50    LET Y=10
90    LET ℂ0=0.2
100   DYNAMIC
150     PRINT Y
200     EQUATIONS
250     DER Y=-2*Y
300     EQUEND
400   DYNEND
```

would cause the values of Y to be printed at intervals of 0.2 in the independent variable. Without statement 90 the results would be printed out at intervals of 1.

ℂ1. Maximum value of independent variable for display

This variable enables the user to control the range of the independent variable over which results are displayed. It has a default value of 20 so that <u>for the display</u> the independent variable varies from 0 to 20. The control variable affects the scaling of the display but otherwise does not affect the problem. It does not determine the range of variation in the problem independent variable, i. e. the 'compute period'.

The following program illustrates the use of the ℂ1 control variable:

```
50    LET Y=10
80    LET C1=0.8
100   DYNAMIC
200     EQUATIONS
250     DER Y=-2*Y
260     DISPLAY Y/10
300     EQUEND
400   DYNEND
```

This will cause a plot of

Y/10

to be displayed against the independent variable over the range 0 to 0.8.
Another use of control variables is illustrated below:

```
20    PRINT 'DECAY CONSTANT'
30    INPUT A
50    LET Y=10
80    LET C1=4
90    LET C0=C1
100   DYNAMIC
200     EQUATIONS
250     DER Y=-A*Y
260     DISPLAY Y/10
300     EQUEND
350     GOTO 20
400   DYNEND
```

Statement 80 will cause the display to correspond to the range 0-4 in the
independent variable, statement 90 will set the communication interval
to the value 4 so that the EQUATIONS section is left after 4 units of the
independent variable. Statement 350 in the DYNAMIC region will then
cause control to go to statement 20 ready for a new value of the constant
A to be input. This is a very convenient way of making the 'compute
period' equal to the range of the independent variable displayed.

The examples included within these notes mainly use the 2 control
variables specified above. The language contains other control variables
used to

(i)   specify the maximum relative error permitted in the integration routine,

(ii)   scale and position the axes used in the display

and   (iii)   to provide automatic scaling for the display.

In the automatic display facility, the equations are solved once, without display, and the maximum values of the variables concerned noted. The equations are solved again and the results displayed in scaled form. A variation of this technique is to make the computer output details of maximum values from a dummy run so that the user can specify the scaling to be used on subsequent runs.

8.8   Interaction

Much attention has been given to providing a simple yet flexible display system in BEDSOCS; displaying solutions in a readily appreciated graphical form is an essential facility in interactive simulation. A second requirement is that parameters, etc. can be readily changed. Just as in BASIC, BEDSOCS allows users to interact by providing a simple method for editing a program, i.e. one or more statements can be changed and the problem re-run. Thus, for example, if on typing the command RUN the solutions obtained indicate that a change should be made, program execution can be interrupted (by depressing a key) and, when the computer has replied with READY, a new value of a particular constant/ parameter can be input by typing the appropriate statement, e.g.

        50   LET A=10   can be replaced by
        50   LET A=5

and the problem re-run. Interaction with a running program can be achieved by use of 'immediately executable statements'. Parameter values can be changed in the middle of a solution much as one might change a value of a constant (by adjusting a pot) in the middle of an analogue computer run. As an example, suppose part way through a run, during the time the equations are being solved, a key is depressed causing an interrupt so that the solution is stopped. The computer will output STOP LINE N where N is the number of the statement about to be executed. The user can type PRINT P where P is any constant/parameter in the equations where upon the computer will respond with the value of P. The user can then assign a new numerical value to P by typing 'LET P = value required' which will immediately cause P to be assigned this new value.

If the user then commands GOTO N (where N is the statement number referred to above) the equations will continue to be solved from the point where the solution was interrupted but with a new value for P. Thus parameters can be changed in the middle of a run.

8.9 Function generation

Unlike the situation within analogue computation, there is no real distinction in digital simulation between methods used to generate functions of the independent variable and of dependent variables. However, in order to generate a function of the independent variable, this variable must be defined by inclusion of the INDVAR statement within the Equations Section. The following example illustrates the representation of an equation involving both types of function:

Model equation

$$\frac{d^2y}{dt^2} + A\frac{dy}{dt} + B \sin y = C \sin 2t$$

Representation

```
EQUATIONS
INDVAR T
DER V = -A*V-B*SIN(Y)+C*SIN(2*T)
DER Y = V
EQUEND
```

In analogue computation the sin y function probably would have been generated by a D. F. G. and the sin 2t function by a 2 integrator-inverter loop. Many types of functions can be included directly in the Representation Set. These include simple functions with abrupt changes, e.g. modulus (as ABS(V)) and Bang-Bang (as K*SGN(V)). However, more complicated functions may require a block of instructions - a subroutine - to define them. In BEDSOCS this is achieved by the use of PROCED blocks. Such a block consists of the following statements:

```
PROCED ⟨LIST 1⟩ = ⟨LIST 2⟩
BASIC STATEMENTS
PROEND
```

154

LIST 1 consists of the output variable (or variables) of the block and LIST 2 the input variables and constants. For example, a program to model the unsymmetrical limiter shown is given below:

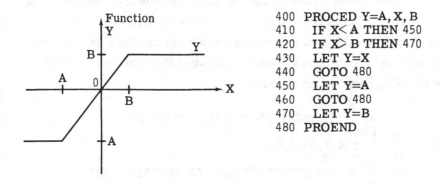

```
400   PROCED Y=A, X, B
410     IF X< A THEN 450
420     IF X> B THEN 470
430     LET Y=X
440     GOTO 480
450     LET Y=A
460     GOTO 480
470     LET Y=B
480   PROEND
```

Fig. 8.7   Unsymmetrical limiter characteristic and
simulation program

Any number of PROCED blocks may be included in the Representation Set.

During the time the equations are being solved, the values of the output variables of each PROCED block are computed from the values of the input variables valid at that time. These evaluations are performed at least once within each integration step. Example 3 at the end of this chapter illustrates how a simple PROCED block is included in a total program.

8.10   Detection of special values in solutions

In many of the problems considered in the notes on analogue computation it is required that when a certain value of a variable occurs some action is taken. Thus in many projectile problems it is necessary to terminate the compute period when a projectile 'hits the ground'. This is easily achieved by <u>continuously</u> comparing height with zero using a comparator and switching modes (COMPUTE→RESET) when the height crosses zero. However, this type of operation is more difficult to perform accurately in digital simulation because of the discrete nature of the digital variables. The variable representing height may cross zero part way through an integration step (or part way through a communication interval) and thus the occurrence of the event may not be detected accurately.

As an example consider the vertical projectile problem discussed earlier (page 145). Suppose it is required to print values of height, velocity and time throughout the flight and also to halt the solution of the equations when Y becomes negative and output the total time of flight. The following program may be used:

```
  5   REM. VERTICAL PROJECTILE PROBLEM.
 10   LET G=9.8
 20   LET K=1.00000E-02
 30   LET Y=T=0
 40   PRINT 'VELOCITY OF LAUNCH. METRES/SEC?'
 50   INPUT V
 70   PRINT 'TIME','SPEED','HEIGHT'
 80   PRINT 'SECS','METRES/SEC','METRES'
100   DYNAMIC
120     PRINT T,V,Y
150     EQUATIONS
155       INDVAR T
160       DER V=-G-K*V*ABS(V)
170       DER Y=V
200     EQUEND
220     IF Y <=0 THEN 350
300   DYNEND
350   PRINT 'TIME OF FLIGHT='
360   PRINT T
400   STOP
```

Results are communicated from the Equations Section to the Dynamic Region each communication interval so that the values of T, Y, V are output at unit intervals in T until Y becomes negative. When this occurs the value of T is output. However, as the instruction testing Y is outside the Equations Section, the test is only performed at each communication point and thus the value of T printed is the value T has at the communication point following the occurrence of Y becoming negative. Clearly T will then only be approximate. The value can be determined more accurately by reducing the communication interval, e.g. using $\mathbb{C}0 = 0.1$ or even $\mathbb{C}0 = 0.01$, but results would then be output for each change of 0.1 or .01 in T, leading to a mass of unwanted details in printed form. The same type of difficulty would be encountered in trying to

156

find the value of the maximum height by printing the value of Y when V becomes negative.

For any given problem it is often possible to find a way round this type of difficulty by extending the model equations, by including special functions or by changing the communication interval as the solutions progress. However, within BEDSOCS two special statements are available, EXIT and HIT, to enable the occurrence of particular events to be detected. Both statements can only be included in an Equations Section as they need to continually interact with the integration routines. The action of EXIT is considered first.

The EXIT statement enables the Equations Section to be left immediately the state (sign) of a variable changes. It thus provides an additional communication point. Control is transferred to the statement following EQUEND. In the following program for the vertical projectile problem, an EXIT (Y < 0) statement is included to enable the total time of flight to be determined:

```
  5    REM. VERTICAL PROJECTILE PROBLEM.
 10    LET G=9.8
 20    LET K=1.00000E-02
 30    LET Y=T=0
 40    PRINT 'VELOCITY OF LAUNCH. METRES/SEC ?'
 50    INPUT V
 90    LET C0=1000
100    DYNAMIC
150      EQUATIONS
155        INDVAR T
160        DER V=-G-K*V*ABS(V)
170        DER Y=V
180        DISPLAY Y/100
190        EXIT (Y< 0)
200      EQUEND
350    PRINT 'TIME OF FLIGHT='
360    PRINT T
370      GOTO 450
400    DYNEND
450    STOP
```

Statement 90 assigns a very large value to the communication interval so that no communication occurs in the run except when the condition of statement 190 becomes true. The Equations Section will be left at the nearest integration step point (using the minimum step length permitted) after Y becomes negative. Thus, as with an analogue comparator, there is a slight amount of uncertainty in the exact point at which the detection of the event occurs.

If it is also required that results are printed throughout the run (by inclusion of a print statement between DYNAMIC and EQUATIONS and by using a suitable communication interval) an additional instruction will be needed between EQUEND and DYNEND to ensure the PRINT T statement is only obeyed when EXIT (Y < 0) becomes true. A program including these features, together with the results obtained, is:

```
  5   REM. VERTICAL PROJECTILE PROBLEM.
 10   LET G=9.8
 20   LET K=1.00000E-02
 30   LET Y=T=0
 40   PRINT 'VELOCITY OF LAUNCH. METRES/SEC?'
 50   INPUT V
 80   PRINT 'TIME', 'SPEED', 'HEIGHT'
100   DYNAMIC
110     PRINT T, V, Y
150     EQUATIONS
155      INDVAR T
160      DER V=-G-K*V*ABS(V)
170      DER Y=V
190      EXIT (Y< 0)
200     EQUEND
210     IF Y> 0 THEN 400
350     PRINT 'TIME OF FLIGHT='
360     PRINT T
370     GOTO 450
400   DYNEND
450   STOP
```

```
RUN
VELOCITY OF LAUNCH. METRES/SEC?
?50
```

TIME	SPEED	HEIGHT
0	50	0
1	26.2811	36.6875
2	12.6975	55.7438
3	2.26663	63.0975
4	-7.39557	60.4869
5	-15.7587	48.7468
6	-21.7587	29.7212
7	-25.9032	5.65709

```
TIME OF FLIGHT=
 7.21833
```

The HIT statement operates in a rather similar way to the EXIT statement. The following example shows how it can be used to determine the maximum height Y1 for the projectile problem.

```
5    REM. VERTICAL PROJECTILE PROBLEM.
10   LET G=9.8
20   LET K=1.00000E-02
30   LET Y=T=0
40   PRINT 'VELOCITY OF LAUNCH. METRES/SEC?'
50   INPUT V
80   PRINT 'TIME', 'SPEED', 'HEIGHT'
100  DYNAMIC
110    PRINT T, V, Y
150    EQUATIONS
155      INDVAR T
160      DER V=-G-K*V*ABS(V)
170      DER Y=V
180      HIT (V< 0)
185      PROCED Y1=Y, V
186        IF V< 0 THEN 189
187        LET Y1=Y
189      PROEND
190      EXIT (Y< 0)
200    EQUEND
210    IF Y> 0 THEN 400
350    PRINT 'MAX HEIGHT', 'TIME OF FLIGHT'
360    PRINT Y1, T
370    GOTO 450
400  DYNEND
450  STOP
```

The HIT statement ensures that the occurrence of $V < 0$ is detected accurately (within the minimum step length of the integration routine) and the PROCED block arranges that the value of Y is assigned to Y1 until V becomes negative at the top of the flight. (This has a similar action to use of a comparator to detect when V becomes negative and a T/S unit to track the height until this occurs and then store the last value tracked.) The results obtained with this program are:

```
>RUN
VELOCITY OF LAUNCH. METRES/SEC?
?50
```

TIME	SPEED	HEIGHT
0	50	0
1	26.2811	36.6875
2	12.6975	55.7438
3	2.26663	63.0975

4	-7. 39497	60. 488
5	-15. 7583	48. 7485
6	-21. 9067	29. 7221
7	-25. 9028	5. 65855
MAX HEIGHT	TIME OF FLIGHT	
63. 3589	7. 21833	

8. 11 Comment regarding iterative computation

The above notes outline the more important features of BEDSOCS and how it can be used to perform operations similar to those performed by analogue, simple interface and memory units. One of the attractive features of digital simulation is the ease with which non-linear functions can be generated. A further feature is the ease with which parameters can be updated between runs by use of simple statements. Unlike the situation with parallel logic analogue computing, no special techniques are required to provide iterative computation features. Thus if a parameter sweep for the velocity of launch is required in the projectile problem, this can be achieved by inclusion of a few simple statements such as:

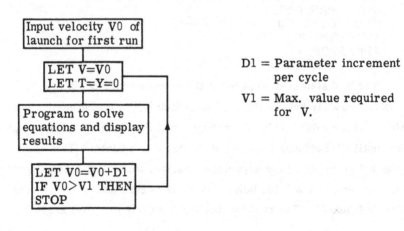

D1 = Parameter increment per cycle

V1 = Max. value required for V.

Fig. 8. 8

The number of runs possible in iteration studies will, of course, be controlled by the amount of computing time available, but BEDSOCS is sufficiently fast with small problems for parameter sweeps, split B. V. and parameter optimisation problems involving up to 2 or perhaps 3 parameters to be studied within a reasonable amount of running time (e. g. typical 2 parameter optimisation within a few minutes), providing great accuracy of solution is not demanded.

The use of BEDSOCS is illustrated by reference to a number of examples, one of which, (5), involving iterative computation. To save space and in order to compare techniques, the examples mainly relate to problems discussed elsewhere in the text. Programs given contain only enough comment to make them understandable; programs should normally be more fully documented.

8. 12   Illustrative examples

(1)   Mass, spring, damper

A simple mechanical system consists of a spring, a mass and a damper suspended from a fixed reference position. If the mass is displaced from its rest position and then released, it will oscillate until the energy is dissipated by the damper. Analyse the effect of different spring constants on the motion of the mass.

Equation:

$$m\ddot{x} = -c\dot{x} - kx$$

where x = position of mass,
m = mass, c = damper constant
and k = spring constant

Program:

```
 10   REM. MASS, SPRING, DAMPER SYSTEM
 15   LET K=1
 20   LET M=5
 25   PRINT 'DAMPER CONSTANT'
 30   INPUT C
 40   LET Y=T=0
 50   LET X=1
 60   LET C1=25
200   DYNAMIC
250     IF T>C1 THEN 25
300     EQUATIONS
310       INDVAR T
320       DER X=Y
330       DER Y=F/M
335       REM. F IS FORCE
340       F=-C*Y*-K*X
350       DISPLAY X
400     EQUEND
500   DYNEND
```

Results:

RUN
DAMPER CONSTANT?2
DAMPER CONSTANT?1
DAMPER CONSTANT?.5
DAMPER CONSTANT?

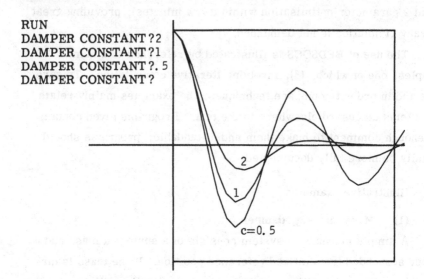

Fig. 8.9

(2)   Vibratory system with Coulomb friction

Example 4(a) of §5.

In this vibratory system the frictional force is assumed to be only dependent on the normal force between the mass and the ground. Frictional force F is therefore a constant force acting in the opposite direction to the motion. Observe the effect of varying F on the solutions, position X, speed V and acceleration A.

In particular note:

(i)   The system comes to rest within a range about X = 0, the size of the range being dependent on the magnitude of F.

(ii) The amplitude of the oscillations decays <u>linearly</u> with time. This is best seen if F is made small.

Equation

If X = distance of the mass from the equilibrium position '0' defined when friction F is zero then

$$m\ddot{X} \pm F + kX = 0 \qquad \text{with } +F \text{ if } \dot{X} > 0$$
$$-F \text{ if } \dot{X} < 0$$

162

Program

```
 5    REM. VIBRATORY SYSTEM WITH COULOMB FRICTION
60    LET M=1
70    LET K=1
80    LET X=1
100   PRINT 'FRICTION F'
110   INPUT F
120   LET V=T=0
200   DYNAMIC
300     EQUATIONS
320       DER X=V
350       DISPLAY X, V, A
360       INDVAR T
370       DER V=A
400         A=-SGN(V)*F/M-K*X/M
600     EQUEND
700   DYNEND
```

Results

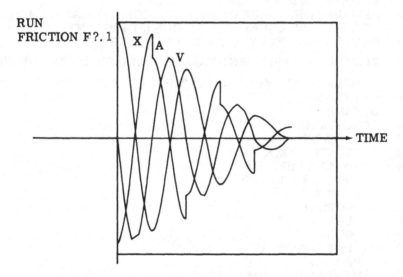

RUN
FRICTION F?. 1

Fig. 8.10   Position, velocity and acceleration characteristics
for Coulomb friction problem

(3)   Movement of a truck between two separated spring buffers.
Use of a deadspace simulator

Example   4(b) of §5

Observe the variations of position x, velocity x and acceleration

163

$\ddot{x}$ against time when $x_0 = 0$, $\dot{x}_0 = .2$, $a = .5$, $k = 1$ and $m = 1$.

Equation

Using $x =$ position of truck, $k =$ spring constant and assuming no friction then $m\ddot{x} = -f(x)$ where $f(x) = 0$ for $-a < x < a$

$$= k(x - a) \text{ for } \qquad x > a$$
$$= k(x + a) \text{ for } \qquad x < -a$$

Program

```
   5   REMARK: MOVEMENT OF A TRUCK
   6   REMARK: BETWEEN TWO SEPARATED
   7   REMARK: SPRING BUFFERS
   8   REMARK: DEAD SPACE SIMULATION
  10   LET K=1
  20   LET X=0
  30   LET V=-.2
  40   LET T=0
  50   LET A=.5
  60   LET N=1
  70   REMARK: C0 IS A CONTROL VARIABLE
  72   REMARK: THE VALUE OF C0 IS THE COMMUNICATION INTERVAL
  74   REMARK: THE EQUATIONS SECTION (STATEMENTS 400 TO 1200)
  76   REMARK: IS EXECUTED UNTIL THE VALUE OF T, THE
  78   REMARK: INDEPENDENT VARIABLE, REACHES THAT OF C0.
  80   REMARK: STATEMENT 1230 IS THEN EXECUTED.
 100   LET C0=C1
 220   DYNAMIC
 400     EQUATIONS
 500       INDVAR T
 600       PROCED F=X, K, A
 610         IF X>A THEN 650
 620         IF X<-A THEN 670
 630         LET F=0
 640         GOTO 680
 650         LET F=K*(X-A)
 660         GOTO 680
 670         LET F=K*(X+A)
 680       PROEND
 700       DISPLAY X, Y, F/M
 720       DER V=-F/M
 730       DER X=V
1200     EQUEND
1230     STOP
1400   DYNEND
```

Results

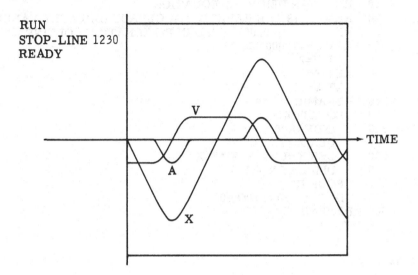

Fig. 8.11

Exercise

Run problem with other larger values of the spring constant and also obtain phase plane plots of solution X against V.

(4)   **Van der Pol's equation**

Van der Pol's equation describes the build up of oscillations in certain types of electronic oscillator.

Equation

$$\frac{d^2x}{dt^2} = u(1 - x^2)\frac{dx}{dt} - x,$$

where u   is a positive constant whose value depends upon the amount of
positive feedback in the circuit (equivalent to negative damping),

x   corresponds to voltage

and $\frac{dx}{dt}$ corresponds to current.

The problem of interest is the way the build up of oscillations (from some initial values of x and $\frac{dx}{dt}$) and the shape (quality in terms of harmonic content) of the oscillations, depends on u.

165

Program

```
10   REM. VAN DER POLS EQUATION
20   REM. C5 IS THE RELATIVE ACCURACY (DEFAULT VALUE
25   REM.        0.001) USED IN INTEGRATION ROUTINE.
30   LET C5=1.00000E-04
40   LET U=2
50   LET X=1
60   LET Y=.5
200  DYNAMIC
300    EQUATIONS
310      INDVAR T
320      DER X=Y
330      DER Y=U*(1-X*X)*Y-X
350      DISPLAY X/4;Y/4
400    EQUEND
450    IF T >= 20 GOTO 600
500  DYNEND
600  STOP
```

Results

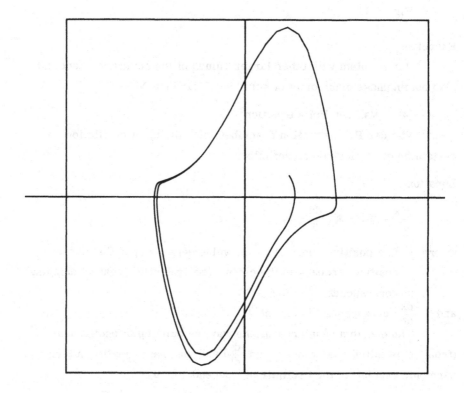

Fig. 8.12   Phase plane plot for Van der Pol's equation

Exercise

Investigate solutions for various values of u and various starting values for $\dot{x}$ and x. Include display control statement to enable suitable range of solutions to be output. Use both a phase plane display and also a display showing the variations of x and $\dot{x}$ against the independent variable.

(5)   **Projectile problem with drag proportional to the square of the speed**

Problem discussed on pages 119 -120. Object is to produce a general program so that for any given angle and speed of launch the horizontal range is determined in printed form and the path of the projectile displayed.

Equations

As given on page 119 but with A used to represent angle θ.

Program

```
10      REM. PROJECTILE.  DRAG PROPORTIONAL TO SPEED SQUARED.
20      LET G=9.807
25      LET P=4*ATN(1)   ....... (i.e.   π)
30      LET C=P/180
40      LET K=1.00000E-02
50      PRINT 'SPEED'
55      INPUT V
60      PRINT 'ANGLE DEGREES'
65      INPUT D
70      LET A=C*D
80      LET X=Y=T=0
200     DYNAMIC
300       EQUATIONS
310        INDVAR T
320        DER V=-G*SIN(A)-K*V↑2
330        DER A=-G*COS(A)/V
340        DER X=V*COS(A)
350        DER Y=V*SIN(A)
360        DISPLAY X/200;Y/150
370        EXIT (Y< 0)
400       EQUEND
410       IF Y> 0 THEN 500
450       PRINT 'HORZ RANGE='
460       PRINT X
470       GOTO 50
500     DYNEND
600     STOP
```

Results
RUN
SPEED?1ØØ
ANGLE?45
HORIZONTAL DISTANCE=16Ø. 474

STOP-LINE 6ØØ

READY
RUN
SPEED?1ØØ
ANGLE?3Ø
HORIZONTAL DISTANCE=169. 227

STOP-LINE 6ØØ

READY
RUN
SPEED?1ØØ
ANGLE?6Ø
HORIZONTAL DISTANCE=127. 714

STOP-LINE 6ØØ

READY

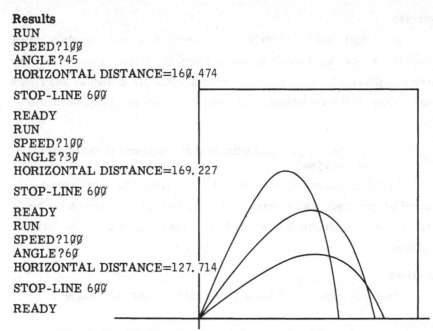

Fig. 8.13   Flight paths for various angle of launch

Extensions

(a) Arrange program to output maximum height reached, time for maximum height, horizontal range and total time of flight.

(b) Modify program so that the speed of launch is automatically adjusted until the horizontal range is within 0. 1 metre of 100 metres. This is most easily achieved by proportional correction using the error in the range to adjust the speed of launch.   Run problem with various values of angles of launch starting with the 45° case.   Some results obtained (45° case) with such a program are shown in Fig. 8.14.

(c) Extend program further by involving two parameter iteration to adjust the speed and angle of launch so that the projectile just clears a wall (height H and distance W from launch point) and reaches a range R within a specified total error (i. e. |error from top of wall| + |range error|).   Build in as much generality as possible into the program so that the user can specify distance and height of wall, range required, iteration gain constants, first estimates for speed and angle of launch, absolute error, etc.   Arrange also that essential data is output when convergence is achieved and that display is scaled to match the problem.   Arrange

168

RUN

DISTANCE = 1ØØ METRES
COMPONENTS OF SPEED OF LAUNCH = 3Ø. 5477 METRES/SEC
SPEED OF LAUNCH = 43. 2Ø1 METRES/SEC

STOP-LINE 8ØØØ

READY

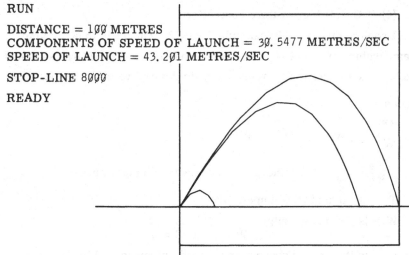

Fig. 8.14   Results of iterative computation showing adjustment of
speed of launch for projectile to achieve a given range

also to draw the wall.   Note: to achieve convergence use the error in
range to control the horizontal component $(V \cos \theta)_0$ and the vertical
miss distance wall error to control the vertical component $(V \sin \theta)_0$ of
the speed of launch.   Some results obtained with such a program are
shown below.

Results

RUN
DISTANCE OF WALL?8Ø
HEIGHT OF WALL?5Ø
RANGE?1ØØ
ESTIMATED SPEED OF LAUNCH?5Ø
ESTIMATED ANGLE?45

TIME	HEIGHT AT WALL	RANGE	SPEED	ANGLE
7.15	5Ø. Ø288	1ØØ. Ø38	63. 7638	58. 67Ø5

STOP-LINE 66Ø

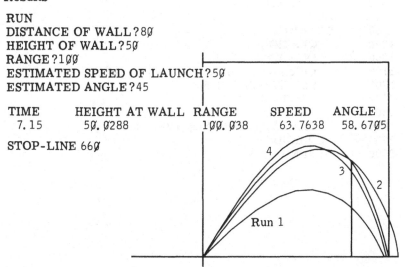

Fig. 8.15   Iterative solutions showing adjustment of speed and
angle of launch for projectile to just clear a wall and
achieve a given range

(6) On/off temperature controller

Problem discussed in example 3 of §12. Object is to determine how temperature of liquid T_1 increases when the heater is first switched on and how the temperature varies about its desired value or set point R.

Equations

$$\frac{dT_1}{dt} = 1.2W - 0.01(T_1 - T_2)$$

$$\frac{5dT_0}{dt} + T_0 = T_1, \quad \text{where } T_0 = \text{measured temperature}$$

T_2 is the ambient temperature

W   is the heater output   W = H   if   E > 0
                                           W = 0   if   E ≤ 0

E   is the error between the desired and measured temperature

$E = R - T_0$

Program

```
  40       REMARK: ON/OFF TEMP. CONTROLLER
 110       INPUT R
 120       PRINT 'HEATER CAPACITY';
 130       INPUT H
 200       LET T2=0
 250       LET T1=T0=0
 300       LET C1=100
 350       LET C0=C1
 400       LET X0=0
 800       DYNAMIC
1000         EQUATIONS
1050         INDVAR T
1100         DER T1=1.2*W-1.00000E-02*(T1-T2)
1200         DER T0=(T1-T0)/5
1300           E=R-T0
1400           W=H*(E> 0)
1600         DISPLAY (T1-R)/100,(T0-R)/100
1700         EQUEND
2000       DYNEND
```

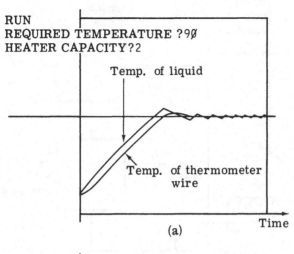

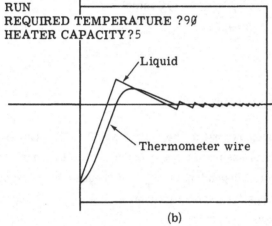

Fig. 8.16   Turn on characteristics for 2 heater capacities

(7)   Endothermic reaction in a stirred tank

A second-order irreversible endothermic reaction takes place in a stirred tank: $2A + \text{heat} \rightarrow \text{products}$ (Fig. 8.17).

Heat is supplied through a steam coil to achieve the required rate of reaction. The temperature T of the steam flowing from the reactor is sensed and transmitted to the controller, where it is compared with the setpoint (desired) temperature T_r. The controller transmits a signal

171

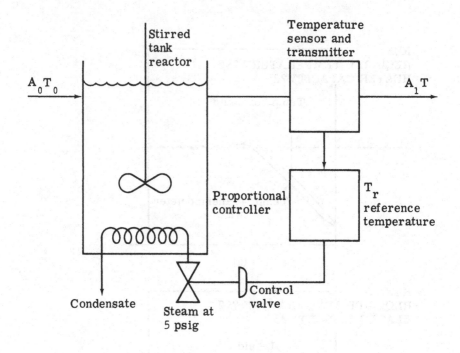

Fig. 8.17   Stirred tank system

to the control valve proportional to the error $e = T_r - T$. The steam
rate through the valve is assumed to be proportional to this error signal;
thus a positive error corresponding to $T_r > T$ causes an increase in
steam flow, while a negative error corresponding to $T_r < T$ causes a
decrease in steam flow.

The object of the simulation is to determine the effectiveness of
the control system in minimising variations in the exiting temperature T
due to disturbances in the entering concentration and temperature A_0
and T_0. The exiting temperature is computed as a function of time by
simultaneous solution of equations (1), (2) and (3). The parameter of
particular interest is the controller gain K_C.

The equations describing this system are:

Material balance
$$VdA/dt = m(A_0 - A) - VA^2 k_0 e^{-E/RT} \tag{1}$$

Heat balance
$$V c dT/dt = mc(T_0 - T) - \Delta H V A^2 k_0 e^{-E/RT} + Q_8 \qquad (2)$$

Controller equation
$$Q_8 = [m_8 + K_c(T_r - T)]\Delta H_\nu \qquad (3)$$

Note that equations (1) and (2) are highly non-linear due to the reaction term which is second-order in concentration and includes the Arrhenius temperature dependency. Solving for highest derivatives and substituting numerical values gives

$$dA/dt = 10^{-3}(1-A) - (1.907 \times 10^{13})A^2 e^{-2.25 \times 10^4 /T} \qquad (4)$$

$$dT/dt = 10^{-3}(575 - T)$$
$$-(0.318) \times 10^{16})A^2 e^{-2.25 \times 10^4 /T} + Q_8/6 \times 10^3 \qquad (5)$$

$$Q_8 = 682 + 960 K_c(600 - T) \qquad (6)$$

Symbols and numerical values

A   reactant concentration in reactor (and outlet), lb-mol/ft^3

A_0 reactant feed concentration = 1 lb-mol/ft^3

c   volumetric specific heat of process material = 60 Btu/ft^3 - R°

E   activation energy = 44,700 Btu/lb-mol

K_c proportional controller gain $\dfrac{lb/sec}{R°}$

k_0 frequency factor in second-order rate expression = 1.907 × 10^{13} ft^3/sec-lb-mol

m   feed (and takeoff) rate of process material = 0.1 ft^2/sec

m_8 steady-state steam flow rate = 0.711 lb/sec

Q_8 steam heat duty, Btu/sec

R   gas constant = 1.987 Btu/lb-mol-R°

T_0 temperature in reactor (and outlet), R°

T   reactor feed temperature = 575°R

T_r temperature setpoint = 600°R

V   reactor volume = 100 ft

ΔH heat of reaction = 10,000 Btu/lb-mol

ΔH_ν heat of vaporisation of steam at 5 psig = 960 Btu/lb

Program

```
10      REM. ENDOTHERMIC REACTION IN A STIRRED TANK
11      REM.                    DISPLAYING RESULTS
50      PRINT 'KC';
60      INPUT K
65      LET C0=100
90      LET C1=2000
100     LET A=.618
110     LET T=600
300     DYNAMIC
400       EQUATIONS
500       DER A=1.00000E-03*(1-A)-(1.90700E+13)*A 2*
                            EXP(-22500/T)
600       DER T=1.00000E-03*(575-T)-(3.18000E+15)*A 2*
                            EXP(-22500/T)+Q8/6000
700       Q8=682+960*K*(600-T)
750       DISPLAY A*1000, T, Q8
800       EQUEND
850       IF C0 > C1  THEN  1000
900     DYNEND
1000    STOP
```

Results   for   KC = .001

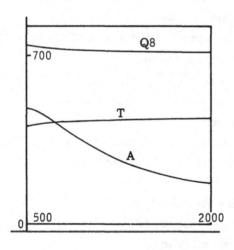

Fig. 8.18   Some results for stirred tank reaction

(8)   Reaction vessel simulation

A reaction takes place between two chemicals A and B to form another, C. The reaction is thought to be of first order and needs one molecule of A and one of B to form one of C.

174

Show how different temperature profiles and rate constants affect the rate of conversion of A and B to C.

The reaction equations are:

$R = K*A*B/M$ Reaction rate (moles/hr.)

$K = 10^{(-K1/(P+273)+K2)}$ Reaction rate temperature term (/hr)

$M = A + B + C$ Total number of moles (moles)

$\dfrac{dA}{dt} = -R$ Reactant A (moles)

$\dfrac{dB}{dt} = -R$ Reactant B (moles)

$\dfrac{dC}{dt} = R$ Reactant C (moles)

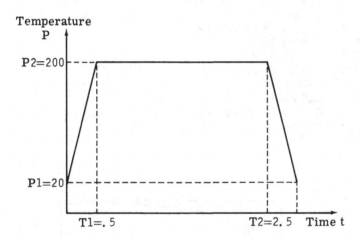

Fig. 8.19   Temperature profile

Study the case for   K1 = 4000

K2 = 10

Initial conditions

at   t = 0, A = 100, B = 100, C = 0

Program

```
2 REMARK; REACTION VESSEL SIMULATION
6 LET T=0
7 LET C=0
9 DATA .5,2.5,3,20,200
```

```
   10  READ T1, T2, T3, P1, P2
   20  DATA 4000, 10, 100, 100
   25  READ K1, K2, A, B
   50  REMARK: STATEMENT 70 USED TO SET
   60  REMARK: THE DISPLAY SCALING
   70  LET C1=T3
  100  DYNAMIC
  140  EQUATIONS
  145    INDVAR T
  150      R=K*A*B/M
  160      K=10↑(-K1/(P+273)+K2)
  170      M=A+B+C
  180    DER A=-R
  190    DER B=-R
  200    DER C=R
  250    DISPLAY A, C, R/5
  510    PROCED P=T, T1, T2, T3, P1, P2
  520      IF T> T1 THEN 550
  530      LET P=P1+(P2-P1)*T/T1
  540      GOTO 590
  550      IF T> T2 THEN 580
  560      LET P=P2
  570      GOTO 590
  580      LET P=P2-(P2-P1)*(T-T2)/(T3-T2)
  590    PROEND
  900  EQUEND
 1005  IF T>=T3 THEN 1010
 1007  DYNEND
 1010  STOP
```

Results

RUN
STOP:LINE 1010

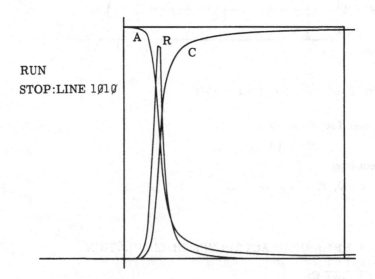

Fig. 8.20   Some results for reaction vessel simulation

9 · Hybrid Computers

9.1 Introduction

Parallel logic and simple interface units were added onto analogue computers to extend the range of problems which could be studied and, to a lesser extent, make more automatic the study of such problems by simulation. For the same reasons, small general-purpose digital computers were added to these parallel logic machines to form full hybrid computers. With such machines the process of setting up, checking and running simulations can be made almost completely automatic and the range of problems that can be efficiently studied is considerably extended.

Many hybrid configurations are possible with varying emphasis on the role of the analogue and digital sections. At one extreme the analogue section may be considered as a special peripheral of the digital to enable rapid integration to be performed. At the other extreme the digital may be regarded as a special peripheral of the analogue to be used to generate multi-variable and time delayed functions.

The construction of a general-purpose hybrid computer is shown in Fig. 9.1. In such a system the digital will probably be a fast (~1 μsec cycle time) mini computer having a word length of 8-16 bits and containing 8-16K words of fast store and (unfortunately) just sufficient peripherals (teletype, reader, punch) to allow program development and running.

The interface consists of two sections.

(i) Monitor and control

This section of the machine enables the digital computer to perform all the operations which would normally be done manually on a parallel logic hybrid and also enables the outputs of all analogue units and the states of the simple interface units to be monitored. The monitor and control interface is partly concerned with the operation of low speed non time critical devices, e.g. servo set potentiometers, relay switches for

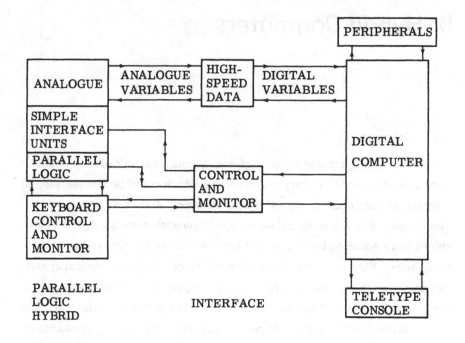

Fig. 9.1   General-purpose hybrid computer

component selection. However, this section of interface is also involved
in high-speed logic operations, e.g. analogue mode selection, reading
comparators, reading logic signals input via the patch panel.

(ii) High-speed data

The purpose of this section of interface is to enable variables
(data) to be transferred rapidly between the analogue model and the digital
computer. The basic units used are Digital to Analogue Convertors
(D. A. C. s), Digital to Analogue Multipliers (D. A. M. s) and Analogue to
Digital Convertors (A. D. C. s).

It will be seen that the digital and interface sections are similar
to those found in process control and other on-line computer control configurations in which analogue and logic signals need to be transferred to
and from a digital computer. Special features of hybrid computer data
interfaces are the comparatively large amplitude and noise-free analogue
signals involved and the very high speed at which data is transferred.

9.2 Hardware

(i) Digital

In the discussion which follows it will be assumed that the word length of the digital computer is 16 bits and it will also be assumed that a number of 16 bit input/output channels are available through which data is transferred to and from the central processor.

(ii) Monitor and control

The control interface enables commands in the form of logic signals to be sent to the parallel logic analogue section. Important operations allowed by computer control are, for example,

(1) Selection of analogue mode (POT SET, I. C. , etc.).

(2) Selection of analogue timescale (integrator gains).

(3) Selection of a specified analogue component (POT 25, AMP 3, etc.) causing its output to be read by the D. V. M.

(4) Potentiometer coefficient setting.

(5) Control of function relay states.

(6) Setting of logic levels on patch panel.

The monitor section enables information about the analogue computer to be read by the digital. Important information of this type is:

(1) Status of analogue machine (mode, timescale, etc.).

(2) Type and number of component selected by the D. V. M. addressing system.

(3) Value of analogue unit output read by D. V. M. This, together with (3) above, enables a particular component to be selected and its output value read.

(4) States of comparators.

(5) States of certain logic signals on patch panel (sense line signals).

The circuitry for these sections of interface is often quite extensive. Fig. 9. 2 illustrates the important features. For reasons of simplicity it is assumed that two input/output buffers are used, whereas in practice it is probable that only a single buffer would be used.

Typically the sequence of operation for the control section is:

(1) The code representing the particular device (e. g. function relay, analogue mode, pot set command) is output.

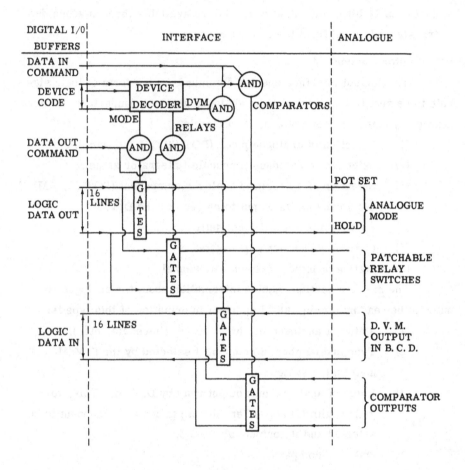

Fig. 9.2   Section of monitor/control interface

(2)   Data (e. g. required mode) is output and presented to the
      gates.

(3)   A DATA OUT enable command is sent causing the data to be
      passed through the appropriate gates, as determined by the

device code in (1) above, and onto the particular device selected.

(4)   A return signal READY or NOT BUSY is sent back to the digital on completion of the operation.

For the monitor section a typical sequence of operation is:

(1)   The code representing the device to be monitored is output.

(2)   A DATA IN enable command is sent causing the data from the device selected to pass through the appropriate gates and be input to the data input buffer.

(3)   The data is read into the computer.

Software for performing the above operations is discussed in §9. 3.

(iii) High-speed data

In Fig. 9. 3 is shown the typical structure of this section of interface. Data words of 12-14 bits length are generally used to match the

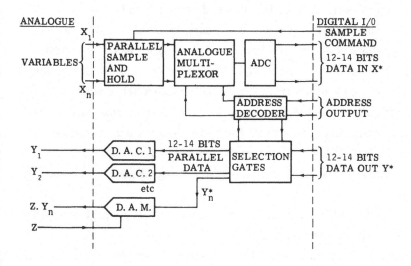

Fig. 9. 3   High-speed data interface. X* represents digital data variable corresponding to analogue variable X. For simplicity A. D. C. convert, busy lines, etc. not shown.

resolution/precision obtainable in the analogue hardware.

Two types of device, D. A. C. s and D. A. M. s, are used to output variables in analogue form from the digital computer and A. D. C. s are used to input values. The operation of all these devices is described in detail in Appendix 1.

(a) Digital to Analogue Convertors

A D. A. C. produces an analogue value Y corresponding to a digital word Y*, the magnitude of Y being arranged to match the dynamic range of the analogue computer. Thus with 10 volt reference machines a D. A. C. is designed to produce a value in the range -10 volts to +10 volts from the digital data word. A typical convertor used for hybrid work will have a response time of about 10 μsec, i. e. once new data is presented to the device the analogue signal will settle to its new value in about this time.

Each convertor is buffered, i. e. data is loaded into the convertor and stored as long as required. Thus the D. A. C. analogue output remains constant except at times when the digital data is updated.

For some applications it is necessary to avoid 'slew' when outputting data via a number of convertors, i. e. it is necessary to update the analogue outputs simultaneously. This is achieved by double buffering. Data is loaded sequentially from the computer into a set of extra buffer stores, one buffer per D. A. C. At a given command all this data is transferred simultaneously using parallel transfer into the normal buffer registers so that all the analogue variables are updated together.

A typical sequence of operation for a group of double buffered convertors is:

(i)   The address of the D. A. C. is output and the particular convertor selected.

(ii) Data is transferred into the extra buffer associated with the D. A. C. selected.

(iii) Steps (i) and (ii) are repeated for all convertors used.

(iv) A master command is output causing all the data to be transferred into the convertors at one instant thus causing the analogue variables to be updated together.

(b) Digital Analogue Multiplier

The D. A. M. combines digital to analogue conversion with multiplication by an analogue variable. Thus if Y* is the digital input word corresponding to an analogue value Y, and Z is the analogue input, the output is ZY. Use of these devices avoids the need for conventional multipliers in some parameter (coefficient) adjustment schemes. Some D. A. M. s provide current output instead of voltage output. These devices, 'electronic pots', need to be connected to amplifier summing junctions.

D. A. M. s, like D. A. C. s, may be single or double buffered.

(c) Analogue Digital Convertors

These devices are very much more complex than D. A. C. s and for reasons of economy it is necessary to time share each A. D. C. between a number of analogue inputs using an analogue multiplexor. Conversion takes rather longer than the time needed to update a D. A. C. ; the longer the word length used, the longer is the time of conversion. Typical execution times are 10 μsec plus 1 μsec per bit.

Slew on data can be avoided by use of parallel sample and hold (i. e. track-store) units connected before the multiplexor and convertor.

A typical sequence of operation for conversion and reading a single analogue input is:

(1) The address of the input required is output to the address decoder of the multiplexor and the particular input selected is connected to the A. D. C.

(2) A command output from the computer causes the sample and hold unit to store the current analogue input (so that the A. D. C. is fed with a constant value while it is converting).

(3) The convertor is made to start converting and when complete a READY signal is sent to the digital computer.

(4) The data is input to the computer.

Various modes of operation of varying degrees of sophistication are possible with modern A. D. C. systems. For example, on receipt of a starting address, S, and finishing address, F, a number, F - S + 1, of inputs may be automatically and sequentially converted over and over again and the data input to the computer. For ultra high-speed operation this data may be continually entered into the computer's store (using direct memory access, data break or cycle stealing techniques) from which it may be accessed by program.

9.3 Software

The type of software needed for hybrid computation depends on the properties of the hardware and its application. The following diagram, Fig. 9.4, shows in a simplified form the general procedure followed when studying problems by hybrid simulation.

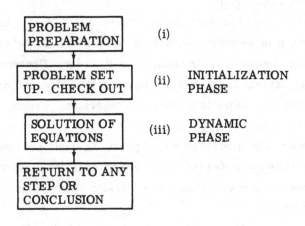

Fig. 9.4

Very different types of software are needed for each of the phases (i), (ii) and (iii).

(i)   Preparation software enables problems to be prepared for analogue/hybrid simulation and aids systematic checking of simulations (i.e. stage (ii)) both statically and dynamically. The software packages used at this stage are both large and complex. They must include digital simulation programs. This stage in the study is often best done using a large computer operating in batch mode.

(ii)   Initialization software is used during the set-up and check-out stages. Because of the complex nature of the hardware (and the high chance of errors occurring) the language in

which the software is written must provide extensive interaction between user and machine. However, the set-up and
debug phase is not time critical and thus a hybrid interpretive language may be used (i. e. a language in which each
instruction is interpreted - and a binary program generated -
at time of execution).

(iii) In the Dynamic phase when the equations are being solved,
high speed of operation may be required depending on the
type of application (e. g. sequential or parallel). Programs
for any high-speed operations must be fully compiled before
execution. The language used can be high level (e. g. FOR-
TRAN) with special hybrid subroutines or low level (assem-
bler/machine code).

Besides the requirements described above two other areas of software are needed:

(iv) Standard Digital software (assemblers, high level languages
for batch and interactive use, editors, drivers for peripherals, operating system software to organise and control
computer operation, etc.).

(v) Hybrid applications software developed for special important
and often-used hybrid applications, e. g. parameter optimisation, split boundary value problems, partial differential
equations.

Problem preparation (i) is discussed in Appendex 2 and hybrid
applications in §10 and §11. The remainder of these notes describe the
software used while setting up, checking out and running hybrid simulations. Discussion will largely be with reference to a hybrid version of
BASIC (which includes the BASIC digital simulation language BEDSOCS)
and it will be assumed that where programs for high-speed operations are
required these will be in the form of fully compiled subroutines. Although
the user usually programs in a high level language the fundamental operation of the machine is governed by assembler language routines and consequently reference to these is made before discussing the high level
language itself.

9.4   Assembler routines for hybrid operations

These routines must cover all the fundamental operations performed via the control, monitor and data interfaces. Many of these operations must be performed at high speed and so very efficient programming is needed. Moreover the programming must allow for checks of correct operation as analogue equipment often does not do what it is told! Thus, for example, a routine designed to switch the analogue section to I. C. mode must not only include instructions to perform the switching to the I. C. mode but must also include a check to confirm that the correct operation has been performed and, if not, take remedial action.

Some subroutines needed are quite extensive and will contain many simpler routines shared by many programs. A good example of a complex routine is that used to set a servo pot to a specified coefficient. Such a routine will include at least the following operations.

(i)   Check that the POT reference number is a permitted number (i. e. check that the POT concerned is in the machine and is available for use) and check that the coefficient requested is less than 1 and is specified to a meaningful number of significant figures (generally 4 with modern computers).

(ii)   Check that the analogue computer is in the POT SET mode. If not switch to correct mode and check again.

(iii) Convert the potentiometer address (e. g. POT 25) into the correct code (e. g. B. C. D.) and output it causing, hopefully, the required pot to be selected. During the time of selection (many milliseconds if relays are used) loop round waiting for completion.

(iv)   Read component selected and check that it is as required, e. g. POT 25 and not AMP 15.

(v)   Convert the potentiometer coefficient (in binary, integer or floating point form) into correct code (e. g. B. C. D.) and output this to the pot setting system.

(vi)   Instruct setting system to begin and loop round (i. e. check BUSY) until complete. This will automatically cause the

D. V. M. to convert as this forms part of the setting up system. If pot will not set in specified time take remedial action (e. g. try again from another value or output error information).

(vii)   Read coefficient on D. V. M.

(viii) Compare coefficient with value required and check if difference acceptable. If not take remedial action.

A subroutine (which may itself contain further subroutines, a process known as subroutine nesting) is needed for each stage in the above procedure. Many of these routines will, of course, be common to other operations, e. g. mode setting, component selection.

The structure and timing of a typical subroutine can be understood by reference to the following example used to control the analogue mode. The program is written in fully annoted symbolic machine code and its operation can be understood by reference to the annotation. The computer is assumed to contain two accumulators 'A' and 'B' and it is assumed that the relevant input/output buffers are called MNCTR (i. e. Monitor/Control) and DATA. Device selection and strobe signals are output from the MNCTR buffer and data (i. e. which mode wanted) via the DATA buffer. A check is made to see if the correct mode is selected by reading status information via the DATA buffer.

COMMENT	BEFORE ENTRY LOAD A ACCUM WITH CODE FOR MODE WANTED I. E. POT SET=1, POT CHECK=2, ETC.		
MODE	NOP		
	STA	REF	STORE CODE FOR MODE IN REF FOR CHECKING
	OTA	DATA	FEED OUT MODE WANTED
	LDA	MODEC	DEVICE CODE FOR ANALOG MODE
	OTA	MNCTR	OUTPUT DEVICE CODE
	ADA	DAOUT	ADD ON DATA OUT STROBE CODE
	OTA	MNCTR	STROBE OUT DATA CAUSING (HOPEFULLY) CORRECT MODE TO BE SELECTED
	CLA		CLEAR A ACCUM
	OTA	MNCTR	RESET TO ZERO
	LDA	STATC	DEVICE CODE FOR STATUS
	OTA	MNCTR	OUTPUT DEVICE CODE
	ADA	DATIN	ADD ON DATA IN STROBE CODE
	OTA	MNCTR	OUTPUT AND HENCE STROBE STATUS DATA INTO DATA CHANNEL

```
CLA              CLEAR
OTA  MNCTR       RESET TO ZERO
LIA  DATA        READ STATUS
AND  MASK        MASK OUT UNWANTED STATUS DATA
CPA  REF         COMPARE MODE FOUND WITH MODE
                 WANTED AND SKIP IF WRONG
JMP  MODE,I      RETURN IF CORRECT
JMP  ERROR       IF WRONG
```

Similar structured routines are used for the high speed data system. The following routine is used to select an analogue input channel, initiate A. D. C. conversion and read the value obtained into the computer. The A. D. C. is assumed to be connected to the digital computer via an input/output buffer called ADC. In this routine no provision is made for checking that the correct analogue channel is selected.

```
COMMENT    ENTER WITH A ACCUMULATOR CONTAINING ADDRESS OF
           ANALOGUE INPUT TO BE READ.  ENTER WITH B
           CONTAINING REPLY CODE.
SBADC      NOP
           OTA  ADC       OUTPUT ADDRESS OF ADC CHANNEL
                          WANTED
           STC  ADC       SET COMMAND OUTPUT BIT OF ADC
                          BUFFER HIGH CAUSING ADC TO CONVERT
           SFS  ADC       WAIT FOR CONVERSION TO FINISH WHEN
           JMP  *-1       FLAG ON ADC BUFFER IS RAISED
                          (AUTOMATICALLY RESETS COMMAND
                          BIT LOW)
           LIA  ADC       LOAD IN DATA I. E. OUTPUT OF ADC
           OTB  ADC       REPLY TO ADC SAYING DATA READ
           JMP  SBADC,I   RETURN
```

9.5 Interpretive language for hybrid operations

The language used to set up, check out and run simulations depends upon the nature (size, complexity, peripherals, etc.) of the hardware available, the use to which it is put and the skill and experience of the users. The language described below is being developed specifically for a small-medium sized hybrid machine in an educational establishment. As the equipment is used by a variety of students and staff, rather than only by highly trained personnel, emphasis is placed on simplicity and flexibility in use.

The prime requirement for a hybrid language for set-up and check-out is that it provides maximum possible interaction between user and machine but at the same time is simple to use and sufficiently automatic so that, if there are no errors, the set-up and check-out is performed rapidly with a minimum of user participation. As at Bradford emphasis is placed on the use of BASIC, an interpretive language, it was therefore decided to produce a special version of BASIC for hybrid operations. [†] Although intended for non-time critical set-up/check-out operations it is sufficiently fast to enable sequential and some simple parallel applications to be studied.

A number of special commands and special BASIC like statements have been added to standard BASIC so that the language contains all the usual features of BASIC. Commands like SETUP, which causes the analogue machine to be set up and statically checked, have been added to the standard BASIC commands RUN, LIST, etc. Most of the standard BASIC statements, e.g. LET X = 2, and also the new hybrid statements, e.g. SET P27 = .125, can be used both normally (i.e. as numbered statements executed in sequence) and as immediately executable instructions. Thus if a LET statement appears as part of a program consisting of a set of numbered statements, it is obeyed in its proper turn. However, if LET X = 2 is input without a statement (line) number it is obeyed immediately rather like a command. Provision of this extension to BASIC enhances on-line interaction.

(i) Initialization phase

The following steps describe a typical sequence of operations followed when using this language to set up and check an analogue problem.

(1) Data is prepared on paper tape using a teleprinter off-line to the computer. Data for each component takes the form of component address followed by a number of set up and/or check values in fields. As the amount of testing needed depends on the type of problem and the wishes of the user, all the fields relating to check values (as opposed to

---

[†] Readers not familiar with BASIC should refer to a standard computer manufacturers handbook on BASIC or to reference 10. The hybrid version of BASIC is similar to that developed at Bangor University.

set-up values) are optional. The general principles can be understood
from the following examples:

P01, .5   means Pot 01 to be set to coeff 0.5.

P15, .25, -.125   means Pot 15 to be set to coeff 0.25 and to have a
                          static test (S. T.) output value of -.125.

Q07, .8, +.8   means manual pot 7 set to coeff 0.8 and to have a
                          S. T. output = +0.8.

A09   means that amplifier (e. g. a summer) A09 is
                          being used in the simulation.

A01, -.5   means amplifier 01 must have S. T. output = -0.5

A05, +.75, -0.1   means amplifier 5 (an integrator) must have an
                          output = +.75 and a derivative input = -0.1 in
                          S. T. mode.

A35, .8, -0.6, +.4   means amplifier 35 (an integrator) must have an
                          output = +0.8 and a derivative = -0.6 in S. T. mode
                          but have an output = +0.4 in I. C. mode.

DAC(7), .5250, -.3   means that DAC7 must be set to .5250 in S. T. mode
                          but must be set to -0.3 in I. C. mode.

ADC(8), .85   means that ADC number 8 must have an input value
                          of .85 in S. T. mode.

C09, 1   means that comparator 9 must be ON (i. e. sum of
                          inputs positive) in S. T. mode.

(2)   Data can be loaded via the paper tape reader by typing the
standard BASIC command PTAPE.

Errors of syntax or illegal values are detected at this stage and
illegal lines output on the terminal. These lines can be immediately
corrected on-line or, in the case of many errors, a new data tape could
be prepared off-line. For example, if a pot coefficient intended to be
.15 was typed as 1.5 then this error is detected as a coefficient must be
< 1 and the line in error printed:

P13, 1.5, .05

The user then corrects the entry by typing

190

P13, .15, 0.5

(3)   Once a correct set of data, forming the SETUP data, is stored the user can command the computer to set up and check out the analogue machine by simply typing the command SETUP. Alternatively, the user could load in a BASIC type program in which SETUP was a statement which when executed could cause the analogue to be set up according to the SETUP table. With the SETUP command (or statement) a number of options are provided to allow great flexibility in use.

(a)   When errors are to be corrected on line the command SETUP is given which causes the following sequence of operations to occur.

(i)   Servo pots are set and any failing to set within tolerance are indicated as soon as the error is detected. The error format used is Address, Coeff Wanted, Error $\times 10^{-4}$. Thus P13, .5, +50 means pot 13 failed to set to 0.5 by an error .0050. The computer waits while the user checks out the error and takes appropriate action. If, for example, the pot has been patched back to front, the user will correct this and again command SETUP causing the setting-up operation to continue. If, however, there appears to be a mechanical fault in the pot concerned, the user can select another pot and type in a replacement command, e.g. REP, P13, P24 causing the details concerning Pot 13 to be transferred to P24 in the set-up table. On commanding SETUP the setting up operation is recommenced.

(ii)   When all servo pots are set the computer will output a message asking the user to set any manual pots to be used in the simulation, e.g. PLEASE SET Q02, .5, Q09, .7. When the user has completed these tasks he/she again types SETUP causing the computer to check the correct setting of the manual pots and continue the setting-up process.

(iii)   The computer completes the setting-up operations by setting DACs, DAMs and relays as required.

(iv)   On completion of set-up, the static test check-out is commenced. In this operation errors are indicated as they

191

appear but the computer does not wait for them to be corrected immediately but completes the total check and then stops. The reason for this is that a single error in the analogue may produce a whole chain of errors and thus all errors must be listed so that the user can check for the first in the chain. The first error the computer detects is very unlikely to be the cause of the trouble as the computer checks through the lists of components in numerical order. Errors are output in format:

Address, Value wanted, Tolerance ($\times 10^{-4}$)
e.g. A09, +.5, -100

Errors in derivative inputs to integrators are output in a similar way, e.g. D35, +.75, -7500 means that the derivative input to amplifier 35 is 7500×10^{-4} too low (this probably means the unit has been patched as a summer instead of an integrator). Incorrect comparator states are indicated as:

Address, Value (1 or 0) wanted, Value found.

At this stage it may be found that some of the errors are due to faulty data rather than incorrect patching or broken hardware. A data entry can be replaced by typing it again correctly at any time when the computer has indicated READY.

(v) When all the static test checks have been made the computer switches the analogue to I.C. mode and performs an initial condition check.

(b) If a hard copy list of all the static test is required on line on the control terminal, the command SETUP, L is given causing all set up and check data (i. e. not just errors) to be listed. Any data line in error is indicated by an asterisk.

e.g.	AMP	,	ST VALUE,	ERROR, (xE-4)	DER VALUE,	ERROR (xE-4)
	01	,	+ .5	, -1		
	02	,	+ .75	, +2		
	05	,	- 0.4	, -1	, +0.2	, -1
*	07	,	+0.35	, +2	, - 0.3	, 124
	15	,	- .75	, -2	,	

192

(c) When only a short amount of time is available on line it is sensible to let the computer perform the setting up and check out as automatically as possible, not stopping for setting errors to be corrected but only to allow for the adjustment of manual pots. This can be achieved by commanding SETUP, A which will cause a full listing of the static test to be output on the paper tape punch for subsequent off line printing.

Notes

A. The checks are all performed using default value tolerances, e.g. ±.0002 for pot coefficients, ±.0003 for amplifier and pot output values and ±.0005 for derivatives. Should the user require other tolerances then a TOLERANCE command must be input before the SETUP command is given, e.g. TOL PC, .0001, TOL PV, .0002, TOL AV, .0002, TOL DV, .0002 would cause a tolerance of ±.0001 to be used for pot coefficients (PC) and ±.0002 for all other values.

B. At the end of the set-up and ST check phases, during which many changes may be made to the SETUP table, there may not be enough time to complete any actual runs. It is then very useful to produce a tape of the current SETUP table which can be used as the input data tape on another occasion. An up-to-date SETUP data tape is obtained by commanding PLIST, S.

(ii) Dynamic operation

Once the setting-up stage is complete and the programmer is satisfied that the simulation is statically correct, dynamic runs, either actual problem solutions or solutions for dynamic check purposes, are commenced. For this stage of operation BASIC statements and hybrid statements in normal program form are used, the program being prepared off line, loaded by the command PTAPE and executed on typing the command RUN. As already mentioned, instructions are usually given in numbered statement form but to allow maximum interaction they can also be given without line numbers if it is required that they are to be obeyed immediately.

Statement/command instructions include:

SET PN = VAL	Set Pot N to coefficient VAL
SET DAC(N) = VAL	Set DAC(N) to coefficient VAL
READ ADD, VAL	Read 'unit' address ADD and assign the value read to VAL. 'Units' include all pots, amplifiers, derivatives, comparators, logic sense lines, A. D. C. s, etc.
TSCALE = TYPE	Set analogue computer timescale to TYPE where TYPE assumes one of

NS ≡ NORMAL SECONDS (INTEGRATOR GAINS × 1)

FS ≡ FAST SECONDS (INTEGRATOR GAINS × 10)

NM ≡ NORMAL MILLESECONDS (INTE-GRATOR GAINS × 1000)

FM ≡ FAST MILLISECONDS (INTEGRA-TOR GAINS × 10000)

MODE = TYPE	Set analogue mode to TYPE where TYPE is any of the standard codes for analogue modes, i. e. PS = POT SET, PC ≡ POT CHECK, ST ≡ STATIC TEST, I. C. ≡ INITIAL CONDITION, OP ≡ COMPUTE, HD ≡ HOLD, PP ≡ REPETITIVE.
WAIT(N)	Wait for N milleseconds before obeying next instruction. $1 \leq N \leq 32,000$.
WAIT FOR(HOLD)	Wait until analogue computer switches into HOLD mode.
WAIT FOR(SEN(N))	Wait until logic sense line N is made True (High or logic 1).

Notes

(i)   The WAIT instructions are useful in making the analogue machine compute for specified periods of time. Thus if it is required that the analogue computer should start in I. C. mode, COMPUTE for 15 seconds and then HOLD the following sequence could be used:

```
110   MODE = IC
120   MODE = OP
130   WAIT(15000)
140   MODE = HD
```

In many simulations the termination of the compute period occurs when some event has happened and a logic signal produced. This logic signal may be used to HOLD the computer directly or sent to the digital computer. Thus the program

```
100   FOR N=1 TO 150
110   MODE = IC
120   MODE = OP
130   WAIT FOR(HOLD)
140   NEXT N
```

could be used to make the computer cycle IC→OP→HOLD→IC→E. T. C. 150 times assuming a logic signal is generated in the analogue/parallel logic hardware to cause the computer to switch from COMPUTE (i. e. OP MODE) to HOLD.

(ii)   If it is required that the precision timer in the analogue machine is to be used to set up the exact times of RESET to IC, COMPUTE and, perhaps, HOLD in an iterative sequence of operation then the MODE = PP instruction can be used.

MODE = PP   will cause the analogue to cycle indefinitely
                   under control of the timer, whereas
MODE = PP(N)   will cause the analogue to perform N
                   iterative cycles.

10 · Sequential Hybrid Computing

10.1 Introduction

Hybrid computers are used to study a very wide range of problems involving the solution of differential equations. The general way in which the computer is used and programmed is described in the next two chapters. Specific applications are considered in the problems given at the end of each chapter.

The ways in which hybrid machines are used can be arranged into two broad groups, sequential and parallel. In SEQUENTIAL computing the digital and analogue sections are operating effectively in series, i. e. the analogue section is operated repetitively and, during the times when the analogue is in its dynamic mode actually solving the model equations, the digital is not performing any calculations or logical decisions. The digital is primarily used to organise the running of the total simulation and perform arithmetic and logic calculations between successive analogue dynamic run periods. In PARALLEL computation, besides being used to organise and control, the digital section is also required to compute actively during the time the analogue is in its dynamic mode of operation. Parallel computing operations are often very time critical in nature, demanding the maximum in the way of speed from the digital section. Sequential operations are generally not so time critical unless very short (~1 msec) analogue run periods are being used.

In practice, interpretive languages are generally only used in the non-time critical set-up and checking phases of a simulation study. For any studies involving high speed of operation, fully compiled programs (FORTRAN or machine/assembler level) are normally used. However, if speed of operation is not of vital importance and when simplicity of use is a major consideration, e. g. within teaching, an interpretive language can be used in a rather restricted way. Thus for ease and consis-

196

tency of presentation all applications, both sequential (§10) and parallel (§11), are described in terms of HYBRID BASIC. It is worth noting that BASIC, because it is interactive in operation, provides an excellent method to check algorithms and that the logic of a program is correct. Once a working program is produced, a FORTRAN version to be used for the serious part of the study is easily written. (N. B. At Bradford, FORTRAN callable subroutines are available to perform all the fundamental hybrid operations which can be performed using HYBRID BASIC.)

The interpretive HYBRID BASIC language enables complex sequences of operations to be performed automatically and the first sequential example illustrates its usefulness in providing automatic control of the analogue machine. The other two sequential application areas considered illustrate how automatic control and the ability to perform complicated logic and arithmetic operations can be applied to the solution of split boundary value and parameter optimisation problems, the latter perhaps being the most important application area of hybrid machines. Space does not allow a full discussion of these applications and therefore the notes must be regarded as a general introduction to the subjects. It is worth noting that many problems involving sequential computation have been studied using analogue machines extensively equipped with parallel logic (gates, counters, etc.). However, the amount of effort and skill needed for such implementations is difficult to justify in terms of the benefits gained and these techniques are best left only for the real enthusiast. Complicated operations are much more easily performed using a general stored program digital computer and the examples below illustrate this point. It will be noticed that in all the examples of sequential hybrid computing the analogue computer is only used to solve the differential equations (a task it performs well and at high speed) while the digital is used for logical control and to perform arithmetical calculations.

10. 2   **Run sequencing**

In some problems, families of solutions of differential equations are required in order to see the effect of variations in certain critical parameters, e. g. to observe the effect of production spreads. Programs to carry out measurements of this type are very easy to write. As an

example, suppose parameters A1 and A2 are known to vary from
A1MIN to A1MAX and A2MIN to A2MAX and suppose about 100 solutions of some equations for y(t) are required to illustrate the effect of
the spread in the values of these parameters. A scheme for solving this
problem is:

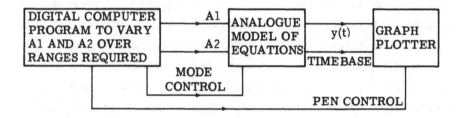

Fig. 10.1

A suitable control program is given below. It is assumed that
for any given values of A1 and A2, the equations will be solved in the
analogue section in a period of about 5 seconds and that, because total
time of running is not important, the values of A1 and A2 are set on
servo potentiometers P01 and P02. Thus each cycle of operation will
involve about an extra second to allow for the setting of A1 or A2 (or
perhaps both); this time will enable the pen to be moved back to the origin
ready for the next solution.

This program will cause 100 solutions of the equations to be made
for 100 combinations of the parameters A1 and A2. Total solution time
will be about 10 minutes. The sequential nature of the operation is clear
from the program. While the digital is in its dynamic phase (updating
values, etc. and setting pots) the analogue is in one of its static modes
of operation (POT SET, IC or HOLD) and while the analogue is in its
dynamic mode, actually solving the equations, the digital is 'waiting' in
a wait or do nothing loop.

Although this sequence of operations could be carried out under
manual control, automatic operation is faster and much less prone to
error. On a parallel logic analogue the operations could, without too

much difficulty, be performed using logical control of memory circuits in a double parameter sweep. However, time would have to be spent patching and checking the generation of the double sweep and this would have to be repeated every time a problem of this type had to be studied. On the other hand the program could be simply stored for future use.

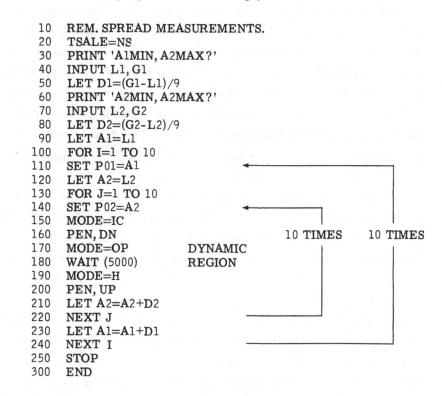

```
10   REM. SPREAD MEASUREMENTS.
20   TSALE=NS
30   PRINT 'A1MIN, A2MAX?'
40   INPUT L1, G1
50   LET D1=(G1-L1)/9
60   PRINT 'A2MIN, A2MAX?'
70   INPUT L2, G2
80   LET D2=(G2-L2)/9
90   LET A1=L1
100  FOR I=1 TO 10
110  SET P01=A1
120  LET A2=L2
130  FOR J=1 TO 10
140  SET P02=A2
150  MODE=IC
160  PEN, DN
170  MODE=OP
180  WAIT (5000)
190  MODE=H
200  PEN, UP
210  LET A2=A2+D2
220  NEXT J
230  LET A1=A1+D1
240  NEXT I
250  STOP
300  END
```

10 TIMES   10 TIMES

DYNAMIC
REGION

10.3   Split boundary value problems

The solution of split boundary value problems by the 'shooting' method and particularly the role of analogue memory units in automatic iteration schemes to match the boundary conditions is discussed at length in §6. The 'numerical' iteration scheme described for all analogue solution, applicable whether the equations are linear or non-linear, is that of proportional correction. In this simple but powerful method the errors in the boundary values (at time other than $t = 0$) are made to control the values of the unknown initial (time $t = 0$) conditions in such a way that the errors decrease to zero and the boundary values are matched.

Clearly, if a stored program digital computer is available, more sophisticated numerical procedures can be employed. However, experience has shown that the proportional correction scheme can be applied to a wide range of problems and there seems little point in using sophisticated methods unless absolutely necessary. This is especially true because most methods require fairly good estimates of boundary conditions to be known in advance if convergence is to be 'guaranteed' and thus interaction by the user is often required at run time. Sophisticated procedures often involve difficult programming and are not likely to be in favour by the average user unless they are available as standard library routines. Most hybrid laboratories contain standard parameter optimisation routines and these can often be used in difficult cases where the boundary value errors are complicated functions of the initial conditions (see Ex. (5) page   ). Some boundary value problems (e. g. civil engineering problems) are difficult to solve because the equations solutions are very 'noisy', i. e. , they are very sensitive to initial condition values. Special techniques, based on the method of decomposition are applicable in these cases.

It should also be noted that there are a number of special techniques for solving linear equations which involve relatively few trial solutions, i. e. give rapid convergence. These methods are generally more difficult to program than the proportional correction method and although they may provide more rapid convergence they lack generality of application as they are not strictly suited for studies involving the solution of non-linear equations.

The shooting method implemented on a hybrid machine can be represented as in Fig. 10. 2.

A guessed set of M initial conditions is set up and the equations solved in the analogue section. The errors in the M boundary conditions (at times other than computer time $t = 0$) are generated to be used to adjust the M initial conditions for the next run. The adjustment calculations are performed in the digital section and the new trial initial values are set up during the time the analogue is in one of its static modes of operation. The trial initial values can be input via potentiometers but,

200

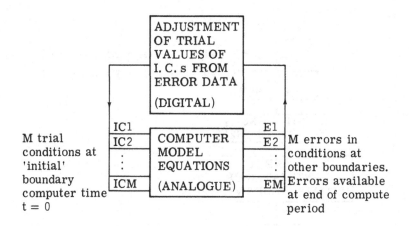

Fig. 10. 2

for higher speed of operation, D. A. C. s (or D. A. M. s if the 'parameters'
to be adjusted are coefficients in an equation rather than initial conditions)
should be used.

In general, each initial value will affect each error and therefore
each error should be used to control each initial value. As explained in
§6, for reasons of simplicity it is best to aim to make each initial value
be controlled by only one error. However, by program it is very easy to
allow for complicated relationships if required.

A general flow diagram of a program for a 2 unknown initial value
problem is shown in Fig. 10. 3. It can easily be extended to many dimensions. V1 and V2 are used for the unknown initial values, E1 and E2
for the errors and G1, H1, G2, H2 for the proportional gains. New
initial values are calculated from the old values using the formulae in
Fig. 10. 3.

A program for the scheme is given on page 203. It is assumed
that the integrator timescales and the length of the compute period are
set manually and that the analogue section switches to HOLD at the end
of this period. V1 and V2 are set on DACs 1 and 2 and errors E1
and E2 read via ADCs 1 and 2.

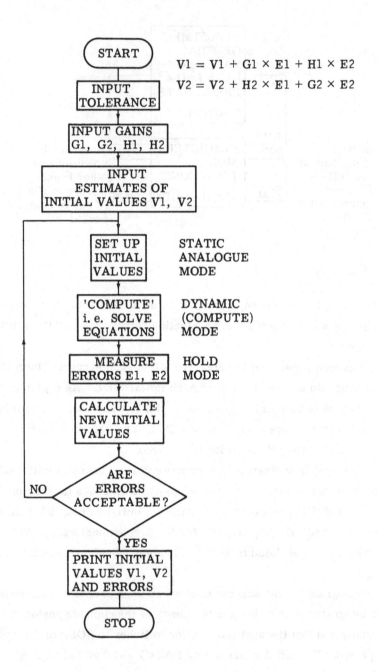

$$V1 = V1 + G1 \times E1 + H1 \times E2$$
$$V2 = V2 + H2 \times E1 + G2 \times E2$$

Fig. 10.3

202

```
 10    PRINT 'TOTAL TOLERENCE?'
 20    INPUT T
 30    PRINT 'ITERATION GAINS ERROR1 TO IC1, ERROR2 TO
                                          IC1?'
 40    INPUT G1, H1
 50    PRINT 'ITERATION GAINS ERROR1 TO IC2, ERROR2 TO
                                          IC2?'
 60    INPUT H2, G2
 70    PRINT 'ESTIMATES FOR INITIAL CONDITIONS IC1, IC2?'
 80    INPUT V1, V2
 90    MODE=IC
100    DAC(1)=V1
110    DAC(2)=V2
120    MODE=OP
130    WAIT FOR(HOLD)
140    ADC(1), E1
150    ADC(2), E2
160    IF ABS(E1)+ABS(E2) < T THEN 200
170    LET V1=V1+G1*E1+H1*E2
180    LET V2=V2+H2*E1+G2*E2
190    GOTO 90
200    PRINT 'V1', 'V2', 'E1', 'E2'
210    PRINT V1, V2, E1, E2
220    STOP
230    END
```

The above program can be used with a wide range of problems involving 2 unknowns. The values (signs and magnitudes) of G1, G2, H1 and H2 must be chosen with reference to the problem itself. (See §6.) Clearly a hybrid scheme of this type is not likely to be any faster in operation than a manual adjustment scheme (if the analogue is run repetitively at high speed) and is probably rather slower in operation than an automatic analogue/parallel logic scheme but it certainly has advantages in generality, ease of running (cf. parallel logic scheme) and the fact that it will provide a log (computer output) of the way the problem was run. Moreover the small effort needed to produce a working program is well worthwhile even for small problems like this if the problem needs be solved for many cases. Efficient use of the hardware is obtained in these cases because of the automation provided by the stored program of instructions.

10.4 Parameter optimisation

Discussion

In many system design problems it is necessary to determine the conditions that must exist for the system to work most efficiently. Also in many production problems it is necessary to find the best conditions for a product to be produced at minimum cost, i. e. most economically. The determination of these best conditions or parameters is called parameter optimisation.

The study of optimisation problems by computers involves three essential steps:

(1) Formation of a model

The system is represented by a model so that the behaviour of the system can be studied by testing the response of the model under varying conditions, i. e. different parameter values. The model generally starts as an analytic model, i. e. a set of algebraic and/or differential equations. These equations are converted into a computer model (analogue/hybrid/digital), and, by inputing various values of the parameters and solving the model equations, the behaviour of the actual system is predicted.

(2) Specification of an objective function

Having derived a model of the system it is necessary to specify in a precise mathematical way a 'figure of merit' or objective function which is a measure of the quality of performance of the system. For any set of parameter values the model equations are solved and the performance of the system determined by calculating this objective function. In order to optimise the system it is necessary to choose the parameters so that the objective function is a minimum or a maximum. In problems involving production the objective function may be the cost per item, in control problems it may be an error criterion and in problems involving machines it may be the efficiency of operation. The calculation of the objective function from the response of the computer model forms part of the simulation and in hybrid systems it may be calculated within either the analogue or digital sections.

The choice of a satisfactory objective function is sometimes the hardest part of the whole problem of optimisation. In engineering problems it is often possible to determine by previous experience whether or not a system is behaving well (i. e. near its optimum) but it is difficult to express this mathematically.

The answer one obtains is generally dependent on the choice of objective function. For example, if it is required to determine the optimum way to move a train from one station to another then (a) minimum total cost, (b) minimum fuel consumption, (c) minimum journey time, could all be meaningful objective functions but the optimum parameters (acceleration time, cruising time, braking time) obtained would clearly depend on choice of objective function. Before it is possible to optimise it is clearly necessary to decide what the system must do. A possible objective function for the train problem might be 'minimum total cost providing journey time does not exceed a certain value'. Sometimes constraints need to be placed on values of parameters used, e.g. in the train problem it may be necessary to specify constraints to take into account passenger comfort (maximum permitted acceleration/retardation). The optimisation of such problems is called constrained optimisation.

(3) Search routine

Having simulated the system including the objective function it is necessary to test the behaviour of the computer model for a wide range of values of the input parameters and, from evaluation of the objective function with each set of values, determine which are the best set. The parameter adjustments sequence used to select these best conditions by repeatedly solving the model equations and computing the objective function is called the search routine. Desirable properties of such routines are that they should give the correct answer with as little analytical and/or computational calculation as possible and be fairly simple to understand.

Very many search routines have been produced but no universal best method has been determined. It is often necessary to match the method to the problem or try many methods with the same problem to ensure the correct answer is found. Much depends on the 'shape' of the objective function, i.e. the way it varies as a function of its parameters, e.g. whether it has a number of minima/maxima and whether or not it contains 'ridges'. Generally, methods giving a high probability of success involve excessive amounts of calculation whereas efficient (i.e. minimum number of trial runs) methods do not necessarily produce the optimum conditions.

To help understanding it is useful to consider objective functions
of two parameters and represent the objective function 'surface' as a
contour map.

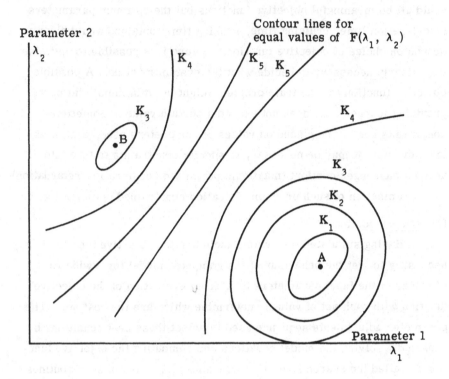

Fig. 10.4

The problem of optimisation is then: starting at any guessed point
$(\lambda_1, \lambda_2)_0$ how to reach the true minimum/maximum A, with as little
calculation as possible and without getting to a false optimum B.

The general process, one of systematic 'trial and error', can be
illustrated as in Fig. 10.5.

When comparing the usefulness of the various search methods
used in optimisation studies, a number of factors must be considered.
Important amongst these are:

     (1)   the simplicity or otherwise of the technique both to program
          and to use,

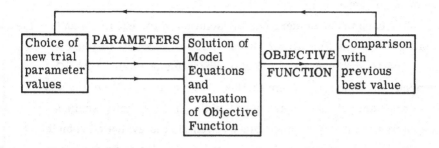

Fig. 10. 5

(2)   the robustness of the method, i. e. whether or not it is
        likely to succeed and locate the optimum even if the error
        surface is complicated,

(3)   the amount of computing time needed to obtain the optimum
        solution.

When problems involving the solution of many complicated differential equations are studied using all-digital techniques, the time taken
to solve the equations for one set of trial parameters and compute the
objective function may be many minutes. The total time of solution, and
hence the cost of the computing time, is chiefly determined by the number
of trial runs which have to be made. Hence good digital computer methods
are generally those which are likely to succeed in a minimum number of
trial runs.

However, when such differential equation problems are studied
by hybrid computer techniques, the time per run is often quite short, from
a fraction of a second to a few seconds, and consequently it is not so
vitally important to obtain the optimum solution in a minimum number of
runs. Thus 'less efficient' methods which are easier to program and
have a high chance of success may be considered. In addition some highly
efficient 'digital computer' methods rely on the precise calculation of
gradients which in turn involve the precise differencing of large and nearly
equal values. Because of the limited resolution of analogue (and interface)
hardware, such methods are not suited for hybrid computer optimisation.

In the notes that follow a few of the simpler methods of search are
considered and programs are developed for some of these methods. Where-

207

ver the term optimum is used it is assumed to refer to the minimum value of the objective function.

For each program derived, the solution of the equations and evaluation of objective function E for any trial set of parameter values is assumed performed under control of a subroutine of HYBRID BASIC statements starting at line number 1000. The exact details of the subroutine program will of course depend on the problem being studied, particularly whether or not the objective function is evaluated completely within the analogue section. However, the subroutine to perform one evaluation will generally consist of the following sequence of instructions:

```
1000 MODE=IC
1010                SET PARAMETER
  .                 VALUES ON D. A. C. s
  .                 AND D. A. M. s
  .
1100 MODE=OP        SOLVE EQUATIONS AND EVALUATE
                    OBJECTIVE FUNCTION E IN
                    ANALOGUE SECTION
1110 WAIT FOR (HOLD)
1120 ADC(N), E      READ OBJECTIVE FUNCTION ON ADC
                    LINE N AND ASSIGN
1990 RETURN         VALUE TO E.
```

GROUP 1

In these methods no information which has been gained from previous function evaluations is used to aid the search (except perhaps in the checking of whether or not an improvement has occurred).

(i) **Global search**

The simplest search technique is to let each parameter vary in steps over its permitted range in such a way that 'all' combinations of parameters are tried. The value of the objective function is calculated with each combination of parameter values and the parameters giving the optimum result are selected. The method is likely to yield the correct result unless too wide a grid or mesh is selected in cases where the objective function contains deep, narrow 'wells'. However, the number of runs needed to yield any reasonable accuracy is enormous, e.g. to localise the position of the optimum to ±1% (i.e. each parameter located to ±1% of its permitted range) even for a 3 parameter problem would involve $(100)^3 = 1$ million runs. Even at 1 second a run this involves a lot of computing time!

The method can be speeded up greatly, with of course a greatly increased chance of failure due to too coarse a grid being used, if the optimum is first approximately located using a coarse grid, and then located more accurately by searching around this approximate position using a medium grid and repeating the process again using a fine grid.

For example the optimum set of parameter values for a 3 parameter problem can be located to within about ±1% by using a 3 stage search, each stage involving the calculation of the objective function 512 times corresponding to 8 trial values of each parameter. However, as the number of parameters involved increases, the number of runs needed increases very rapidly and even this successive localisation technique is not attractive.

Exercise

Write a program to perform a global search for 3 parameters in 3 stages of localisation to enable the optimum parameter values to be located within ±1%.

(ii) Series of one parameter searches

Another obvious method of searching is to perform a series of one parameter searches (in which all but one parameters are held constant) each parameter being varied in turn until a 'local' minimum is found. The method is illustrated in Fig. 10.6 for a function of two parameters.

The single parameter searches can be performed using any efficient numerical procedure (e.g. some form of bisection) providing that, for hybrid applications, it does not involve the calculation of derivatives. During the initial part of the search the one parameter minima need only be found approximately but, as the search progresses, greater accuracy of location is required.

Although this type of search should involve far fewer trial runs

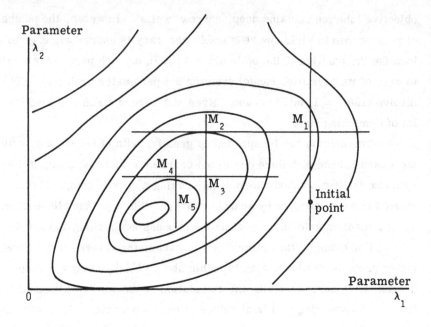

Fig. 10.6 Series of one parameter searches

M_1, M_2, M_3 etc. are local one parameter minima.

than a global method, it may locate a local rather than a global optimum. Starting from a number of different initial points should reduce the risk of this occurring.

However, the method has not found much favour as it is often very inefficient (i.e. gives very slow convergence) in the presence of 'ridges' in the objective function surface.

Exercise

Write a routine for finding the minimum of a function of one parameter and include this routine in a program to perform a 4 parameter search. To locate the one parameter minima a simple 'step and bisect' algorithm could be used, i.e.

Starting at a value λ_0, step λ in steps of $\Delta\lambda$ calculating $E(\lambda)$ at each point, until the function E no longer improves. When this happens step in the opposite direction with a half amplitude step size (i.e. replace $\Delta\lambda$ by $-\frac{\Delta\lambda}{2}$) until the objective function again no longer improves (or a maximum of 4 steps have been performed). At this stage halve the step size again and step in the opposite direction. Stop the search when the step size has reduced to a specified magnitude.

(iii) **Random searches**

In random searches the basic method is to vary the parameters in a random way, calculate the objective function for each combination of trial parameters and select that combination which gives the best objective function. Very many variations of the basic technique are used, e. g. in which each parameter is varied in turn, in which all parameters are varied together, in which the properties (e. g. variance) of the random generator producing the random steps are varied as the search progresses, etc. The method can be arranged to minimise the chance of selecting a local optimum by performing a random search with a very large average step size about any optimum found.

The number of runs needed to locate the optimum depends not only on the starting point chosen but also on chance and thus this number is very variable.

A popular form of the method is the creeping random search. In this technique the search is started from a trial initial point. Random changes are made in all parameter values and should a combination of parameters be produced which gives a better objective function value, i. e. an improvement, the random search is restarted about this new point. The technique is illustrated in Fig. 10. 7 for a 2 parameter search. Unsuccessful trials are marked 'x' and successful ones 'o'.

A variation of this method is to arrange that once an improved point is located, random (or other) steps are taken in the direction of the improvement until no further improvement is obtained.

Random search techniques have been applied successfully to parameter optimisation problems in at least 6 dimensions. The ability of the method to avoid local optima is an important characteristic. The efficiency of the search in terms of the number of function evaluations made is very dependent on the average step size used. If too small a step is used, initial convergence is poor but convergence near the optimum is good. If too large a step is used, although initial convergence may be good, convergence near the optimum is generally poor as the majority of trial points chosen will be well away from the optimum. Thus it is necessary to arrange that the average step size is varied depending on the progress of the search (e. g. on the ratio of successful to unsuccessful trials).

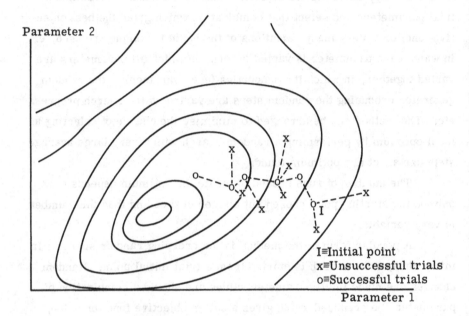

Fig. 10. 7 Creeping random search

(Area of search from current best point restricted to part of field.)

A program to perform a simple creeping random search is given below for the case of 2 parameters L1 and L2 which are both assumed to lie in the range [0, 1]. A random number generator[†] RND(0) is used to generate a random number between 0 and 1. This is then used to produce a random positive or negative step in parameter L1, the average

[†] The action of the random number generator statement RND(0) for a particular implementation needs to be examined carefully. Normally on the command RUN it will generate the same sequence of random numbers starting with a certain value. Thus 'random' searches can be re-run following exactly the same sequence. If this is to be avoided, additional instructions must be used to randomise the starting point.

amplitude of the step being determined by the input scaling factor P. The same technique is used to produce a random step in parameter L2. The function is evaluated at this trial point. If the combination of parameters chosen randomly gives an improvement, the parameter values, together with the corresponding function value, are output and the search continued from this new point. If no improvement is obtained, only the trial parameter values are output. No provision is made to stop the search but simple tests are made to ensure that only permitted values of the parameters (i. e. in range 0 to 1) are used.

The search program is very simple, involving less than 20 computational statements, i. e. those other than those used for remarks, printing headings, etc. and the number could be further reduced by combining some together, e. g. statements 95, 100 are equivalent to LET L1=B1+2*P*(RND(0)-0.5). To set up even a simple 2 parameter random search using a parallel logic hybrid machine involves a considerable amount of skilled programming especially if the random steps have to be generated from shift registers set up as pseudo random sequence generators.

```
 10  REM CREEPING RANDOM SEARCH
 20  PRINT 'FRACTION OF PARAMETER RANGES TO BE
                        SEARCHED INITIALLY'
 30  INPUT P
 40  PRINT 'INITIAL VALUES PAR1, PAR2?'
 41  INPUT L1, L2
 42  REM. B1 AND B2 USED FOR BEST PARAMETERS TO DATE.
 43  LET B1=L1
 44  LET B2=L2
 60  PRINT 'PAR1', 'PAR2', 'FUNCTION'
 70  REM EVALUATE AND PRINT INITIAL FUNCTION
 80  GOSUB 1000
 85  REM. E0 USED FOR BEST FUNCTION VALUE TO DATE.
 90  LET E0=E
100  PRINT B1, B2, E0
110  REM. GENERATE NEW TRIAL VALUE OF PARAMETER 1.
120  LET X=RND(0)
130  LET L1=B1+2*P*(X-.5)
140  IF L1< 0 THEN 120
150  IF L1> 1 THEN 120
155  REM. GENERATE NEW TRIAL VALUE PARAMETER 2.
160  LET Y=RND(0)
170  LET L2=B2+2*P*(Y-.5)
```

```
180  IF L2< 0 THEN 160
190  IF L2> 1 THEN 160
200  REM EVALUATE FUNCTION
210  GOSUB 1000
220  IF E< E0 THEN 240
221  REM. NO IMPROVEMENT. PRINT AND TRY AGAIN.
222  PRINT L1, L2
230  GOTO 120
239  REM. IMPROVEMENT. UPDATE BEST VALUES.
240  LET E0=E
250  LET B1=L1
260  LET B2=L2
270  PRINT B1, B2, E0
280  GOTO 120
1000 etc SUBROUTINE TO EVALUATE FUNCTION
2000 END
```

Exercises

(1)   Extend the above program so that the search stops after N unsuccessful trial evaluations occur consecutively, where N is input before the search begins.

(2)   Extend further so that after a sequence of N unsuccessful trials steps is made, the average step size is decreased by a factor of 10 (i. e. change P automatically) and the search continued until a further sequence of N unsuccessful trials is obtained. This will considerably increase the efficiency of the search and enable the optimum to be located more accurately.

(3)   Extend the program further so that when a minimum is obtained, the search is restarted with such large trial step values that 'all' points in parameter space are examined. Should a point of improvement be found, which will imply the optimum previously found was a local and not a global optimum, arrange that the search is started again.

(4)   Extend the program to deal with up to 5 parameters and arrange that at the end of the search the ratio of the number of unsuccessful to successful trials is output.

(5)   Modify the method of search so that as soon as an improved point is found, random amplitude steps are made in the direction of the improvement until no further improvement can be obtained. Arrange for the general random search to continue from this best 'unidirectional' ran-

dom search.

GROUP 2

Derivative methods

There are a number of search methods used which involve the calculation not only of the objective function at a point but also the partial derivatives of the function with respect to the parameters. In problems for which hybrid computers are used, the calculation of the objective function itself involves the solution of a set of differential equations and each partial derivative must be calculated by differencing values of the objective function at neighbouring points. Either central difference or one-sided difference formulae may be used in these calculations, the latter, i. e.

$$\frac{\partial F}{\partial \lambda_i}(\lambda_1, \ldots \lambda_i, \ldots \lambda_n) \simeq \frac{F(\lambda_1, \ldots \lambda_i + \Delta\lambda_i, \ldots \lambda_n) - F(\lambda_1, \ldots \lambda_i, \ldots \lambda_n)}{\Delta\lambda_i}$$

involving fewer function evaluations.

To obtain reasonably accurate estimates of these partial derivatives implies that $\Delta\lambda_i$ for $i \in [1, n]$ must be small. Unfortunately the values of the functions at λ_i and $\lambda_i + \Delta\lambda_i$ may be large but differ only by a small amount. Relatively large errors may be introduced in calculating these differences particularly in analogue/hybrid computer systems with their inherent lack of precision/resolution.

All methods of optimisation do of course involve the taking of differences to find out whether or not a new objective function is better or worse than a previous one but:

(a) these differences are generally large except near the optimum point,

(b) often knowledge of the sign of the difference is all that is required.

In gradient methods involving the calculation of derivatives, the actual value of the magnitude is used and it is for this reason that these methods are not favoured for use in hybrid optimisation studies.

In the following notes a particular variation of the simplest of these methods, the so-called modified steepest descent technique, is described primarily because of its educational rather than practical value. It is instructive to set up a search involving this method and to observe the search path, particularly with functions containing 'long narrow valleys'. The method converges slowly in these cases, the search running back and forth across the valley, unless a fortuitous starting point is selected.

It is interesting to note that the steepest descent method can be programmed on a parallel logic hybrid. A particularly elegant implementation of the technique is described in ref. 6; the program to carry out the search is stored in only $(3 + n)$ bistable elements, where n is the number of parameters involved.

(iv) Steepest descent and modifications

The basic search technique is illustrated below, for the case of 2 parameters.

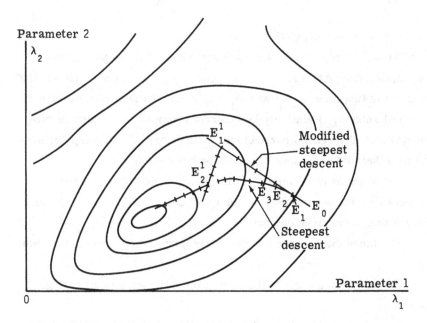

Fig. 10.8 Steepest descent and modified steepest descent

E_0, E_1, E_2 etc., are points of exploration for normal method and E_0, E_1^1, E_2^1 are points of exploration for the modified method.

The objective function is calculated for some trial initial values of parameters (λ_1, λ_2), point E_0 on diagram. Small changes $\Delta\lambda_1$, $\Delta\lambda_2$ (not shown) are made in turn to parameter values λ_1 and λ_2 and the objective function calculated twice more, and partial derivatives $\dfrac{\partial F}{\partial\lambda_1}$ and $\dfrac{\partial F}{\partial\lambda_2}$ estimated by differencing.

The direction of the steepest descent path is calculated from these derivatives and a step made along that direction by an amount proportional to the slope itself, i. e. change in the parameter values at this update stage $\Delta\lambda = -k$ grad E, where k is a constant. At the new point E_1 the gradient is calculated again and a further step made. The process is repeated until the gradient becomes zero at a minimum value.

The process is inefficient in the sense that too many function evaluations are needed per update step (particularly so if central difference formulae are used).

A simple modification to the method called the modified steepest descent is to arrange to step, after each gradient evaluation, along the direction of maximum slope until the objective function worsens and then to recalculate the gradient. A maximum number of steps (e. g. 8 for a two parameter problem) is permitted at each update stage to avoid problems introduced where the gradient is small but the function is not near an optimum (e. g. along the top of a ridge). Once an optimum has been located approximately using one-sided difference formulae to evaluate the partial derivatives, it can be located a little more accurately by using central difference formulae.

Steepest descent methods are easy to program as is illustrated by the following program for a 2 parameter modified steepest descent search.

A maximum of $C = 8$ update steps is allowed between derivative evaluations. To fix the position of the minimum accurately it is necessary that the explore steps used in the derivative evaluations are small. To minimise the introduction of errors when differencing, due to limited resolution of the analogue equipment, it is advisable to measure the error criterion by means of the D. V. M. monitor in the analogue section of the computer. This generally provides greater precision (typically 15 to 16 bits) than is usually available in fast A. D. C. systems (typically 12 bits).

```
  5 REM. MODIFIED STEEPEST DESCENT. 2 PARAMETERS.
 10 PRINT 'GAIN K'
 20 INPUT K
 30 PRINT 'EXPLORE STEPS D1, D2 FOR DERIVATIVE
                                  CALCULATION'
 40 INPUT D1, D2
 50 PRINT 'INITIAL GUESS L1, L2'
 60 INPUT L1, L2
 65 PRINT 'PAR1', 'PAR2', 'FUNCTION'
 70 REM, CALCULATE FUNCTION AT CENTRAL POINT
 80 LET C=0
 90 GOSUB 1000
100 LET E0=E
105 PRINT L1, L2, E
109 REM. CALCULATE PARTIAL DER H1 W. R. T.  PAR1.
110 LET L1=L1+D1
120 GOSUB 1000
130 LET H1=(E-E0)/D1
140 LET L1=L1-D1
149 REM. CALCULATE PARTIAL DER H2 W. R. T.  PAR2.
150 LET L2=L2+D2
160 GOSUB 1000
170 LET H2=(E-E0)/D2
180 REM. UPDATE STAGE.
190 LET C=C+1
200 IF C> 7 THEN 80
210 LET L1=L1-K*H1
220 LET L2=L2-K*H2
230 GOSUB 1000
240 IF E< E0 THEN 250
241 REM. STEP BACK 1 PLACE TO BEST POINT TO DATE.
                                  EXPLORE AGAIN.
242 LET L1=L1-K*H1
243 LET L2=L2-K*H2
244 GOTO 80
245 REM. IMPROVEMENT. HENCE TRY ANOTHER STEP.
250 LET E0=E
260 GOTO 190
1000 SUBROUTINE TO EVALUATE FUNCTION etc.
1990 RETURN
2000 END
```

Exercises

(1)   Extend the program above so that the scaling of the objective function evaluated in the analogue section can be adjusted to keep the objective function always reasonably large, e. g. as the objective function decreases to 0. 2, change the scaling amplitude factor by 5 so that the objective function increases to 1.   This technique helps to reduce the errors associated with the calculation of the differences.

(2)   Extend the program to n parameters, where $n \leq 5$,
allowing a maximum of 2^{n+1} steps at the updating stage.

GROUP 3

In this group of direct search methods not involving derivative
evaluations, the new set of trial parameter values are extrapolated from
current and past values. Well-known methods in this group include
Simplex and its extension Hyplex, extensively used in linear programming and related problems, Partran and the pattern search technique
of Hooke and Jeeves. This last method has been shown to be particularly
appropriate for hybrid optimisation and it is the only method of this group
considered in these notes.

(v) Hooke and Jeeves

The method can best be understood by reference to the diagram,
Fig. 10.11, and the flow charts. The search comprises two basic operations repeated over and over again:

(a)   A simple exploration about a pattern point to determine the
'best' direction in which to 'move'.

(b)   A pattern move from a base point using knowledge gained in
(a).

In a two parameter problem the explore stage from a pattern point P1,
P2 is as shown in the flow diagram, Fig. 10.9, and the total search is
as shown in Fig. 10.10.

The progress of a typical search using the above algorithm is
shown in Fig. 10.11. Where a series of successful pattern moves are
made, the steps taken using formulae $P1 = X1 + (X1 - B1)$,
$P2 = X2 + (X2 - B2)$ become larger and larger, the direction of the
pattern move increasingly approximating to the best direction possible.

The magnitude of the initial step sizes can be made unequal and
the search is normally stopped when the step sizes, D1 and D2, have
reduced below a specified fraction of their initial values.

The program on page 222 directly relates to the flow diagrams,
Figs. 10.9 and 10.10. In addition provision is made to stop the search
when the step size has reduced below a certain value. For reasons of
space, PRINT statements have been reduced to a minimum but normally

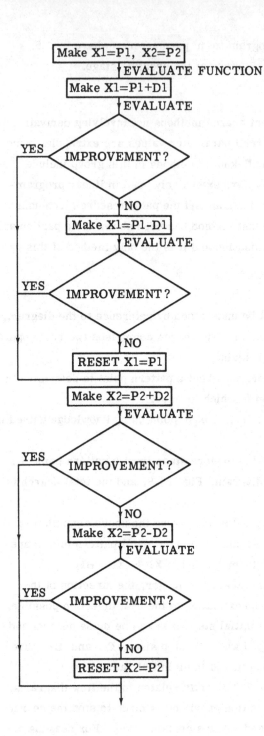

Make X1=P1, X2=P2
↓EVALUATE FUNCTION
Make X1=P1+D1
↓EVALUATE

YES   IMPROVEMENT?

↓NO
Make X1=P1-D1
↓EVALUATE

YES   IMPROVEMENT?

↓NO
RESET X1=P1

Make X2=P2+D2
↓EVALUATE

YES   IMPROVEMENT?

↓NO
Make X2=P2-D2
↓EVALUATE

YES   IMPROVEMENT?

↓NO
RESET X2=P2

X1, X2 represent trial parameter values used. D1, D2 are the steps made in the parameters. After completion of this algorithm X1, X2 will be the 'best' values about P1, P2 for the parameter values. The number of function evaluations needed will be from 3 to 5 and the 'best' values obtained for X1, X2 will be one of nine possible combinations: P1 or P1 ± D1, P2 or P2 ± D2. Note this includes X1=P1, X2=P2.

Fig. 10.9

220

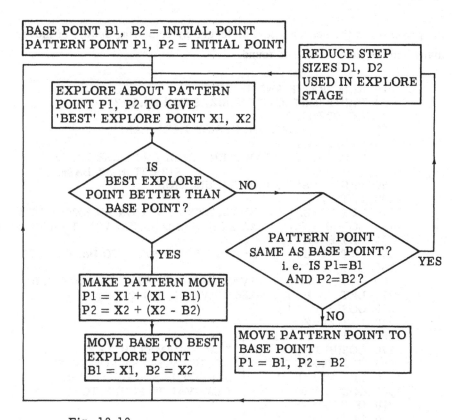

BASE POINT B1, B2 = INITIAL POINT
PATTERN POINT P1, P2 = INITIAL POINT

REDUCE STEP SIZES D1, D2 USED IN EXPLORE STAGE

EXPLORE ABOUT PATTERN POINT P1, P2 TO GIVE 'BEST' EXPLORE POINT X1, X2

IS BEST EXPLORE POINT BETTER THAN BASE POINT?

NO

PATTERN POINT SAME AS BASE POINT? i. e. IS P1=B1 AND P2=B2?

YES

YES

MAKE PATTERN MOVE
P1 = X1 + (X1 - B1)
P2 = X2 + (X2 - B2)

MOVE BASE TO BEST EXPLORE POINT
B1 = X1, B2 = X2

NO

MOVE PATTERN POINT TO BASE POINT
P1 = B1, P2 = B2

Fig. 10.10

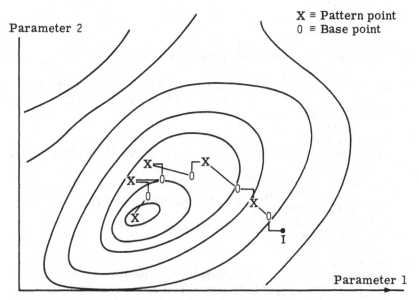

X ≡ Pattern point
0 ≡ Base point

Parameter 2

Parameter 1

Fig. 10.11   Hooke and Jeeve's pattern search

the progress of the search would be logged by outputting details of moves made and the function values found.

```
 10  REM. HOOKE AND JEEVES.
 20  PRINT 'INITIAL STEP SIZES FOR D1, D2?'
 30  INPUT D1, D2
 50  PRINT 'INITIAL VALUES OF PAR1, PAR2'
 60  INPUT B1, B2
 70  REM. B1, B2 PARAMETER VALUES AT BASE B1, B2.
                               FUNCTION AT BASE B0
 80  PRINT 'PAR1', 'PAR2', 'FUNCTION'
100  LET X1=B1
110  LET X2=B2          EVALUATE FUNCTION AN EXTRA TIME
120  GOSUB 1000         AT START AND ASSIGN VALUE OBTAINED
130  LET B0=E           TO B0.
150  LET P1=B1          SET PATTERN POINT TO BASE POINT
160  LET P2=B2
200  LET X1=P1          EVALUATE AT PATTERN POINT AND
210  LET X2=P2          ASSIGN VALUE TO X0.
230  GOSUB 1000
240  LET X0=E
260  LET X1=P1+D1
270  GOSUB 1000         FOR PARAMETER 1 EXPLORE
280  IF E<X0 THEN 380   ABOUT PATTERN POINT AND
290  LET X1=P1-D1       SELECT BEST POINT.  ASSIGN
300  GOSUB 1000         BEST VALUE FOUND TO X0.
310  IF E<X0 THEN 380
330  LET X1=P1
340  GOTO 410
380  LET X0=E
410  LET X2=P2+D2
420  GOSUB 1000
430  IF E<X0 THEN 520   FOR PARAMETER 2 EXPLORE
440  LET X2=P2-D2       ABOUT PATTERN POINT AND
450  GOSUB 1000         SELECT BEST POINT.  ASSIGN
460  IF E<X0 THEN 520   BEST VALUE FOUND TO X0.
480  LET X2=P2
490  GOTO 550
520  LET X0=E
550  REM. CHECK IF BEST EXPLORE POINT IS BETTER THAN
                               BASE.
560  IF B0< X0+1.00000E-05 THEN 700
580  LET P1=2*X1-B1
590  LET P2=2*X2-B2     UPDATE PATTERN POINT.
610  LET B1=X1
620  LET B2=X2          UPDATE BASE POINT.
630  LET B0=X0
640  GOTO 200
700  REM. CHECK IF PATTERN POINT=BASE POINT.
710  IF ABS(B1-P1)+ABS(B2-P2)< 1.00000E-07 THEN 900
720  GOTO 150
```

```
900  REM. REDUCE STEP SIZE.
910  LET D1=D1/10
920  LET D2=D2/10
930  PRINT D1
940  IF D1>1.00000E-04 THEN 200
950  PRINT 'BEST VALUES TO DATE PAR1, PAR2, FUNCTION'
960  PRINT B1, B2, B0
990  STOP
1000 SUBROUTINE TO EVALUATE OBJECTIVE FUNCTION E
1010 PRINT X1, X2, E
2000 RETURN
6000 END
```

Exercise

Extend the above program to 5 parameters. Add in PRINT statements and headings so that a log of the progress of the search is made.

10.5 General comment

In problems involving parameter optimisation, it is generally not sufficient just to obtain the optimum conditions because in practical problems the variation of the function about the optimum is also of importance. Without this information it is not possible to say how critically parameters must be set in order to produce near optimum conditions/performance. There is little point in specifying to a design engineer that the optimum parameter value is 0.1457 if ±25% variations about this value only result in a +1% change in the objective function. Thus once the optimum has been obtained, simple one parameter sweeps (each parameter varied in turn) should be made centred on the optimum point. The one advantage of the global search method is that all this data is generated during the search (and should be output or stored for reference).

10.6 Examples

(i) Split boundary value problems

(1)   Derive a hybrid computer simulation for the problem discussed in Ex. 4 of §6.

(2)   Set up a model of the 'projectile over the wall' problem discussed in §6 (problem 2) but assume frictional drag is proportional to the square of the speed, i. e. simulate in the analogue section the equations given in §7. Arrange within the analogue model to store the height of the

projectile as it crosses over the wall and arrange to switch the analogue to HOLD when the projectile 'hits the ground'.

Use this model as the basis for a general hybrid computer study which will enable the user to specify the position and heights of the wall and the horizontal range required and to obtain from the computer the required speed and angle of launch. Use the program in the text as the basis for boundary value matching but include statements which will use the error in the range to control the horizontal component, i.e. $(V \cos \theta)_0$ of the speed of launch and the miss distance above the wall to control the vertical component $(V \sin \theta)_0$. The values of V_0 and θ_0 for each successive run should be calculated from these miss distance errors within the digital section.

(3)   Write a general computer program to match the boundary conditions when studying beam deflection problems (Ex. 7 of §6) on a hybrid computer. Arrange that the length of the COMPUTE period, corresponding to the length of the beam, be determined by a WAIT statement. Write the program to handle any combination of boundary conditions corresponding to the different ways a beam may be supported, clamped or left free at its ends. This can be done by:

(a)   assigning 4 variables to the initial conditions at one end (i.e. the start) of the beam for the deflection, slope, moment and shear and by assigning 4 variables corresponding to the possible errors in the boundary conditions at the other end of the beam.

(b)   Linking each of these initial conditions to each error (16 iteration constants involved).

(c)   Arranging that for any particular case all but 2 of these constants are made zero.

Write the program so that it can be used by a person having little knowledge of digital computing. Arrange that the equations are solved at high speed while the boundary value matching is taking place and that once this is completed the model is slowed to normal seconds timescale and the variables (deflection, etc.) recorded in turn on an X-Y graph plotter. To select variables for recording assume that whichever ampli-

fier is selected by the analogue addressing system is automatically joined
to the Y input of the recorder.

(ii) Parameter optimisation problems
Notes

The examples given below are of simple problems involving the
adjustment of only one or two parameters. It is well worthwhile studying
these simple problems before getting involved in multi-dimensional optimisation in order to gain experience of different types of search methods.
(With one or two parameters the progress of a search can be readily
observed on a simple display or pen recorder.) A more extensive problem involving optimisation is given in §11.

Because of the relative complexity of a hybrid system it is important to check initially the operation of any optimisation routine by finding
the minimum value of a simple algebraic function evaluated entirely
within the digital section of the hybrid. A simple example could be the
function

$$E = 0.25 + 2(L1 - 0.5)^2 + 0.5(L2 - 0.5)^2$$

which has a minimum of 0.25 at $L1 = 0.5$, $L2 = 0.5$.

A much more demanding example for study is
$E = 100(y - x^2)^2 + (1 - x)^2$ which was introduced by Rosenbrock as a
test for search procedures.

(4)   The movement of the needle of a simple moving coil voltmeter in response to a positive input voltage $V(t)$ applied from time
$t = 0$ is:

$$\frac{d^2X}{dt^2} + A\frac{dX}{dt} + Bx = C.V(t),$$

where X is the deflection angle of the needle, B and C are fixed constants and A is a design constant or parameter that can be adjusted in
order to control the damping of the movement. It is required to find the
optimum value of the damping so that the needle movement will follow
most closely the input forcing function $V(t)$ for various types of function.
As a measure of performance the integral $\int_0^T [X - \frac{C}{B}. V(t)]^2 dt$ is to

be the objective function, where T is sufficiently large to allow time for the meter to fully respond to the input.

Prepare a hybrid simulation for this problem in which the parameter A is input to the model via a D. A. C. and the objective function input to the digital section via an A. D. C.

Incorporate a routine in the program to record a plot of the optimum response X(t) against t.

Assume when V(t) is a constant 10 volts the deflection X is 1 radian. Take B = 10, C = 1 and consider the case when V(t) is a step of 5 volts amplitude applied at time t = 0, and also the case when V(t) is a single triangular waveform of 10 volts peak amplitude and 10 seconds duration.

(5)   Set up any split boundary value problem involving 2 unknown initial conditions. Introduce an objective function $E = |E1| + |E2|$, where E1 and E2 are the errors in the boundary conditions and try to fit the boundary values (i. e. make E go to 0) using various optimisation routines starting from various initial points. Check the efficiency of the routines by checking how many function evaluations (runs) are needed before E is less than a specified value. Note how slow all these routines are when compared with a well set up proportional correction iteration scheme such as that described in §6. (Solving split B. V. problems by parameter optimisation has been likened to using a sledge-hammer to crack a nut! However, both are effective.)

Notes

(a)   The projectile over the wall problem of §6 (problem 2) is a suitable simple example for this study.

(b)   E may be calculated from E1 and E2 using analogue hardware or digital program.

(c)   It may be necessary to limit some of the problem variables to avoid overloading.

(d)   Deliberately limit the value of E and note the effect of this on the various search routines.

(6)   Set up the gated step control problem, example 1(vii) of §12, and determine the optimum values of a and b using a hybrid technique with a number of search routines.   Carefully check the effect of the requirement that b, the switch-off time, is always greater than the switch on time a.   Where needed modify the search routine to allow for this constraint on the parameters.

11 · Applications Involving Simultaneous Computation

11.1 Introduction

The sequential computing operations described in §10 essentially automate and make more efficient the process of running hybrid simulations; they do not extend the range of problems that can be studied as, clearly, even large optimisation studies can be, and have been, carried out by manual adjustment of parameters. The following notes describe some simultaneous/parallel hybrid computing operations in which both analogue and digital sections are computing at the same time and data is continually being transferred between these sections. Some of these operations, like sequential operations, make more efficient and easier the use of hybrid computers without extending the range of problems that may be studied. Others, e.g. the generation of functions of many variables, genuinely extend the range of applications.

Fig. 11.1 shows the essential features involved in simultaneous computation.

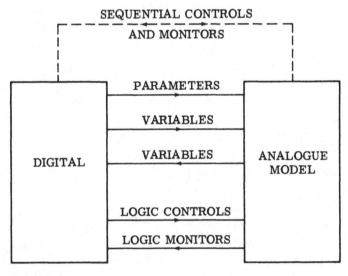

Fig. 11.1

During the time the analogue section is in the COMPUTE mode actually solving the model equations, data, in the form of analogue parameters and variables and logic signals, are being transferred continually between the digital and analogue sections and digital operations (calculations, storing of data, etc.) are being performed. The types of hybrid operations being performed at this time are very varied.

For example:

(i)   analogue variables X, Y, Z may be read into the digital via A. D. C. s, a function F(X, Y, Z) calculated and its value returned to the analogue via a D. A. C. ,

(ii)   an analogue variable X may be read into the digital, delayed by a time T, and fed back to the analogue,

(iii)   the behaviour of a chemical process, modelled in the analogue section, may be monitored continually by the digital and when certain conditions occur (e. g. representing danger hazards) the digital section made to change certain parameters (e. g. valve settings) in the analogue model.

The hardware needed to enable these types of operation to be performed has already been described in §9. The software needed to use effectively this hardware is both extensive and complex. The prime difficulty is that to make best use of the high speed capabilities of the analogue units, many simulations need to be operated at high speed and thus the generation of functions, etc. , within the digital must be performed at very high speed. Invariably the speed at which a simulation may be run is determined by the rate at which the digital can operate and the rate at which data can be transferred via the interface.

Time delay in hybrid loops is the major source of error in problems involving parallel computation. The effect of delay error can be most easily calculated by considering a sine-cosine generator loop in which the sign reversal is introduced by the digital section of the machine (Fig. 11. 2).

If no delay is introduced by ADC sample and conversion, digital processing (i. e. multiplication by -1), and DAC update then the equation for X is

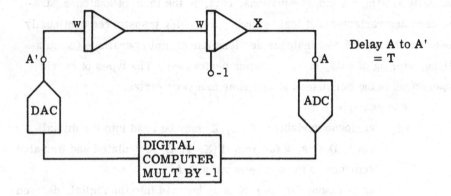

Fig. 11.2

$$\frac{d^2X}{dt^2} + w^2X = 0 \quad \text{with} \quad X_0 = 1$$

and thus

$$X = \cos wt.$$

However, if a relatively small delay T is introduced (Tw $\ll$ 1) then it can be shown that X obeys the equation

$$\frac{d^2X}{dt^2} - Tw^2\frac{dX}{dt} + w^2X = 0 \quad \text{approximately,}$$

i. e. the effect of the delay is to introduce a negative damping term $-Tw^2\frac{dX}{dt}$ into the equation.

The solution of this equation with $X_0 = 1$ for small values of Tw is $X = \exp(+\frac{Tw^2t}{2})\cos wt$ approximately or, neglecting quadratic and higher order terms in t in the series expansion for the exponential term, $X \simeq (1 + \frac{Tw^2t}{2})\cos wt$. After 1 complete cycle, i. e. $t = \frac{2\pi}{w}$ seconds, the amplitude of the 'cosine' waveform will have increased by about 100 πwT percent.

Thus if T is only 1% of the period of waveform, i. e. $T = \frac{2\pi}{100w}$, then the cosine waveform amplitude will have increased by about $2\pi^2 \simeq 20$ percent after 1 cycle!

230

The approximation formula can also be worked in reverse. For example, if $w = 1$ giving a period of 2π seconds and an increase of only 0. 1% in the amplitude of the cosine waveform is allowed per cycle then $100\pi T < 0.1$ or $T < \frac{1}{\pi}$ m sec $\simeq 300\mu$sec.

This illustrates the seriousness of the problem of time delay in hybrid loops and the reason why fast interface units and fast digital computation is required and why the analogue machine generally has to be operated in slow speed (Normal Seconds or 10 times as fast) in parallel hybrid simulation problems.

It is comparatively easy to organise and program a hybrid problem in which only one operation is performed repetitively in the digital section while the analogue is in its COMPUTE mode. However, it is difficult to organise and program the digital if it has many different tasks to perform, some repetitively and some not, throughout the COMPUTE period. For example, it may be necessary to generate a number of functions, including time delayed functions, repetitively throughout the analogue COMPUTE period while at the same time monitoring a number of logic variables and performing various logical control operations. When this type of requirement occurs, it is usual to have to write a special program, in which all these operations are carefully interlaced, in machine/assembler level instructions if speed of operation is absolutely vital or in a fully compiled high level language (e. g. FORTRAN with hybrid subroutines) if speed is not quite so critical.

In the following notes some of the most frequently used hybrid operations are discussed in a very general way but detailed examples involving hybrid Fortran programs are not given. Instead, for the sake of simplicity and compatibility, hybrid operations are given in terms of fully compiled CALL routines included in the hybrid version of BASIC developed at Bradford primarily for use in teaching applications. Use of these 'easy to use' routines enables small but realistic problems to be studied which involve simultaneous computation. Finally an example is given which involves both use of sequential and simultaneous hybrid computing.

231

11.2 Simultaneous hybrid operations

(i) Data logging

In data logging, the digital computer is organised to sample and store values of a number of variables throughout the analogue COMPUTE period and subsequently output them in tabulated numerical form. Thus it can be used instead of a multichannel graph plotter if the solutions are wanted in tabular form, e.g. for further processing. It enables higher accuracy to be obtained than is usual with multipen recorders (not single channel recorders which are often as accurate as the analogue computer solution itself) and is more automatic in operation. It is, perhaps, the simplest of all simultaneous operations as it involves transfer of data in one direction only. However, if many variables are to be sampled at once, slew may be a problem unless of course the A.D.C. system is provided with parallel sample/hold. Assuming parallel sample and hold, samples could be taken of N variables approximately every N times the length of time needed to sample, convert, read and store one value. Thus with a sample, convert, read and store time of 25 microseconds, ten variables could be logged every 0.25 millisecond if the digital computer were assigned completely to this task. This speed of logging is not likely to restrict the rate at which the analogue model equations can be solved, e.g. with a 1 millisecond integrator timescale, 40 sets of 10 samples could be made in a typical COMPUTE period of 10 milliseconds.

(ii) Function generation

Many techniques are available to generate functions of the independent analogue variable time and of dependent analogue variables. The methods available, particularly for functions of dependent variables, are very varied and powerful and have been discussed in §4, §5 and §7. Whenever possible it is advisable to generate functions by analogue hardware; it is a waste of a powerful digital facility to commit it to perform a simple but repetitive operation such as the continuous generation of $\cos \theta$ from θ.

However, there are situations when it is necessary or expedient to use the digital computer to generate functions, because:

232

(a) no analogue units are available to do the operation as the computer does not contain the hardware required,

(b) the analogue hardware needed for such an operation is extensive, perhaps difficult to use, and is better and perhaps necessarily employed performing other operations,

(c) the operation cannot be performed satisfactorily (or at all) by analogue hardware.

Functions to be generated can be broadly classed into those which are known in an analytical algebraic form, e. g. $f(x) = \exp 2x$, and those expressed in 'tabular' form for which an analytical form is not known. 'Tabular' functions arise as the result of experimental measurements/observations.

Within a hybrid system, functions can be generated by table look up or by direct evaulation and it is not obvious which technique should be used. Clearly either algebraic or tabular form functions can be generated by table look up techniques, the algebraic functions being converted by direct calculation at a number of points into tabular form prior to the dynamic phase of the simulation. Functions generated by table look up obviously require fast access (e. g. core) store. Both types of function can also be generated using direct evaluation throughout the COMPUTE period. In this case, prior to the simulation, the tabular functions and the more difficult algebraic functions need to be approximated to by analytical (polynomial, rational function) expressions, an operation which may be difficult if the function involves many variables. In any specific case, the method chosen will depend on how quickly the function needs to be generated and what overhead in the way of immediate access store is involved. Whichever method is used it is important to realise that the usual digital software routines for evaluation of functions (e. g. $\cos \theta$ from θ) or for performing interpolation invariably produce far more precision than is usable in a hybrid system. Thus it is invariably best to write special routines to generate the functions to the equivalent of the precision obtainable in the analogue/interface units. As 12 bits including sign is approximately equivalent to ±5 parts in 10^4 (i. e. ±. 0005 in a number whose maximum value is 1), function evaluations to 4 significant places is all that is generally required. Clearly function evaluation to this precision involves only a fraction of the time needed for evaluations to 9, 10 or more significant figures often used in digital computer calculations.

Whichever method is used, time is involved in sampling, working out the new function value and returning it to the analogue machine. Thus the function that is returned is time delayed w. r. t. the input sampled variables. The effect of this delay in determining the speed at which the analogue problem can run has already been considered for a sine-cosine loop (§11.1).

A further general point is that, ideally, function values should only be updated when they require to be changed. Thus, if on sampling a number of variables, they are found not to have changed significantly, time should not be wasted in evaluating the function but the computer should be allowed to move on to some other operation, e. g. generating another function. The numerical analysis involved and the special programming to carry out this type of operation at very high speed makes use of very special skills and is not likely to be tackled by the general or occasional user.

Direct evaluation

From the sampled analogue value or values, the function is evaluated in the digital section using a numerical procedure (generally in the form of a polynomial approximation to the function). The input variables are effectively in fractional number form, as all analogue variables are normally less than or equal to one, and thus special routines can be used to evaluate the polynomial approximation at high speed. For many simple functions of one variable (e. g. $\cos \theta$) polynomials of degree 4 will give sufficient precision. Evaluation of such polynomials, if calculated in nested form, i. e. $F(X) = aX^4 + bX^3 + cX^2 + dX + e = X\{X[X(aX+b)+c]+d\}+e$ involves only 4 operations of multiplication and 4 additions. With modern small fast (~ 1 μsec cycle time) machines, and allowing for A. D. C. sampling and D. A. C. update time, total function evaluation can be achieved in about 100 μsec even if floating point hardware is not used.

Table look up

Table look up has the disadvantage that it requires fast access storage. However, if sufficient storage is available so that interpolation between values is not needed, the method can give very fast generation of functions. In a one μsec cycle time machine, table look up of this type can be performed in about 10 μsec giving a total loop time (one variable in via ADC one variable out via D. A. C.) of about 40 μsecs.

If interpolation is used (probably essential for functions of more than 1 variable), the time involved will depend on the precision required and the number of table entries available as both of these will affect the sophistication of the interpolation (linear, quadratic, etc.) used. The additional time involved would also depend on the availability or otherwise of fast arithmetic instructions.

Note regarding generation of functions of the independent variable, time.

Functions of time can be treated just like any other functions of a single variable if the analogue section includes a unit to generate an analogue variable proportional to time, i. e. a timebase. However, if the total hybrid installation contains a real time clock controlling both the analogue and digital sections, the functions can be generated and output directly to the analogue without the need to sample an analogue timebase. Timing information is obtained from the real time clock, i. e. the functions are updated at times specified by digital timing pulses.

(iii) Time delay simulation

Time delay simulation is a special type of function generation in which a function **X** is required to be delayed in time but otherwise to be unchanged.

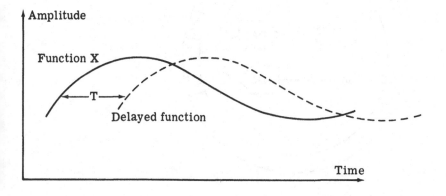

Fig. 11. 3

The form of the function is not known prior to the simulation, i.e. the function is a dependent computer variable otherwise it could be directly generated using the technique for generation of explicit functions of time (§4). Time delays are required in simulations of systems in which 'information' is transported from place to place (e.g. motion of a concentration profile in a liquid along a pipe) or in which there are delays due to the processing of information.

Very many methods have been used to simulate this type of delay, some in which the delay is constant and some in which it can vary. A summary of some of these methods is given in ref. 5. All the methods are approximate and involve the use of special hardware (e.g. tape record/playback) or involve use of many analogue units (Pade' filters). A hybrid machine is able to perform this type of operation very well using a sample, delay, playback technique. To delay a function X by a time T, samples can be made of the function via an A.D.C. at intervals of T/N and placed cyclically into N store locations, i.e. once all stores are filled in order new values are stored starting again from the beginning of these store locations. The value in the store location effectively displaced by T from the current point of writing is read back at each sample time and output via a D.A.C. The method is illustrated in the diagram below.

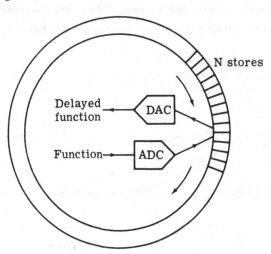

Fig. 11.4   The write and read pointers move from store to store at each sampling point.

In this type of delay simulator involving a fixed number of stores, the duration of the delay is controlled by controlling the sampling interval, i. e. delay = N ×interval. In some situations it may be convenient to use a variable number of stores with a fixed sampling interval, e. g. if a function is to be delayed by various times T_1, T_2, T_3 etc. , to give a number of delayed functions.

The minimum delay possible for an N point approximation is N × time needed to read via an ADC, store, collect from store and output via a D. A. C. With a typical set-up involving 100 stores and 50 μsec 'overheads' per sample point, the minimum delay possible would thus be 5 milliseconds, assuming the digital computer was fully dedicated to this one simple task.

11. 3   Parallel operations within BASIC

Although it is not possible to use an interpretive language directly in simultaneous computing due to the amount of time needed to interpret each instruction as well as execute it, special assembler language routines can be built into such a language to perform certain important operations, e. g. function generation. With a suite of such routines, some of the important techniques of simultaneous computation can be very simply demonstrated and used. Although of limited use for serious hybrid work, the availability of such routines is useful within a teaching environment in which BASIC and extensions to it is the language used for introduction to digital computing, digital simulation and hybrid computing. The detailed design and operation of the routines is influenced by the nature of the hardware available. The routines described below were developed for a system in which precise timing signals are available from a timer within the interface section of the machine.

The routines themselves, with simple examples of use, are given below. It will be noticed that they all contain instructions to switch the analogue section to the COMPUTE mode at an appropriate time and some also assume that the routine is to be terminated when the computer is switched by logic control to HOLD.

237

(1) Data log

CALL($1, V, S, I, T/P$)

where V = Number of variables to be logged (1 to 8).

   S = Number of times at which samples are to be taken.

   T/P = Output device for results. T ≡ teletype, P ≡ punch.

   I = Interval as a multiple of 0. 1 msec at which samples are
      to be taken.

Action

   (a)   Switches analogue to IC mode. Samples and stores in an
       array the values of the variables input on the appropriate
       number of A. D. C. lines.

   (b)   Switches to COMPUTE.

   (c)   After interval 0. 1 × I msec, sample values and store in an
       array.

   (d)   Repeats (c) until the appropriate number of samples have
       been taken.

   (e)   Prints or punches results as sets of 3-figure fractional
       numbers, e. g. . 375.

Speed of sampling

   Depends on number of variables to be sampled at each sampling
time. For 8 variables sampling interval must not be less than 0. 5 msec.

(2)   Generation of a function of time

CALL($2, N$) for input of data and

CALL($3, D, I$) for running.

Action CALL($2, N$)

N values of a function are read on paper tape and stored in a one dimen-
sional array.

CALL($3, D, I$)

   (a)   Switches analogue to I. C. mode and outputs first value on the
       D. A. C.   attached to channel D.

   (b)   Switches analogue to COMPUTE mode.

   (c)   After delay of 0. 1 × I msec outputs next value via D. A. C.

   (d)   Repeats (c) until all values output.

   (e)   Switches analogue to HOLD.

238

Speed

Minimum time of updating of function value is 0.1 msec.

Use

Generation of complicated functions of the independent computer variable without need for extensive analogue or parallel logic hardware, e.g. loading distributions for beams.

(3) Function of one dependent variable

CALL(4, N)

CALL(5, A, D)

Action   CALL(4, N)

N pairs of values read via paper tape reader and stored in $2 \times N$ array. Each pair of values correspond to one point on the function curve.

CALL(5, A, D)

(a)   Switches analogue to I.C. mode. Variable on A.D.C. channel A read and function value output on D.A.C. channel D.

(b)   Switches analogue to COMPUTE mode.

(c)   Variable input to A.D.C. read and new function value output via D.A.C.

(d)   Step (c) repeated until analogue switched to HOLD by logic.

Speed

Function updated every 0.4 msec.

Use

Generation of functions of 1 variable specified in tabular form. Routine includes simple linear interpolation between points.

(4) Function of 2 variables

CALL(6, N)

CALL(4, A1, A2, D)

Natural extension of (3) to 2 variables. A1, A2, A.D.C. addresses. D = D.A.C. address and N = number of (triple) data points.

(5) Generation of trigonometrical functions

CALL(8, A, D1, D2).

Action

(a)   Switches to I.C. mode.

Samples value of θ input on A.D.C. channel A, outputs sin θ and cos θ on D.A.C. channels D1 and D2.

(b)   Switches to COMPUTE mode.

(c)   Samples value of θ and outputs sin θ and cos θ.

(d)   Repeats (c) until analogue switched to HOLD by local logic.

Speed

Value of θ sampled, functions generated and output every 0.5 msec.

Use

Generation of sin θ and cos θ for $-\pi < \theta < +\pi$, where θ scaled as $(\frac{\theta}{3.49})$ with θ measured in radians. †

(6) Axes rotation, etc.

CALL(9, A1, A2, A3, D1, D2)

Action

Similar to (5) but 3 variables sampled on A.D.C. channels A1, A2, A3, i.e. θ, X and Y and 2 variables output via D.A.C.s D1 and D2.

D.A.C. (D1) output = X.cos θ + Y. sin θ

D.A.C. (D2) output = X. sin θ - Y. cos θ

If Y = 0 and X made equal to R then polar to cartesian conversion achieved.

Speed

Values updated every 0.5 msec.

Use

General-purpose routine for use in axes rotation and polar to cartesian coordinate transformation.

(7) Time delay

CALL(10, A, D, T, V)

where A = A.D.C. input channel number.

D = D.A.C. output channel number.

T = Delay as a multiple of 0.1 msec.

V = Initial output value.

Action

(a)   Switches to I.C. mode and outputs initial value V.

---

† Scaling chosen to be compatible with analogue hardware D.F.G.s.

(b)   Switches to COMPUTE mode.

(c)   Waits T/100 then samples and stores value of A. D. C. input.

(d)   Repeats (c) 99 times.

(e)   Outputs first value read after time T and samples and
       stores input variable.

(f)   Continues to output values sampled earlier and continues to
       sample and store next input values until analogue is switched
       to HOLD by local logic.

(8) Maximum value

CALL(11, A, V)

Action

Switches analogue to COMPUTE mode and samples value of variable input on A. D. C. channel A repetitively throughout compute period
and, when the analogue is switched to HOLD by local logic patching,
assigns to V the maximum value of the variable input.

Speed

Variable sampled every 50 μsec. Hence input variable should not
change within 50 μsec by more than the error permitted in the estimate
of the maximum value.

Use

Detecting and storing the maximum value of a variable. Particularly useful when derivative information relating to the variable is not
available in the analogue simulation and so the maximum value needs to
be estimated by direct methods (or perhaps methods involving use of
approximate differentiation circuits).

11. 4   Hybrid optimisation problem involving sequential and parallel computation. Motion of a railway coach.

The following is a typical example of a problem in vehicle dynamics
which can be efficiently studied using a hybrid computer. The problem
itself is discussed and then suggestions are given as to how the problem
could be simulated and the test runs performed in order to achieve optimum design performance.

241

(i) Problem and model equations

The problem concerns the behaviour of a railway coach as it travels across a joint between rails. The object of the study is to determine optimum values of various parameters in the coach's suspension system. These optimisation studies are to be performed for various coach speeds. A measure of the roughness of the ride can be estimated by computing the maximum value of the vertical acceleration of the coach as the wheel runs over the joint and the optimum design will be that combination of parameters, for a given speed, which minimises this value. The coach is assumed to have 4 wheels and the diagram (Fig. 11.5) shows the suspension system for one of the corners of the coach.

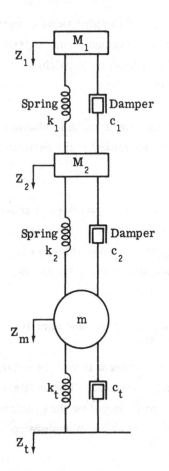

M_1 = Primary mass ≡ one quarter the mass of the coach.

M_2 = Secondary mass.

m = mass of the wheel and half-axle.

Z_1, Z_2 and Z_m are the vertical displacements of the masses from their equilibrium positions.

Z_t is the dynamic track profile.

k_1, c_1 are the coach (primary) suspension spring and damping constants.

k_2, c_2 are the secondary suspension spring and damping constants.

k_t, c_t are the effective wheel/track 'spring' and 'damping' constants.

Fig. 11.5   Suspension system

The 'exact' model equations for such a system will be complicated. However, if it is assumed that the system can be sufficiently well represented by a linear model in which the force exerted by each spring is proportional to the extension or compression of the spring and the force introduced by each damping effect is proportional to velocity, then the controlling equations are:

$$M_1 \ddot{Z}_1 = -k_1(Z_1 - Z_2) - c_1(\dot{Z}_1 - \dot{Z}_2) \qquad (11.1)$$

$$M_2 \ddot{Z}_2 = +k_1(Z_1 - Z_2) + c_1(\dot{Z}_1 - \dot{Z}_2) \qquad (11.2)$$
$$-k_2(Z_2 - Z_m) - c_2(\dot{Z}_2 - \dot{Z}_m)$$

$$m\ddot{Z}_m = +k_2(Z_2 - Z_m) + c_2(\dot{Z}_2 - \dot{Z}_m) \qquad (11.3)$$
$$-k_t(Z_m - Z_t) - c_t(\dot{Z}_m - \dot{Z}_t)$$

The dynamic track profile Z_t for a dip of depth Z may be represented as:

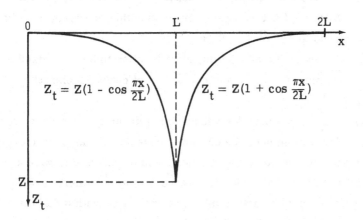

Fig. 11.6 Dynamic track profile characteristic. (Vertical scale greatly exaggerated)

Thus if the coach is travelling at a speed V then

$$Z_t \text{ (time)} = Z(1 - \cos \frac{\pi V}{2L} \tau) \text{ for } 0 < \tau < \frac{L}{V}$$

$$= Z(1 + \cos \frac{\pi V}{2L}\tau) \quad \text{for} \quad \frac{L}{V} < \tau < \frac{2L}{V}$$

$$= 0 \qquad\qquad \text{for} \quad \tau > \frac{2L}{V}$$

where time τ is measured from the point when the wheel is a distance L before the track joint.

The function Z_t and its time derivative $\dot{Z}_t$ are forcing functions for equation (11. 3).

For a given type of wheel and track and a given mass for the coach then M_1, m, k_t and c_t are fixed constants in the system while M_2, k_1, c_1, k_2 and c_2 are all constants which may be adjusted to optimise the system performance, i. e. they are design parameters. Thus for each value of speed V, the design involves the optimum choice of 5 parameters. Clearly, for reasons of physical realisability, these parameters must be in certain specified ranges, i. e. there are certain simple constraints on the parameter values. In addition to these constraints there is a further constraint on a problem variable because, for reasons of safety, the wheel must not leave the track, i. e. upward acceleration of the wheel = $-\ddot{Z}_m < g$. Allowing for a margin of error then this constraint may be further tightened to be $-\ddot{Z}_m < 0.5g$.

As already mentioned the objective function to be minimised is the maximum value of the vertical component of coach acceleration, i. e. $\max |\ddot{Z}_1|$.

The model equations derived assumed linearity. However, certain elements of the system could be chosen to have non-linear characteristics. Thus, for example, the primary damper could be selected to have a velocity squared characteristic, i. e. force $= c_1 u|u|$ (where $u = \dot{Z}_1 - \dot{Z}_2$). Alternatively, it could be selected to be a linear type with a definite limit to the maximum damping force it could exert,

$$\text{i. e.} \quad \text{force} = c_1 u \quad \text{for} \quad u < u_L$$
$$= c_1 u_L \quad \text{for} \quad u > u_L$$

The addition of selected possible non-linear elements further extends the 'dimension' of the design problem.

244

(ii) **Simulation:**   The role of the analogue and digital sections.

In a study of this type it is not always obvious where some parts of the system should be simulated, i. e. in the analogue or digital section. Clearly the digital should be used for control of the sequential optimisation and the analogue to model the differential equations. However, the forcing functions could be produced in either the digital or analogue sections and the objective function evaluated in either of these two sections. The forcing functions Z_t and $\dot{Z}_t$ can be generated efficiently by analogue hardware (with simple use of comparators and switches to switch between parts of the functions as the wheel crosses the track joint) and thus there is little point in involving the digital in this operation. However, it is difficult to determine the maximum value of the coach acceleration, i. e. $\max |\ddot{Z}_1|$ by analogue hardware as the time derivative of $\ddot{Z}_1$, i. e. $\dddot{Z}_1$, does not appear directly in the model equations and hence in the simulation. Thus either special peak reading analogue circuits (ref. 7) or a method based on use of an approximate differentiation circuit (page 279) will have to be used. This type of operation can be performed very easily and at high speed by a digital computer operating in a 'sample and update maximum mode' (ref. CALL (11, A, V), page 241).

The total simulation could, therefore, be as shown in Fig. 11. 7.

Notes

(1)   The analogue simulation will be a little unusual as it will be necessary to generate the highest derivatives of both Z_1 and Z_m, i. e. $\ddot{Z}_1$ and $\ddot{Z}_m$, directly in the model as both must be measured. Thus summers will have to be used to produce $\ddot{Z}_1$ and $\ddot{Z}_m$ from the terms on the R. H. S. of equations (11.1) and (11.3) whereas $\ddot{Z}_2$ will not be generated explicitly but equation (11.2) written and simulated in the form

$$-\frac{d}{d\tau}(-\dot{Z}_2) = \text{R. H. S.}$$

(2)   The length of the COMPUTE period must allow for the possibility of the maximum of $|\ddot{Z}_1|$ occurring when the wheel is a considerable distance past the track joint, e. g. a time period equivalent to a distance $x = 4L$ could be used.

(3)   The coach velocity V is only going to be changed occasionally, i. e. after each optimisation study and thus the low speed set up sys-

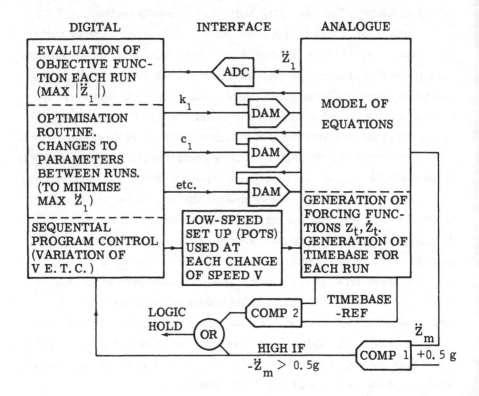

DIGITAL	INTERFACE	ANALOGUE

EVALUATION OF OBJECTIVE FUNCTION EACH RUN (MAX $|\ddot{Z}_1|$)

OPTIMISATION ROUTINE. CHANGES TO PARAMETERS BETWEEN RUNS. (TO MINIMISE MAX $\ddot{Z}_1$)

SEQUENTIAL PROGRAM CONTROL (VARIATION OF V E. T. C.)

ADC $\ddot{Z}_1$

k_1 DAM

c_1 DAM

etc.   DAM

LOW-SPEED SET UP (POTS) USED AT EACH CHANGE OF SPEED V

MODEL OF EQUATIONS

GENERATION OF FORCING FUNCTIONS $Z_t, \dot{Z}_t$. GENERATION OF TIMEBASE FOR EACH RUN

LOGIC HOLD   OR   COMP 2   TIMEBASE -REF

HIGH IF $-\ddot{Z}_m > 0.5g$

COMP 1 $\ddot{Z}_m$ +0. 5 g

Fig. 11. 7

tem could be involved whenever a change is to be made in V. Changing V will necessitate changes in the forcing functions and also in the length of the COMPUTE period required. The length of the COMPUTE period can be easily fixed by controlling the TIMEBASE rate.

(4) Each COMPUTE period could be terminated by switching into HOLD whenever the TIMEBASE has reached the reference value or as soon as the constraint $-\ddot{Z}_m < 0.5g$ is violated. Whether or not the constraint has been violated can be checked by the digital computer reading the state of COMPARATOR 1 and thus, if required, the particular run concerned can be rejected in the optimisation study.

(iii) General comments

As there is only one true hybrid time critical operation (evaluation of max $\ddot{Z}_1$) the analogue and hence the total simulation could be run at high speed, e. g. the analogue model could be in NORMAL MILLISECS timescale (i. e. 1000 times faster than normal seconds) and COMPUTE periods arranged to be between about 5 and 50 msec (depending on the speed V). Thus on average 20 or so runs could be made per second, allowing for the time needed to select and change parameter values between runs. Thus many thousands of runs could be performed in a few minutes and a total optimisation (involving adjustment of 5 parameters) should be achieved in a few minutes (this assumes that all goes well in the optimisation). If about 10 values of velocity are to be used, the total running time for the simulation could, at least theoretically, be as short as 1 hour. This could only be achieved by use of an efficient overall organising and controlling program.

Such a program should ensure that an adequate record of the runs are made for reference purposes. In particular the progress of each search should be logged (parameter values and objective function value) for subsequent output if required and optimum solutions recorded, i. e. once a set of optimum parameters have been obtained for a given value of V, analogue recordings against time of all important variables Z_1, $\dot{Z}_1$, $\ddot{Z}_1$, etc. should be made automatically at low speed on an X-Y or chart recorder or recorded in digital form (using a data log program) for later use. Finally the digital section should output, again preferably in graphical form, summary results in an easily interpretable form, e. g. graphs showing the variations in the optimum values of the parameters and also in the optimum values obtained for the objective function as functions of speed, V.

Although a considerable amount of effort is needed to produce an efficient total program for such a simulation study, this effort is well worth while if the problem has to be studied many times over. A pleasing feature of a hybrid simulation of this type is that it still retains one of the important properties of an analogue computer, i. e. the parallel nature and high speed of the solution of the model equations. Thus the behaviour of the model can be observed on an oscilloscope display and the model itself can be easily extended (e. g. inclusion of non-linear damping) and the total study re-run. In this hybrid simulation, high efficiency is achieved by the logical control/organising capability of the digital section married to the high-speed capabilities of the analogue section to solve the model equations.

(iv) Suggested values for a simulation study

M_1	3000	kg	
M_2	1000	kg	
m	400	kg	(Range 100-1500)
k_1	50	kN/m	(Range 20-80)
c_1	such that damping coefficient $\simeq 0.3$ (range 0-1)		
k_2	500	kN/m	(Range 50-1000)
c_2	such that damping coefficient $\simeq 0.3$ (range 0-1)		
k_t	30	MN/m	
c_t	such that damping coefficient $= 0.05$		
Z	2 cms		
L	3 m		
V	0-250 km/hr		

12 · Simulation in Control

12.1 Introduction

Perhaps the single most important application of simulation is in the study (design and testing) of feedback control systems. In the following notes:

(i)   the principles of operation of control systems are explained and some of the phraseology used is introduced.

(ii)   model equations for a few systems are derived,

and   (iii)   computer simulations for a number of systems are produced and the techniques for determining the behaviour of computer models discussed.

The notes end with a set of simple examples chosen to illustrate the wide range of systems possible and the applicability of simulation techniques.

The notes are written so that a knowledge of Laplace Transforms is not required but, where expedient, equations are given in Laplace Transform form as well as in differential form. This should make the notes more easily understandable to persons already familiar with control system theory.

12.2 Note on the role of simulation

Simulation is not normally used in the initial design of a control system. Rather it is used as a tool to confirm the correctness of the design and to optimise the design by determining the behaviour under varying conditions. The basic design is carried out from theoretical considerations. At this stage many approximations and simplifications have to be made. Once a basic design is produced of a system believed able to meet a certain specification, computer models are made and tested to confirm the correctness or otherwise of the design. The computer model is made to represent the actual proposed system as completely as possible (i. e. it should not include the simplifications which had to be introduced in order to carry out the initial design) and performance checks made under a wide range of operating conditions (inputs, loads, random noise). In particular the effect of varying certain critical adjustable design parameters (e. g. amplifier gain) is observed and the parameter values selected to give the best performance.

In certain situations the actual control system is already in existence (e. g. biological systems; muscular control of limb positions) and the object of the simulation is to find a model which adequately represents the system. Again the initial design of the model is done from theoretical considerations, using observations on the behaviour of the system, etc., and simulation is used in the adjustment of the model parameters so that the model behaviour matches that of the system as closely as possible.

12.3   An example of a control system

In Fig. 12.1 is shown a simple motor generator set used to produce electricity.

Fig. 12.1

Normally it would be required that the output voltage across the load should remain constant (as set initially by the throttle control valve). Clearly the regulation of the system will be very poor as the output voltage will fluctuate for a wide range of causes, e. g. variation in the load itself, engine and dynamo efficiency (which change with temperature and aging), variation of fuel quality. The variation of the output due to these and other causes can be greatly reduced by the addition of 'feedback' to the system. This feedback may be introduced manually or automatically:

(i)   an operator could be employed to monitor the output voltage and adjust the throttle control accordingly,

(ii)   an automatic means could be introduced to achieve regulation:

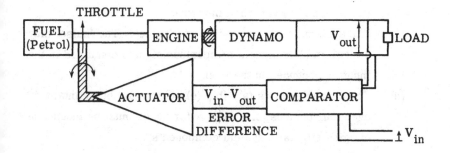

Fig. 12.2

In this system the 'output' voltage across the load is continuously compared with the 'input' voltage V_{in}, i. e. the set point or demanded (required) value of V_{out}, and an error voltage produced. This error voltage is used to adjust the throttle and so control the flow of fuel in such a way as to minimise the error. Should any change occur either within (e. g. engine efficiency) or outside (e. g. load) the system which causes the output voltage to depart from its required value then immediate automatic action is taken to reduce this departure from normality. Note, information (value of V_{out}) is fed back from the output of the system to the input (V_{in}) to produce an error which is used to control the output. This is the essential characteristic of a control system. Systems with feedback are called closed loop and those without are said to be open loop.

Many control systems are power amplifying devices. Electro-mechanical systems of this type are called servomechanisms or servos, e. g. servo-assisted car steering.

12.4   General comments

(i)   Desired characteristics of control systems

(a)   Precise operation.

In the example considered above the output must equal the input as closely as possible. If the supply is to be controllable then this characteristic must be true for all values of the input set point.

(b) Fast operation.

The system must respond quickly to any change in demand (i. e. permitted variation in input).

(c) The system should not respond to 'noise'. The 'noise' may be true random signals or spurious signals contained in the input or produced in the loop.

(d) The characteristics (a), (b), (c) above must be maintained over long periods, i. e. the performance must be independent of aging effects in system components.

(ii) Essential parts of unit feedback single input-output systems

The essential parts of many 'following type' control systems (e. g. the example above in which the output should 'follow' any changes in the input) can be shown thus:

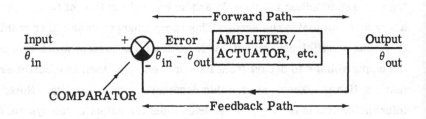

Fig. 12. 3

The dimensions of the input and output signals must be the same (e. g. both are voltages in the example considered) so that they can be compared and the difference or error produced.

(iii) Transducers

Variables which need to be controlled must be measured. Devices which measure and produce a signal (generally voltage or current) proportional to the controlled quantity are called transducers. When such devices are included in a system they are best thought of as belonging in the forward path:

252

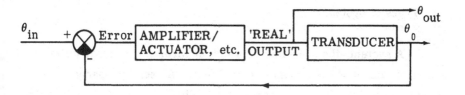

Fig. 12.4

In this case θ_0 indicates a value proportional to the real output but of the same dimensions as θ_{in}. A simple example of this occurs in rotary speed control systems. The actual variable to be controlled is the speed of a motor. This speed is measured by a tachometer to produce a voltage (ideally proportional to speed). This voltage is compared with an input voltage to give an error used to drive (via an amplifier) the motor. Transducer characteristics can affect system performance and so must be included at the design stage and in the simulation.

(iv) **Optimum systems**

When the parameters of a system are set up so that the performance, as judged by some performance or error index, is best then the system is said to be optimised. (It may not of course be the best system for the job!) The optimum values of system parameters are very dependent on what is required of the system and the nature of the input. Choice of a suitable performance index in optimisation studies is often difficult as it may be hard to express mathematically what is required of the system. The integral squared error (I. S. E. or $\int error^2 . dt$) is a much-used error criterion particularly appropriate when determining the performance of a system to a random input. For other inputs, step changes, ramps, etc., other measures of performance may be more meaningful, e. g. $\int |error| dt$, (IAE); $\int t |error| dt$, (ITAE). In studies of head damage (to dummies) in car crashes an accepted Head Injury Criterion is $\int_0^T |A|^{2.5} . dt$, where A is the resultant head acceleration and T the time period over which it is measured.

In general an optimum system is one that $\begin{array}{c} \text{maximises} \\ \text{minimises} \end{array}$ } the appropriate measure of $\dfrac{\text{performance}}{\text{error}}$ }.

(v) Types of systems

Linear

A system, the behaviour of which is governed by linear differential and algebraic equations, is said to be linear. A useful property of such a system is that the output response to a number of separate inputs is the sum of the responses to each input individually.

Linear with constant system parameters

These systems, in which the essential parameters do not vary with time, are governed by linear constant coefficient differential equations. The design of such systems is frequently done using Laplace Transform and/or frequency response methods. Very many methods are available for the design of such systems, e. g. Bode, Nyquist, Root Locus. Interactive computer programs (which may include simulation packages) are available to facilitate such design.

Non-linear

All real systems are non-linear although the amount of non-linearity in some systems may be so small that they may be considered linear.

Most non-linearities have an adverse effect on system performance, e. g. backlash in gear boxes. Such undesirable non-linearities are called parasitic. Non-linearities are however sometimes designed into systems to enhance performance. The chief objection to non-linearity is that it makes system design difficult. Such systems are generally 'linearised' using perturbation techniques and the system designed around a linearised model. The effect of including non-linear elements, i. e. making it more realistic, can be checked by simulation.

(vi) Stability

Often when a closed loop system is formed (and even if no input is applied) the output will contain fluctuations which increase with time (or the output may oscillate at a constant amplitude). Such systems are unstable. The instability is caused by the feedback action being of wrong 'phase' and, instead of reducing the error, increases it. In such systems the output variable increases in amplitude (as an oscillation or otherwise)

254

until non-linear limiting occurs; any inputs then have little or no effect. In certain types of mechanical systems instability must be avoided as violent oscillations may damage the control system itself or the load attached to it. The problem of control system design is how to make a closed loop system match some performance criterion without introducing instability. In fact systems have to be designed with a certain stability margin otherwise the output variables may contain ringing (slowly decaying oscillations) when sudden changes of input are made.

(vii)   Compensation

In order to achieve adequate stability and optimise system performance (and also to overcome other limitations) certain additional 'compensating' elements have sometimes to be included in the loop. These have the effect of modifying the total loop characteristic. For linear systems such elements may be included anywhere in the loop but are frequently inserted after the comparator:

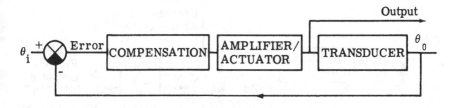

Fig. 12.5

A compensator much used in chemical engineering control systems is the so-called 3 term controller which produces a signal from the error proportional to the sum of the error itself, the time integral of the error and the time derivative of the error.

Compensation may also be affected by using more than one feedback signal. For example certain electro-mechanical positional control systems are stabilised by the action of velocity feedback added onto the normal positional data:

255

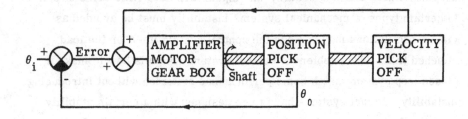

Fig. 12.6

The above is an example of a multi-loop system. It contains both proportional and derivative action.

12.5   An example of a linear control system used to control the position of a load

(i) System

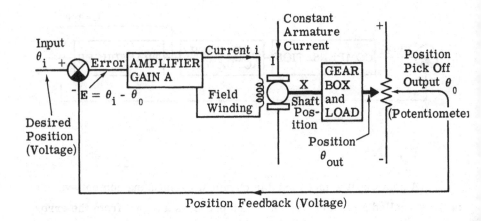

Position Feedback (Voltage)

Fig. 12.7   Positional control system

The output voltage θ_0 produced from the potentiometer indicates the position θ_{out} of the load. X is the angular position of the motor shaft. If $\theta_0 \neq \theta_i$ an error voltage E is produced which should drive the load via the amplifier, motor and gearbox and so make θ_0 change in such a way that the error decreases. The output should therefore follow

256

any variations in the input.

(ii) Equations

Assuming:

(i)   The armature current is constant.

(ii)   The time constant of the field winding can be neglected.

(iii)   The friction on the output shaft is proportional to speed.

(iv)   All system components obey linear equations (e. g. backlash in gearbox neglected, saturation in amplifier neglected).

Then the equations for the system are:

$$E = \theta_i - \theta_0 \tag{12.1}$$

$$i = A. E \tag{12.2}$$

Field current in motor = output current from amplifier.

The torque produced by the motor is proportional to $i \times$ armature current and so torque

$$T = K. i, \tag{12.3}$$

where K is a constant as the armature current is assumed to be constant.

This torque is used in overcoming friction, assumed proportional to the angular velocity of the motor shaft, and also used in accelerating the load, i. e.

$$\text{Torque} = T = F. V + \frac{d}{dt} (JV), \tag{12.4}$$

where

$$\frac{dX}{dt} = V, \tag{12.5}$$

F is the friction constant and J the inertia of the motor, gearbox and load referred to the motor axle.

As θ_0, the voltage indicating load position, is proportional to X

$$\therefore \quad \theta_0 = C. X, \tag{12.6}$$

where C, a constant, includes the gearbox reduction ratio and the potentiometer voltage/position ratio.

Equations (12.1) to (12.6) are all in a form directly suitable for analogue or digital simulation except (12.4) which needs to be rewritten as:

$$\frac{d}{dt}(JV) = T - F.V. \tag{12.7}$$

(iii) Laplace Transform representation

Equations (12.1) to (12.6) could also be expressed in Laplace Transform form: e.g. (12.4) would become $\overline{T} = F\overline{V} + Js\overline{V}$ (assuming inertia J is constant), where s is the Laplace Operator and $\overline{T}$ and $\overline{V}$ the transformed variables. Rearranging this equation gives

$$\overline{V} = \frac{1}{F + Js} \cdot \overline{T}$$

where $\frac{1}{F + Js}$ is the Transfer Function representing the output to input relationship $\overline{V}$ to $\overline{T}$.

The overall system would then be represented in a 'transfer function block diagram' form as:

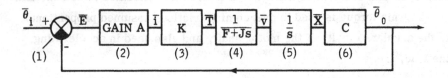

Fig. 12.8. The numbers refer to the equations relating to each block, e.g. block (4) relates to equation (12.4)

(iv) Analytical solution

If all the equations are combined, as would be done for analytical solution, the overall equation, written in standard form with the forcing function on the R.H.S., relating θ_i and θ_0 becomes:

$$\frac{d^2\theta_0}{dt^2} + \frac{F}{J} \cdot \frac{d\theta_0}{dt} + \frac{CKA}{J} \cdot \theta_0 = \frac{CKA}{J} \cdot \theta_i, \tag{12.8}$$

where J is assumed constant.

This equation is a special case of the equation for a <u>quadratic</u>

system and it is worth examining its solution for various values of the constants.

The equation can be conveniently expressed in the form

$$\frac{d^2\theta_0}{dt^2} + 2. \xi. w_0 \frac{d\theta_0}{dt} + w_0^2. \theta_0 = w_0^2. \theta_i, \qquad (12.9)$$

where $w_0^2 = \frac{CKA}{J}$ and $2. \xi. w_0 = \frac{F}{J}$.

For reasons which will become clearer later ξ is called the damping coefficient (in this case dependent on the friction) and w_0 the natural frequency of oscillation.

If it is assumed that $\xi = 0$ (no friction) and a unit step 'demand' is applied at time $t = 0$ then

$$\frac{d^2\theta_0}{dt^2} + w_0^2 \theta_0 = w_0^2. 1 \text{ for } t \geq 0. \qquad (12.10)$$

It may be shown that the solution of this equation, assuming the system is initially at rest, i.e. $\theta_0 = 0$ and $(\frac{d\theta}{dt})_0 = 0$ is $\theta_0 = 1 - \cos w_0 t$.

This solution, together with the input step, is shown in the following diagram

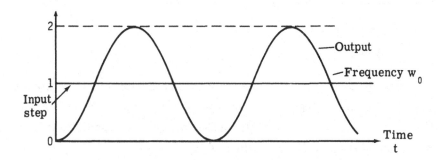

Fig. 12.9

Thus the output is seen to oscillate at an angular frequency w_0 about the intended output position '1' and the system is unstable. Changing the gain of the amplifier will not help stability, it will only change the frequency w_0 of the oscillation.

$$[w_0 = \sqrt{\left(\frac{CKA}{J}\right)}] \; .$$

However, if ξ is assumed to be positive (and less than 1) the solution of the equation, again for a unit step input, becomes

$$\theta_0 = 1 - [\cos wt + \frac{\xi}{\sqrt{(1 - \xi^2)}} \sin wt]\exp(-\xi w_0 t), \qquad (12.11)$$

where $w = w_0 \sqrt{(1 - \xi^2)}$.

This damped oscillatory motion is shown diagramatically:

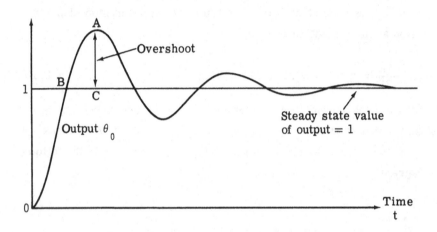

Fig. 12.10

As the amplitude of the oscillations decays with time the system is stable. It is interesting to note that it is the friction present ($\xi \propto F$) in this system that produces stability. (The energy in the oscillations is converted into heat by the frictional forces.)

Important characteristics of control systems are

(a)   the magnitude of the first overshoot to a step input, i. e. AC,

and   (b)   the time taken for the system to respond to the step. (This may be expressed in various ways, e. g. time 0 - B; time for output to rise 10-90% of its final value.)

For quadratic systems, the lower the value of ξ (for a given w_0) the greater is the overshoot, the 'faster' is the response but the longer the time before the output settles to its required value. In practical situations

260

systems are often designed to overshoot a little ($< 15\%$) in order to
try to achieve a fast response and many designers of complex high order
systems aim to make them predominantly quadratic in character. For
this reason the simulation and behaviour of quadratic systems is examined
extensively in the subsequent notes and examples.

In Transfer Function form a quadratic system may be represented
as:

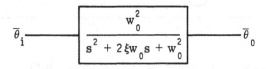

$$\bar{\theta}_i \quad \longrightarrow \quad \boxed{\dfrac{w_0^2}{s^2 + 2\xi w_0 s + w_0^2}} \quad \longrightarrow \quad \bar{\theta}_0$$

Fig. 12.11

This is derived directly from equation (12.9).

(iv)   Simulation

When simulating control systems by analogue means it is generally
best to derive the equations in simple form (e.g. (12.1) to (12.6)) and use
a unit for each equation. In this way very close correspondence is kept
between parts of the original system and parts of the computer model.
Changes can be very easily made to parameters and whole sections can
be replaced if required. More 'efficient' (in terms of computer hardware)
simulations are sometimes possible but such simulations may lack the
close 'direct' one to one correspondence which is of such great value.
Minimum hardware configurations do sometimes have to be used if the
problem is getting too large for the computer concerned.

The order in which units appear in the model should be the same
as in the original system. (With linear systems the order of units in the
forward path could be reversed without affecting the final output but this
would lead to lack of correspondence.)

The ease with which unscaled computer diagrams may be derived
from properly constructed simple algebraic and first order differential
equations can be seen from the following diagram derived for equations
(12.1) to (12.6) of the positional control system example in which the

inertia J is assumed to be constant:

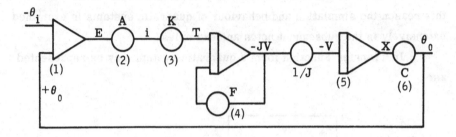

Fig. 12.12. Computer diagram for system shown in Fig. 12.7
and in block form in Fig. 12.8

Notes

If the inertia J is variable a multiplier (set up to divide) would have to be used instead of the pot '$\frac{1}{J}$'.

If all the intermediate variables do not need to be monitored then pots can be combined together and the order of units slightly changed to simplify the structure, e.g. the pots A, K, $\frac{1}{J}$ and the integrator producing $-JV$ could be rearranged, viz.:

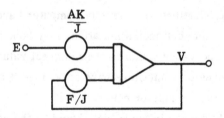

Fig. 12.13

Again if the value of X is not specifically required the order of the last two items could be reversed:

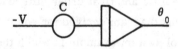

Fig. 12.14

262

However, it is best in general to retain as much correspondence as possible between the original system and the model. The model may have to be slightly modified when scaling is introduced in order to avoid very small pot settings or high gains.

Scaling can best be performed on the simple equations derived for the system. Maximum values of variables i, T, V, X, etc., will depend on the magnitude and nature of the input signal. If the simulation is well planned the scaling should be suitable for a wide range of input signals.

Certain simple systems (e.g. quadratic) appear in many simulations and it is useful to derive well-scaled simulations for such systems. Larger systems can then be constructed by linking together these blocks. This scaling is considered in the following section and the positional control system discussed above is studied further in example 8 at the end of these notes.

12.6 Simulation of a 1st order lag

The equation $T\dfrac{d\theta_0}{dt} + \theta_0 = \theta_i$, where θ_i = input and θ_0 = output, governs the behaviour of many simple 'time lag' systems. Three systems giving rise to this equation are:

(i) Lagged thermometer

If T_W = Temperature of wire inside case

and $\quad T_A$ = Temperature surrounding the casing

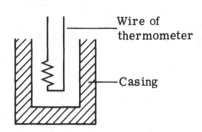

Wire of thermometer

Casing

Fig. 12.15

then the rate at which heat passes through the casing is proportional to the temperature difference $T_A - T_W$. Thus the rate at which the temperature of the wire increases is proportional to this difference, i. e.

$$\frac{dT_W}{dt} \propto T_A - T_W$$

or

$$T \cdot \frac{dT_W}{dt} + T_W = T_A \,,$$

where T, a constant having dimensions of time, is the time constant of the thermometer system. T_A is the input θ_i and T_W the output θ_0 of the system.

(ii) Resistor capacitor low pass filter

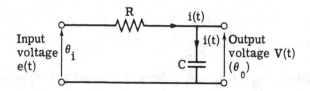

Fig. 12.16

The voltage $V(t)$ is the input voltage $e(t)$ minus the voltage drop $R. i(t)$ across the resistor R, i. e.

$$V(t) = e(t) - R. i(t).$$

Also for the capacitor $i(t) = C \dfrac{dV(t)}{dt}$. Thus

$$RC \frac{dV}{dt} + V = e,$$

or

$$T \cdot \frac{dV}{dt} + V = e,$$

where T is the time constant RC.

The equation is of standard form where θ_i is the input and θ_0 the output of the system. This circuit is extensively used to reduce the high-frequency noise signals often present on analogue signals from measuring

264

instruments in process control systems, but a time lag is introduced by its use.

(iii) Series resistance - inductance circuit

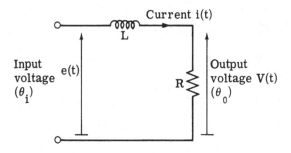

Current i(t)

Input voltage $e(t)$ (θ_i)

L

R

Output voltage $V(t)$ (θ_0)

Fig. 12.17

For any input $e(t)$ the current $i(t)$ is given by

$$L\frac{di}{dt} + Ri = e$$

and the output voltage $V = Ri$. Thus

$$\frac{L}{R}\frac{dV}{dt} + V = e,$$

or

$$T \cdot \frac{dV}{dt} + V = e,$$

where the time constant $T = \frac{L}{R}$. This is of standard form if $V \equiv \theta_0$ and $e \equiv \theta_i$.

Response of simple lag to a unit step

If θ_i is a step of unit magnitude applied at time $t = 0$ then

$$T\frac{d\theta_0}{dt} + \theta_0 = 1 \text{ for } t \geq 0.$$

Assuming the initial value of θ_0 is zero then

$$\theta_0 = 1 - \exp(-\frac{t}{T}).$$

This 'exponential rise' response is shown in Fig. 12.18. The output 'LAGS' behind the input and for a step input the output will rise to

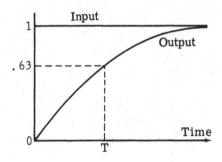

Fig. 12.18

about 63% of its final output in a time T (the time constant of the system).

Simulation

The equation $T\dfrac{d\theta_0}{dt} + \theta_0 = \theta_i$ can be written in the form $-\dfrac{d\theta_0}{dt} = -\dfrac{1}{T}.\theta_i + \dfrac{1}{T}.\theta_0$ and thus, given $-\theta_i$, θ_0 may be produced:

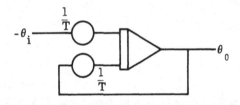

Fig. 12.19

The circuit is correctly scaled if simulated thus as θ_0 can never exceed θ_i (θ_0 follows the input θ_i). Thus if θ_i is correctly scaled the output must also be correctly scaled regardless of input variations.

12.7   Simulation of a quadratic system

The basic equation is

266

$$\frac{d^2\theta}{dt^2} + 2.\,\xi.\,w_0\,\frac{d\theta_0}{dt} + w_0^2\theta_0 = w_0^2.\,\theta_i,$$

where θ_i is the input and θ_0 the output of the system. This may be simulated in a variety of ways. However, the method which is best in the sense that a maximum of information (on the error, output θ_0 and 'velocity' $\frac{d\theta_0}{dt}$) may be output from the simulation is as follows:

Let error $E = \theta_i - \theta_0$, therefore

$$-\frac{d}{dt}\left(\frac{\dot{\theta}_0}{w_0}\right) = 2.\,\xi.\,w_0\left(-\frac{\dot{\theta}_0}{w_0}\right) + w_0 E,$$

where

$$-\frac{d\theta_0}{dt} = -\dot{\theta}_0 = w_0\left(-\frac{\dot{\theta}_0}{w_0}\right).$$

Hence:

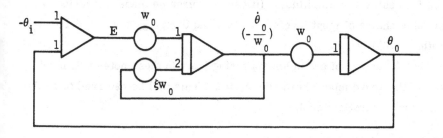

Fig. 12.20

Scaling

If a step of unit magnitude is applied at the input the output cannot exceed 2 units in magnitude (see diagram on page 259) and the error cannot exceed 1 unit. Thus θ_0 and E should be scaled as $\left(\frac{\theta_0}{2}\right)$ and $\left(\frac{E}{1}\right)$.

The maximum rate of change of θ_0, i.e. $\dot{\theta}_0$ will occur when the damping is minimum, i.e. when $\xi = 0$. When this is so, the output $\theta_0 = 1 - \cos w_0 t$ and $|\dot{\theta}_0| = |w_0 \sin w_0 t| \le w_0$. Thus $\dot{\theta}_0$ should be scaled as $\left(\frac{\dot{\theta}_0}{w_0}\right)$. The scaled simulation is therefore:

267

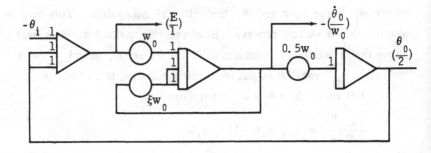

Fig. 12. 21

Although this amplitude scaled system is derived assuming a step input it will also be suitably scaled for a large variety of inputs not exceeding 1 machine unit amplitude. (It can of course be made to overload by suitable choice of input forcing function and damping, e. g. $\theta_i = \cos w_0 t$ with $\xi = 0.$)

A number of examples appearing later in these notes will involve use of the above model in which $w_0 = 1$. This will be referred to as the standard quadratic model.

12.8 Simulation of transfer functions

When control system characteristics are specified in terms of (Laplace Transform) transfer functions they may be simulated using a technique involving algebraic manipulation:

The integrator equation is $-\dfrac{d \text{ output}}{dt} = \text{input}$. Thus

$$-s \, . \, \overline{\text{output}} = \overline{\text{input}} \text{ (assuming zero initial output),}$$

or

$$\frac{\overline{\text{output}}}{\overline{\text{input}}} = \frac{-1}{s},$$

i. e. the integrator has a transfer function of $-\dfrac{1}{s}$.

Therefore, if a transfer function can be written in terms of combinations of $-\dfrac{1}{s}$ it may be simulated using appropriate combinations of integrators (plus pots and perhaps summers).

268

For example, the transfer function of a simple lag

$\dfrac{\bar{\theta}_0}{\bar{\theta}_i} = \dfrac{1}{1 + sT}$ may be simulated thus:

Cross multiply: $(1 + sT)\bar{\theta}_0 = \bar{\theta}_i$.

Divide by sT: $\dfrac{\bar{\theta}_0}{sT} + \theta_0 = \dfrac{\bar{\theta}_i}{sT}$.

Rewrite $\bar{\theta}_0$ in terms of $-\dfrac{1}{s}$

and factorise: $\bar{\theta}_0 = (-\dfrac{\bar{\theta}_i}{T} + \dfrac{\bar{\theta}_0}{T})(-\dfrac{1}{s})$.

Therefore:

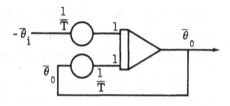

Fig. 12.22

A system having a quadratic transfer function

$$\dfrac{\bar{\theta}_0}{\bar{\theta}_i} = \dfrac{w_0^2}{s^2 + 2\xi w_0 s + w_0^2}$$

may be simulated thus:

Cross multiply: $\bar{\theta}_0(s^2 + 2\xi w_0 s + w_0^2) = w_0^2 \bar{\theta}_i$.

Divide by s^2: $\bar{\theta}_0(1 + 2\dfrac{\xi w_0}{s} + \dfrac{w_0^2}{s^2}) = \dfrac{w_0^2 \bar{\theta}_i}{s^2}$.

Rewrite $\bar{\theta}_0$ $\bar{\theta}_0 = \dfrac{w_0^2(\bar{\theta}_i - \bar{\theta}_0)}{(-s)^2} + \dfrac{2\xi w_0 \bar{\theta}_0}{(-s)}$

and factorise $\therefore$ $\bar{\theta}_0 = (\dfrac{w_0}{-s})[\dfrac{w_0}{-s}(\bar{\theta}_i - \bar{\theta}_0) + 2\xi\bar{\theta}_0]$.

Hence:

269

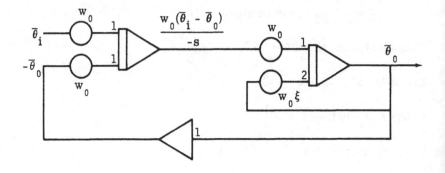

Fig. 12.23

In both examples the integrator is used as a building block having a transfer function $(-\frac{1}{s})$. The integrator is also used to perform summation. Although this technique is often used it has some serious limitations:

(a) The simulation is often more difficult to scale than if it is derived from the differential equation form. This is true partly because in 'generalising' the problem by use of transfer functions it is easy to lose sight of the original problem.

(b) Simulations derived naturally this way (although often efficient in terms of the number of units involved) do not necessarily produce very meaningful 'intermediate variables'. The simulation derived for the quadratic above conveys no direct information on the error $\theta_i - \theta_0$ or the 'velocity' $\dot{\theta}_0$ (i.e. $s\bar{\theta}_0$ in Laplace terms). The reader is left to see how the final expression for $\bar{\theta}_0$ may be manipulated so that it produces the much better simulation shown earlier, Fig. 12.21.

Thus on general-purpose analogue computers there appears to be no obvious advantage in simulating systems via the use of transfer functions. (This is not true for simulators in which transfer functions are simulated by direct use of resistors and capacitors connected around operational amplifiers.) If the technique is used it is important to try to involve the use of simple, easily simulated blocks. Thus the system of Fig. 12.24 should be simulated as in Fig. 12.25 (perhaps with the blocks in a different order):

270

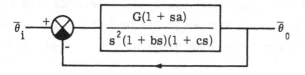

Fig. 12.24

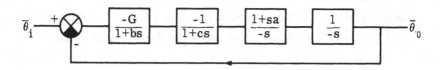

Fig. 12.25

where each block is simulated using one integrator (plus other units for the block $\frac{1 + as}{-s}$) rather than as:

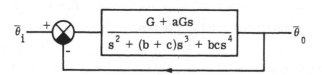

Fig. 12.26

(or even worse if the closed loop transfer function is derived and simulated in polynomial form!). Simulations derived other than by the simple block approach are almost impossible to scale and in addition simple changes to constants (a, b or c) may involve the re-setting of many pots. Close correspondence between model and system is lost and changes to the original system (other than simple coefficient changes) will involve the rederiving of a complete new analogue model.

The authors believe that, in general, simulations should be derived directly from the system differential equations rather than via transfer functions. An exception to this rule is the derivation of simulations for time delays (Padé filter approximation example 6). In addition as transfer functions only apply to linear systems (or the linear parts of non-linear systems) their usefulness in realistic simulations is severely restricted.

12.9 Measurement of behaviour of analogue computer models

The behaviour of control systems is normally required to be known for a range of input functions, e.g. steps, ramps, sinewaves. In simulation tests these functions may be generated either externally to the computer (by standard signal generators) or by units within the computer itself. The latter method is generally most convenient because:

(i) The signals are automatically synchronised to the computer, i.e. they start at the right time.

(ii) Should the timescale of the model be changed the 'frequency' of the test signals automatically changes by the same amount.

(iii) The amplitudes of the signals are in machine unit form.

As integrator 'integrating' inputs only become connected when the computer is switched into the COMPUTE mode, a constant present in the I.C. mode will automatically become a step applied at time = 0 when the computer is switched to COMPUTE. Thus in the examples that follow steps appear as constants. This important point is illustrated further in example 1 below.

The circuit on page 66 of §4 is very useful for generating triangular and square wave inputs of controlled frequency. A very useful way to present the response of a system to a square wave input is illustrated in Fig. 12.27.

12.10 Examples

The following examples have been selected to show the wide range of application of simulation techniques and also to teach some of the simpler ideas of control. No large models are included (although they are involved in most important applications) because the principles and techniques can be understood by use of simple models, particularly of 2nd order quadratic systems. Readers are left to select particular examples

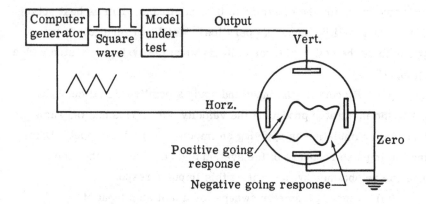

Fig. 12. 27

to match their interests and the type of equipment available. The examples were derived initially for analogue/hybrid computer simulation but can, of course, be investigated using digital simulation techniques.

(1) **Behaviour of a quadratic system**

     Set up a standard quadratic system as in the diagram Fig. 12. 21 with $w_0 = 1$.

     (i)   Apply a step unit input (i. e. a constant of 1 machine unit amplitude) and record the output and error against time (0-10 seconds) for $\xi = 0[0.1]1$. From the curves obtain a plot of the percentage overshoot due to a step input as a function of the damping coefficient. ($\xi = 0.5$ should give 16-17%.) Also plot 10-90% rise time as a function of ξ.

     (ii)   Apply a ramp input 0.1t, observe effect of different values of ξ and record case $\xi = 0.5$. Note the 'velocity lag', i. e. the way the output does not exactly follow the 'constant velocity' input demand. Explain why this is so.

     (iii)   Note how the response to the ramp 0.1t can be obtained by integrating (via a gain of 0.1) the response of the system to a unit step. Consider why this is so and use the technique to obtain the response to a quadratic input $0.01t^2$ from the step response.

     (iv)   Apply a unit step input and compute the error criteria

(a) $\int_0^{10} Error^2 dt$ (ISE)   and   (b) $\int_0^{10} |Error| dt$ (IAE)

for various values of damping. With each criterion determine the optimum value of ξ for the criterion to be a minimum. This is best obtained using a fast repetitive mode of operation. Which, in general, do you suppose to be the better of these criteria when the system is tested with a step input?

(v)   Disconnect the input and apply a positive initial condition input to the integrator producing the velocity $-\dot{\theta}_0$. This has the same effect in the simulation as applying an impulse $\delta(t)$ at the input. Determine the impulse response of the system and observe that the step response can be obtained by integrating this impulse response.

(vi)   Obtain parameter sweeps for a unit step input of:

(a) I. S. E.   (b) I. A. E.

(c) percentage overshoot   (d) rise time

as functions of ξ, $0 \rightarrow 1$.

If the computer is switched to HOLD when θ_0 goes through its first maximum, the value of the error at this time is the % overshoot/100.

(vii)   Characteristics (c) and (d) above show that a fast response is accompanied by excessive overshoot, i.e. when ξ is small. A method of overcoming this is to switch the input step signal off for a short period shortly after it is applied, (a very common intuitive technique used in manual control). If the times of switching off and on are carefully adjusted for a system with little damping, the response can be made to appear:

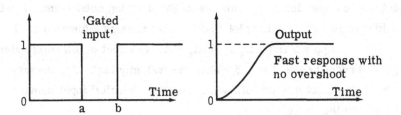

Fig. 12.28

Set up a simulation of a quadratic system including a circuit to gate the step and another to compute I. S. E. or I. A. E.

N. B.   The error is the difference between the actual step (not the gated step) and the output.

For $\xi = 0$ adjust a, b until the error criterion is a minimum and check the output appears as in the diagram. This '2 parameter' system can best be optimised when operating the computer in a fast repetitive mode and displaying the error criterion via a last value circuit on the D. V. M.   Repeat for other values of ξ. Consider carefully the practicability of the technique as a means of achieving fast response with little or no overshoot.   (For $\xi = 0$, $a \simeq 1.05$ and $b \simeq 2.1$ seconds for optimum response.)

(2)   Effect of limiting on step response

(i)   Set up a simple quadratic control model with $\xi = 0.5$ and include a ± limiter (soft (slow turn on) or hard (sharp turn on)) to limit the error to about ±0.2. Note the difference in the responses obtained with/without limiting as the step amplitude is increased $0.1 \rightarrow 1$.   A convenient way to do this is as follows:

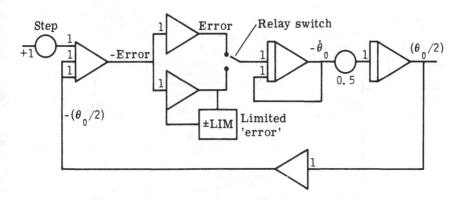

Fig. 12.29

The relay switch can be used to switch the limiting in or out of the model.   If possible the computer should be operated in high-speed REP-OP, the switch state changed at the end of each compute period and the output $(\theta_0/2)$ displayed against time.

Note how the performance index (ISE or IAE) is worsened by the action of limiting when the step amplitude is > 0.2.

275

(Reference to the example on page 256 shows that limiting included this way is equivalent to saturation in the amplifier driving the motor.)

(ii) A saturating amplifier sometimes has a transfer characteristic approximating to a cubic of the form

$$\text{output} = a.\,\text{input} + b(\text{input})^3$$

where a is a positive and b a negative constant. Simulate this characteristic instead of the ± limiter in the system of the previous example and note that the same adverse effect on performance is produced (use a = 1, b = -0.5).

Also observe effect of making b positive (=0.5) and consider if it would be worth trying to 'design in' this type of non-linearity into a control system.

(3) **On/off temperature control system**

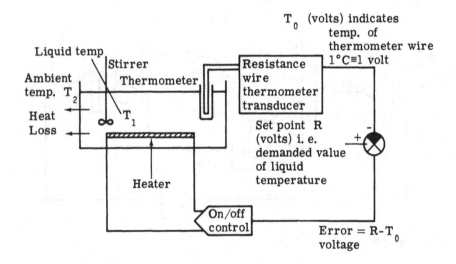

Fig. 12.30

The above shows a simple on/off control scheme used to control the temperature T_1 of liquid in a small tank. The heater produces either H or zero kilowatts depending on whether the error $E = R - T_0$

is positive or negative. The thermometer system introduces a lag (of time constant L) into the measurement of the liquid temperature T_1. The equations are therefore:

Thermometer

<u>Static</u> T_0 (volts) $\equiv T_1$ (degrees centigrade)

<u>Dynamic</u> $L\dfrac{dT_0}{dt} + T_0 = T_1$ (1)

        (Transfer Function $\overline{T}_0 = \dfrac{\overline{T}_1}{1 + Ls}$)

Comparator   Error $E = R - T_0$ (2)

Tank $\dfrac{dT_1}{dt} = k.\,W - \alpha(T_1 - T_2)$ (3)

        (Newton's Law of Cooling. k, α constants)

        where $W = H$ if $E > 0$

                $W = 0$ if $E < 0$

Simulation

      Assume $H = 3$, $k = 1.2$, $\alpha = 0.01$, $L = 5$ and $T_2 = 0$ kilowatt, second, degrees centigrade units.

      Include timescale speed up factor of 10 or 20. Determine:

(i)   Response from cold (i.e. $T_1 = 0$, $T_0 = 0$) to a step demand $R = 75$ volts ($\equiv 75°C$). Observe T_1, T_0 and Error E.

(ii)   Note effect on turn on response of varying

       (a) heater output

       (b) heat loss 'α'

       for various values of R (20 < R < 80).

(4) Liquid level control scheme

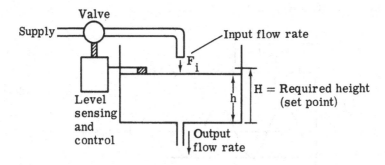

Fig. 12.31

The above diagram shows a system by which the level, h, of liquid in a tank is controlled. The object of the control is to ensure that the height equals the required height H whatever the output flow rate. The general equations are:

$$A\frac{dh}{dt} = F_i - F_0,$$

where A is the cross-sectional area of the tank.

Error $E = H - h$

Flow rate F_i through valve is a function of Error E.

Case 1

Assume the output flow is what naturally flows via an orifice due to pressure, i.e. $F_0 = K\sqrt{h}$, where K depends on the size of the hole.

(a) Investigate the effect of <u>proportional control</u>, i.e. $F_i = G.E$, where G is the gain.

Observe the way in which the tank fills when the system is initially switched on and note how the size of the steady state error depends on the size of the hole and the magnitude of gain G.

(b) Show how the steady state error may be eliminated by use of <u>integral control</u>, i.e. $\frac{dF_i}{dt} = G.E$, where G is the gain.

Note the effect of variations in G and K on the transient switching on response.

Case 2

Assume the output flow rate is determined by demand and that integral action control is used. Investigate the effect of various demand patterns assuming the system starts in steady state with $h = H$. In particular note effect of demands:

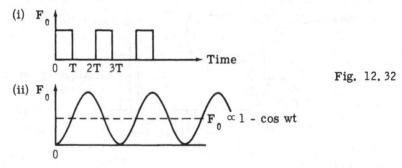

Fig. 12. 32

278

Note: For purposes of simulation assume $H = 1$, $h < 2$, $A = 1$, $0.2 < K < 2$, $G < 5$, $T = 2$ and $w = 2$.

(5) Simulation involving use of a 3 term controller

Many chemical engineering control systems make use of '3 term controller' compensators to 'optimise' the performance characteristic. The input X and output Y variables of such a controller obey the equation

$$Y = K(X + T_d \frac{dX}{dt} + \frac{1}{T_r} \cdot \int X.\, dt),$$

where K is the controller gain, $\frac{1}{T_r}$ the reset rate and T_d the derivative time constant.

It is seen that simulation of this device would involve the use of a differentiator. However, analogue computers do not usually contain devices to differentiate as such devices would be 'noisy', i.e. they would amplify high frequency components of noise and other spurious signals (e.g. mains hum), present in the computer variables. Integrators reduce these spurious signals (cf. numerical differentiation and integration). If a differentiator has to be used it is usual to simulate it approximately by implementing the relationship

$$(1 - a) \frac{dX_0}{dt} + X_0 = \frac{dX_i}{dt}$$

or in Transfer Function form as

$$\frac{\bar{X}_0}{\bar{X}_i} = \frac{s}{1 + (1 - a)s},$$

where a is as near to (but less than) 1 as noise considerations permit. ($a \simeq 0.95$ to 0.98.) A simulation for this relationship is:

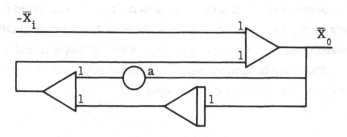

Fig. 12.33

279

(i)   Derive a computer simulation of a 3 term controller in which the above circuit is incorporated.

(ii)   Build this controller into a model of a simple process:

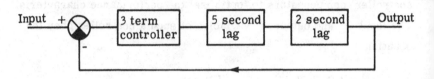

Fig. 12. 34

and generally investigate the effect of proportional action, proportional plus integral and proportional plus integral plus derivative action on the response of the system to a simple step input. In particular note how integral action reduces the steady state error present if proportional gain is used alone but that integral action may make the system unstable. This tendency to instability can be corrected by derivative action.

(iii)   As (ii) above but include a further 1 second lag in the forward path so that the system is unstable unless derivative action is included.

(6) Effect of time delay

Many models (e. g. economic models) need to include the effect of time delay or transport delay. Such time delay can best be simulated using a full hybrid computer in a 'function collect, store and playback mode'. The delay is introduced by the digital computer (an operation it is well able to perform!). However, time delay may be simulated approximately by means of analogue units using Padé filter approximations. Using Laplace transform theory a pure time delay Y has a transfer function e^{-Ts}. This may be approximated by rational functions of various order. For example, in second order form

$$e^{-Ts} \simeq \frac{1 - \frac{1}{2}.\,Ts + \frac{1}{12}.\,T^2 s^2}{1 + \frac{1}{2}.\,Ts + \frac{1}{12}.\,T^2 s^2}$$

which may be simulated:

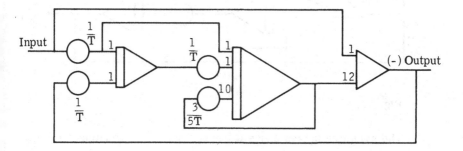

Fig. 12. 35

The above simulation is valid providing the input to the delay unit does not change too rapidly (for sinusoidal input of angular frequency w then wT needs to be less than about 2). Step inputs cannot be used.

Simulate a standard quadratic control system in which $\xi = 0.5$ and include the above approximation to a delay T in the feedback path. Test the response of the overall system to a step input for various values of T(0. 1-5) being careful to observe and record the delay simulator's input (i. e. the output of the system) and its output. Note the quality of the approximation and observe the effect of the delay. Note. It is useful to include a system without delay as a reference or use the switching technique discussed in example 2 to switch the delay unit in and out of the feedback path.

(7) **Simulation of a sampled data system**

Digital computer control systems are essentially sampled data in character, i. e. variables are sampled at intervals, new control actions calculated and corrections applied. Unless the sampling is sufficiently frequent, control may be adversely affected. The effect of the sampling itself may be simulated by means of a track store. It is shown below included in a simple second order model in which $\xi = 0.5$:

281

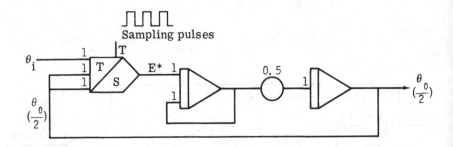

Fig. 12. 36

The sampling pulses cause the error E* to be updated at regular intervals.

Model the above system using a unit step input and note the effect of the sampling interval on (a) the response and stability of the system, and (b) the way the actual response is affected by the times of sampling in relation to the time at which the step is applied. This second effect means that the response is not exactly predictable unless the sampling rate is high compared to the time of the system response.

Important notes:

(i) It is essential that the occurrence of the sampling pulses is not synchronised to the time of application of the step input if this latter effect is to be observed.

(ii) For reason (i) above the sampling pulses could be obtained from a generator external to the computer and the computer operated at high speed in REP-OP to show the effect of the sampling. Alternatively, the sampling pulses could be derived from a monostable driven by the logic square output from the triangular/square wave oscillator described in §4.

If this is done the oscillator must be made to free run, i. e. the integrator used must be in COMPUTE mode all the time irrespective of the mode of the rest of the computer model.

(iii) The sampling pulse must be sufficiently wide to allow the

282

T/S unit to track the new error information. With modern T/S units, a few microseconds should be sufficient.

(iv)   The period of the sampling should be adjustable from a few (2 or 3) to tens of samples in the response time of the system.

(8)   Position control system

Simulate the system described by equations (12.1) to (12.6) in the text and referred to on pages 257-261 for the case $C = 1$, $K = 1$, $J = 1$, $F = 0$ (no friction) and $0.1 < A < 10$.

(i)   Check that when gain $A = 1$ the response to a unit step is $1 - \cos t$. Note that the effect of change of gain A is to change the frequency of the oscillation. The same effect would have been produced if the inertia J was varied (or K or C).

For $A = 1$ observe the effect of increasing friction and determine the value of F for the overshoot to be 10%.

(ii)   In practice it is not generally possible to control friction. Instead a signal proportional to velocity is derived from a tachometer attached to the motor shaft and fed back in addition to the positional data to compensate (or in some cases stabilise) th response by effectively controlling the amount of damping. In the real system the voltage output from the tachometer is produced by changes in shaft position X and therefore 'appears' after X:

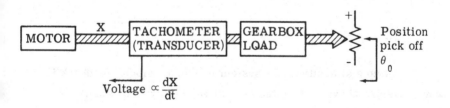

Fig. 12.37

However, if the system is simulated in this order a differentiator will be needed to obtain $\frac{dX}{dt}$ from X. For reasons explained in Example 5 this would have to be simulated in approximate form as analogue computers do not normally contain differentiators. The simulation for the

283

motor should already contain a unit producing an output proportional to velocity and this can be used instead:

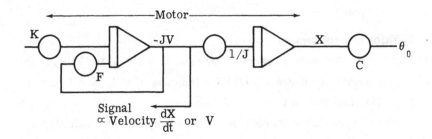

Fig. 12.38

The velocity feedback signal may be introduced into the system in a number of ways. One convenient method is to subtract it from the usual error and input $\theta_i - \theta_0 - \alpha.V$, where α is a constant, into the amplifier driving the motor:

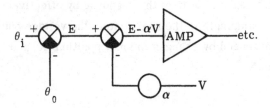

Fig. 12.39

Set up a simulation of a system including velocity feedback in the way suggested above. Make the natural velocity friction small $(F \sim 0.1)$ and observe the way that for any given value of A the response overshoot may be controlled by the amount of additional velocity feedback applied.

(iii)   In deriving system equations no account was taken of the field time constant. This cannot always be ignored. If the amplifier has controlled voltage gain A and the field winding has an inductance L and resistance R then:

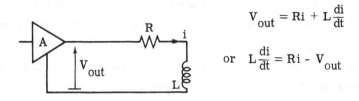

$$V_{out} = Ri + L\frac{di}{dt}$$

or $$L\frac{di}{dt} = Ri - V_{out}$$

Fig. 12.'40

Thus equation 12.2 should be replaced by

$$\frac{di}{dt} = \frac{R}{L} \cdot i - \frac{A}{L} E$$

and a lag of time constant $\frac{L}{R}$ must be included in the simulation. The total simulation including the field winding time constant and also velocity feedback becomes:

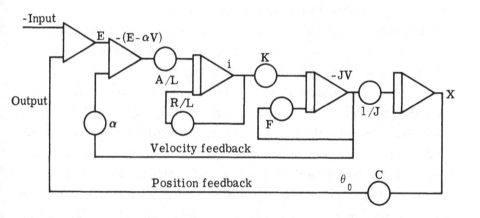

Fig. 12.41

Set up the above system and apply a step input.

(a)   Initially make $F = 0$ (no friction), $\alpha = 0$ (no velocity feedback) and $R/L = 0.5$, and note that the system is unstable for all values of gain A.

(b)   If a small amount of friction is included $(F \sim 0.1)$ note that the system is unstable unless A is made very small.

285

(c)　Add on velocity feedback and note how for any value of A the system can be made stable if α is made sufficiently large.

(iv)　From the results obtained in (i), (ii) and (iii) above it will be noticed that the performance, as judged by response time/overshoot or by an error criterion of the type $\int |\text{error}| dt$, will continually improve as the gain A increases. This is not so for variation of friction F (or velocity feedback α) which, for any value of gain A, has a clear optimum value. Thus it would seem that A should be made as large as possible to give the best response. In practice a large value of A would mean that for even small errors

(a)　the output of the amplifier would limit (saturate) and the amplifier would be unable to supply the large amount of current which the equation implies should flow,

(b)　if the amplifier were able to supply an almost unlimited amount of current then the field winding would become overloaded and perhaps burned out.

Thus in order to avoid misleading conclusions which may be reached by considering linear theory approximations to control systems, it is vital to include some of the non-linear limitations.

Modify the simulation to include a ± limiting summer to represent the amplifier. Optimise the system (by adjusting A, α) for a small step input. Increase the magnitude of the step until considerable limiting occurs. Note change in response and re-optimise. Non-linearity of this type makes it very difficult to design a system able to handle a wide range of inputs. In practice it may be necessary to use a low gain, and resulting 'poor' performance for small inputs, in order to obtain a predictable and acceptable performance over a wide range of amplitudes.

(v)　Effect of backlash. A further non-linearity which may affect performance is hysteresis backlash in the gearbox between motor, load and position pick off. This characteristic is represented in Fig. 12.42. Assuming the gearbox starts in the symmetrical slack position, a small rotation 'a', i.e. $0 \rightarrow A$ of the input shaft is needed before the output shaft follows the input (AB). As soon as the input shaft starts to rotate the other way at B the output will remain fixed in position until the slack

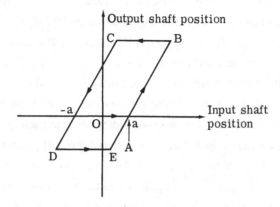

Fig. 12.42

'2a' is taken up at C. The output will then follow the input until the direction of input rotation is changed at D.

Hysteresis is one of the more difficult non-linearities to simulate. Clearly as the output for any input depends on how that output point was approached, memory is implied in the characteristic. Thus a simulation will involve use of integrators or track store units. A very efficient way to simulate hysteresis is:

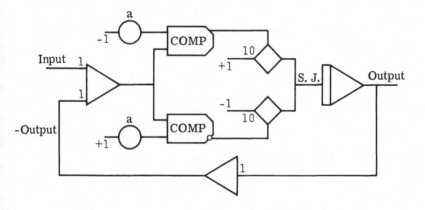

Fig. 12.43

The gain of the integrator must be such that the integrator output can follow any variations in the input along the sections AB, CD. Normally this will be achieved if the integrator gain is made 10-100 times that of the integrators used in the rest of the simulation so that the hysteresis simulator can keep pace with the fastest changes in its input.

Set up the system of (ii), (iii) or (iv) and include a hysteresis nonlinearity between X and θ_0. Observe the response for square wave and sinewave inputs (see page 273 for method to display response) of various amplitudes. To check operation of hysteresis circuit prior to the simulation proper, apply a triangular waveform or sinewave to the hysteresis simulator and display output against input. The basic hysteresis loop display should be obtained providing the peak to peak input amplitude is larger than the slack '2a'.

(vi) Velocity squared feedback. Set up the simulation case (ii) with $F = 0$ but replace the velocity feedback by a signal proportional to $\dot{X}|\dot{X}|$, i.e. a signal taking the sign of $\dot{X}$ but proportional to $\dot{X}^2$ in magnitude. Observe the response to a step input and compare it with that obtained with normal velocity feedback for a similar overshoot. Consider the usefulness (or otherwise) of applying this or other types of non-linear feedback (e.g. feedback $\propto X|\dot{X}|$).

Appendix 1 · Analogue and Hybrid Computer Hardware

A1.1 Introduction

The following notes provide a simple description of the way in which analogue and hybrid computer units work and how they perform various mathematical operations on computer variables. The equations are derived assuming ideal components and only a little discussion of errors is included.

Most computer units (other than pots) include one or more electronic operational amplifiers and a number of fast mechanical relay switches and/or electronic switches. Units are described under three headings: linear, non-linear and hybrid. Circuits are given showing the connections of the components within integrators, etc. , depending on the computer mode.

Although descriptions are specifically related to units contained in 10 volt reference computers, the principles of operation apply to machines with other reference voltage levels. The magnitude of computer variables are expressed in volts instead of machine units. To make the printing clear, capital letters are used for voltages and currents; this does not imply that they are constant in magnitude.

A1.2 Linear analogue units

(i) Potentiometer

Unlike other computer units, the output-input relationship for a potentiometer depends on the load R_L to which the output is joined. If there is no load on the potentiometer (i. e. R_L infinite) and if the setting of the pot is adjusted until the resistance between the arm A and low L terminals is $k \times R$, where R is the total resistance, then the output voltage = k times the input voltage. With a load resistance of R_L and

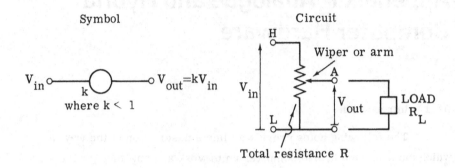

Symbol

Circuit

V_{in} ○———○ $V_{out} = kV_{in}$
k
where k < 1

H
Wiper or arm
A
V_{in}
V_{out}
LOAD R_L
L

Total resistance R

Fig. A1.1 Potentiometer

assuming the resistance between the A and L terminals of the pot is adjusted to μR then

$$V_{out} = \frac{\mu R_L}{R_L + \mu(1-\mu)R} \; V_{in} \; ,$$

i. e. to multiply by 'k' the pot must be adjusted until

$$\frac{\mu R_L}{R_L + \mu(1-\mu). R} = k.$$

This shows clearly why it is necessary to ensure each pot has its correct load while it is being set. Special circuits are used to ensure that each pot is correctly loaded when the computer is in the POT SET, (PS) mode. Should the load on a pot be changed at any time then the pot must be reset.

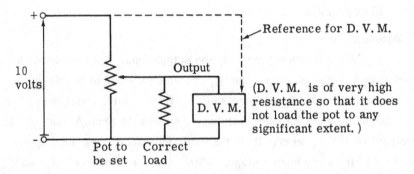

+

Reference for D. V. M.

10 volts

Output

D. V. M.

(D. V. M. is of very high resistance so that it does not load the pot to any significant extent.)

-

Pot to   Correct
be set   load

Fig. A1.2 Potentiometer setting

When the computer is in the PS mode and a particular pot is selected, 10 volts (1 machine unit) is automatically joined to the input of the pot and the output of the pot joined to the D. V. M. (Fig. Al. 2).

The pot is adjusted until the output voltage is the required fraction, k, of the input voltage (10 volts). The precision with which a pot can be set depends on the basic resolution of the pot itself and on the resolution of the D. V. M. The accuracy depends on the accuracy of the D. V. M. including the zero offset error, i. e. the meter reading when the input is zero. The effect of offset error is greatest when the coefficient, k, is least.

(ii) Operational amplifier

Symbol

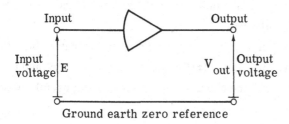

Fig. Al. 3

High gain operational amplifiers form the basis of all amplifier computing units, i. e. all analogue units other than pots. The following are the basic properties of such amplifiers valid providing the output voltage lies within the permitted range of ±10 volts (±1 machine unit) of zero:

(i)   The amplifier amplifies direct (constant or varying) voltages applied to its input.

(ii) The amplifier is essentially linear, i. e. its output voltage is linearly proportional to the input voltage.

(iii) When the input voltage is zero the output is very small, ideally zero, i. e. the amplifier has no significant voltage offset.

(iv) The gain of the amplifier is -A where A is very large, ideally infinite. Thus $V_{out} = -A.E.$
The amplifier includes a sign change. If the input voltage goes positive the output goes negative and vice versa.

(v) Because the gain A of the amplifier is very large, the input voltage is always very small (virtually zero) whatever the magnitude of the output voltage. The amplifier input is said to be a <u>virtual earth</u> and will be taken to be at zero voltage in much of the subsequent analysis.

(vi) The input impedance (resistance) of the amplifier is very large (ideally infinite) and thus very little current (ideally none) flows into or out of the input of the amplifier.

(vii) The output impedance of the amplifier is very low and it can drive many other units without its performance being adversely affected.

The above properties are valid providing the output voltage lies within the normal dynamic range (±10 volts or ±1 mu of zero) and providing the input does not vary above a certain 'maximum useful operating frequency'.

(iii)   Inverter (sign reverser)

Symbol   Circuit

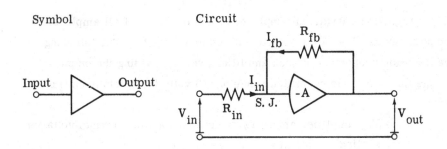

Fig. A1.4

V_{in} = Input voltage V_{out} = Output voltage
R_{in} = Input resistor R_{fb} = Feedback resistor
I_{in} = Input current I_{fb} = Feedback current
S.J. ≡ summing junction (or amplifier input junction).

Assuming a perfect amplifier, i. e. no current into amplifier input, infinite gain A so that amplifier input junction (S. J.) is a virtual earth, etc. then

$$I_{in} + I_{fb} = 0 \qquad \text{Kirchoff's Current Law}$$

$$I_{in} = \frac{V_{in}}{R_{in}} \qquad \text{Ohm's Law}^{\dagger}$$

$$I_{fb} = \frac{V_{out}}{R_{fb}} \qquad \text{Ohm's Law}^{\dagger}$$

so that $-V_{out} = \dfrac{R_{fb}}{R_{in}} \cdot V_{in}$

If $R_{fb} = R_{in}$ (usually 10^4 or 10^5 ohms) then $\underline{\underline{-V_{out} = V_{in}}}$

($\dagger$Note: Due to the amplifier input junction being virtually at zero voltage, the voltage across the feedback resistor is the same as the output voltage and the voltage across the input resistor equals the input voltage.)

If the effect of finite amplifier gain A is included, the equations need to be slightly modified. As the output voltage is V_{out}, the 'error' voltage E at the amplifier input junction is $-\dfrac{V_{out}}{A}$. Thus:

$$\frac{V_{in} - E}{R_{in}} = I_{in}$$

$$\frac{V_{out} - E}{R_{fb}} = I_{fb}$$

$$E = -\frac{V_{out}}{A}$$

and $I_{in} + I_{fb} = 0$. Hence

$$-V_{out} = \frac{R_{fb}}{R_{in}} \cdot \frac{A}{A + 1 + \dfrac{R_{fb}}{R_{in}}} \cdot V_{in}$$

For a unity gain inverter where R_{in} is nominally equal to R_{fb} then:

$$-V_{out} = \frac{R_{fb}}{R_{in}} \cdot \frac{A}{A + 2} \cdot V_{in} \cdot$$

With constant or slowly varying inputs, the gain A is very large $(> 10^7)$ so that $\frac{A}{A+2}$ is very nearly 1. The gain of the inverter is then almost entirely dependent on the exact values of the feedback and input resistors. (The amplifier characteristics are 'designed out'.) Resistors are manufactured to a tolerance of about $\pm 0.005\%$ at best and thus the actual gain of a unity gain inverter (i. e. R_{fb} nominally equal to R_{in}) incorporating such resistors is usually correct to within $\pm 0.01\%$ of 1 (i. e. 1 part in 10^4). At higher frequencies the gain of the inverter becomes increasingly affected by the amplifier characteristics, particularly gain and phase response. An inverter using a quality amplifier is likely to introduce a dynamic gain error of about 1% if the input is a sinewave of frequency 1 KHz. In addition the transfer characteristic for high frequency inputs worsens as the amplitude of the output waveform increases.

(vi)   Summer

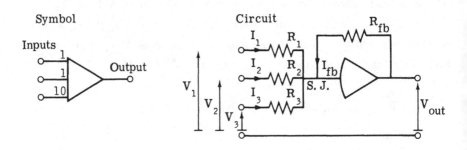

Fig. A1.5

The circuit of a summer is similar to that of an inverter except that the input network consists of a number of resistors. Assuming an ideal amplifier then:

$$(I_1 + I_2 + I_3 + \dots) + I_{fb} = 0,$$

$$I_1 = \frac{V_1}{R_1}, \; I_2 = \frac{V_2}{R_2}, \; \text{etc.}$$

$$\text{and } I_{fb} = \frac{V_{out}}{R_{fb}}$$

$$- V_{out} = R_{fb} \left(\frac{V_1}{R_1} + \frac{V_2}{R_2} + \dots \right).$$

Summation is essentially achieved by the addition of currents at the amplifier input or summing junction (S. J.). The amplitude of the total current in the feedback resistor (and hence the output voltage) equals the total current input via the resistors R_1, R_2, etc.

The ratios $\frac{R_{fb}}{R_1}$, etc., are chosen to have values 1 or 10 to give gains of 1 or 10 at the inputs to the summer.

Thus, if $\frac{R_{fb}}{R_1} = 1$, $\frac{R_{fb}}{R_2} = 1$, and $\frac{R_{fb}}{R_3} = 10$ then

$-V_{out} = V_1 + V_2 + 10V_3$.

Again, like the inverter, the accuracy of the transfer characteristic depends on the values of the resistors.

To ensure correct loading of the potentiometers while they are being set in the PS mode it is arranged, by relay switching, that the input resistors are joined to earth (zero reference):

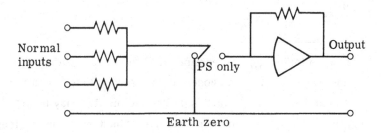

Fig. A1. 6 Summer

In all other modes the input resistors are joined to the amplifier input junction so that the unit operates as a summer.

(v)   Integrator

The circuit for an integrator is similar to that of an inverter except that the feedback resistor is replaced by a capacitor used to accumulate and store charge.

Assuming an ideal amplifier then:

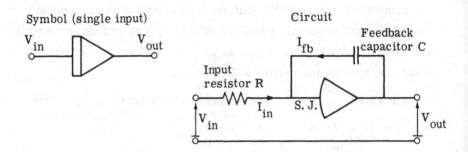

Symbol (single input)

V_{in} V_{out}

Circuit

Feedback
capacitor C

I_{fb}

Input
resistor R

I_{in} S. J.

V_{in}

V_{out}

Fig. A1.7

$$I_{in} + I_{fb} = 0,$$

$$I_{in} = \frac{V_{in}}{R},$$

and $I_{fb} = C \dfrac{dV_{out}}{dt}$ using Coulomb's Law.

Hence $-\dfrac{dV_{out}}{dt} = \dfrac{1}{RC} \cdot V_{in}$

The gain factor $\frac{1}{RC}$ determines the rate of integration. For normal seconds operation RC is chosen to be 1 second to give a gain of 1. ($R = 10^5$ Ohms and $C = 10^{-5}$ farads.) The factor RC may be set, by trimming the value of the capacitor, and maintained over long periods of time to within $\pm 0.01\%$ of its nominal value providing close control is kept of the environment, particularly temperature, of the components.

For the multiple input case, in which a number of input currents are added together as in the summer,

$$-\frac{dV_{out}}{dt} = \frac{1}{C} \cdot \left(\frac{V_1}{R_1} + \frac{V_2}{R_2} + \dots \right).$$

The factor $\frac{1}{C}$ is common to all inputs and is used to control the basic time scale on the integrator, e.g. to speed up the integration rate by a factor of n the value of C must be decreased by a factor n. The gains of different inputs are controlled by the choice of the relative magnitudes of R_1, R_2, etc.

Initial condition

The equation for the integrator may be expressed as $V_{out} = -\frac{1}{RC} \int . V_{in} . dt$. Assuming that integration starts at time 't = 0' when the computer is switched from I. C. to COMPUTE then

$$[V_{out}]_0^t = -\frac{1}{RC} \int_0^t V_{in}. dt$$

or

$$V_{out}(t) = -\frac{1}{RC} \int_0^t V_{in}dt + V_{out}(0),$$

where $V_{out}(0) \equiv$ the initial output voltage (or the initial voltage across the capacitor).

Special circuits are used to enable the capacitor to be charged to any desired initial voltage in the I. C. mode. The details depend on the type of computer used, but basically the unit is operated as a unity gain inverter in this mode with the capacitor joined either between the output and the summing junction, or the output and earth.

Hold

In the HOLD mode the input resistors (or resistor) are not joined to the summing junction and no current flows in or out of the capacitor. The voltage across the capacitor (and hence the amplifier output) therefore, remains constant.

In practice a certain amount of current 'leaks' in or out of the capacitor resulting in drift. Great care is needed in choice of capacitor and amplifier, positioning of components with respect to power supply rails, general cleanliness, etc., to achieve acceptable drift rates for computational purposes. Rates as low as 1 millivolt (i. e. 0. 01% of 1 machine unit) per 100 seconds are achieved with integrators in normal seconds timescale. ($C = 10^{-5}$ farad.) This drift rate is equivalent to a leakage current of less than 10^{-10} amps or a leakage resistance (across the capacitor) of more than 10^{11} ohms!

Complete circuit

The circuit below shows the integrator connections in the various modes of operation. During the PS mode the input resistors (including the IC input resistor) are returned to earth or zero to ensure correct loading on the potentiometers. In the IC and HOLD modes the normal input resistors are joined to zero whereas, in the ST mode, the input resistors are connected to a special amplifier so that the 'derivative', i.e. total input of normal inputs, may be measured. In ST and IC modes the initial condition resistors are joined so that the capacitor is charged to the required initial voltage.

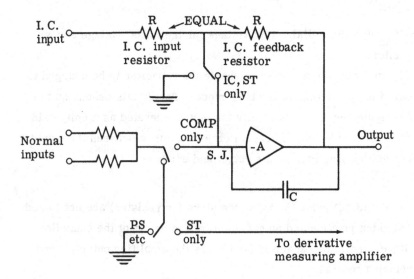

Fig. A1.8 Circuit of integrator

The rate at which the capacitor may be charged up in the IC mode depends on the value of the IC feedback resistor 'R'. In some machines where it is necessary to achieve rapid charging (-short reset periods) the capacitor is joined between amplifier output and earth so that the full output current of the amplifier (rather than the current through R) is used to charge the capacitor.

On the diagram the switches are drawn as electromechanical devices. In modern machines some of these switches are electronic in order

298

to achieve rapid switching between modes.

A1.3   Non-linear analogue devices

Diodes (see §5) are used extensively in circuits to simulate non-linear functions. In some circuits (e. g. zero limiter) only one diode is used but others (e.g. DFG) involve use of very many of these devices.

(i)   Zero limiter

The basic circuit and characteristic of a simple unity gain positive zero limiter incorporating one silicon diode is:

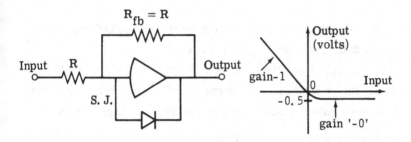

Fig. A1.9

For positive outputs the diode is reverse biased and has very high resistance. The total feedback resistance is that of resistor R_{fb} so that the gain is -1.

As the input voltage goes positive the output voltage goes negative until, at about -0.5 volt, the diode conducts and becomes low resistance. The effective feedback resistance becomes very low compared with the value of the input resistance R so that the gain becomes almost zero. Thus the output is limited to positive values only.

The characteristic obtained may be described as that of a soft zero limiter because of the 'gradual' diode conducting characteristic.

This 'gradual' limiting effect and 0.5 volt offset from zero can largely be removed by including a second diode in a balance circuit (see Fig. A1.10).

When the input is negative the amplifier output X goes positive and drives the actual output positive via D2. The gain in this mode is

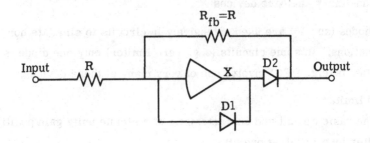

Fig. A1.10

$-\dfrac{R_{fb}}{R} = -1$ nominally, as the same current must flow via both input resistor R and feedback resistor R_{fb} (D1 is cut off).

When the input is positive, X is driven to about -0.5 volt (D1 conducts) and D2 is reverse biased and cut off. No current can therefore flow via the feedback resistor and so the output voltage is zero.

(ii) **Diode function generations** (D.F.G.s)

The differences between fixed function and variable functions D.F.G.s is explained in §5.   Both types essentially consist of an operational amplifier together with resistance-diode networks as input and/or feedback elements:

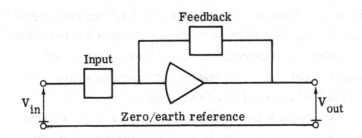

Fig. A1.11

To generate a particular function the current through one (or both) of these networks is made a non-linear function of the voltage across it, so that the output voltage is the required non-linear function of the input voltage. Thus if a squaring unit is required, an ordinary resistor can be used for the feedback component and a special diode resistor network in which the current is proportional to the square of the voltage used for the input component. The current through the feedback resistor and hence the output voltage is then proportional to the square of the input voltage and a squaring characteristic is obtained. A square root circuit can be produced by using a square law network as the feedback element and a resistor for the input network.

The error in function generators of this type depends on the complexity of the function itself, how well the device is set up initially and the stability of the characteristic with temperature and aging effects. Normally they are considered to be 0.1% devices, i.e. devices in which errors are likely to be 0.1% of 1 machine unit or about 10 times as great as the errors usually associated with linear units.

(iii) Multipliers

The problem of multiplying two variables together accurately, quickly and economically, is one of the classic problems of electromechanical and electronic engineering. At least a hundred different methods have been tried. In analogue computation three methods have been extensively used: servo, electronic time division and quarter square. The last of these three is the standard method used in many modern machines because of its fast operation.

The QUARTER SQUARE multiplier has as its inputs $+X$, $-X$, $+Y$ and $-Y$ and it outputs XY using two squaring D.F.G.s and a summing amplifier by implementing the relationship:

$$XY = \frac{1}{4}[(X + Y)^2 - (X - Y)^2]$$

With reference to Fig. A1.12:

Current $I_1 \propto -(X + Y)^2$

Current $I_2 \propto +(X - Y)^2$

and $I_{fb} = -(I_1 + I_2)$

Therefore, the output Voltage $\propto (X + Y)^2 - (X - Y)^2$

i.e. $\propto XY$

A quarter square multiplier effectively uses three operational amplifiers as both signs of X and Y are needed and an amplifier is

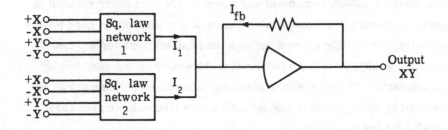

Fig. Al. 12

required as the output device.

The accuracy of a multiplier depends largely on how well it is initially set up and how stable are the squaring network characteristics. As for D. F. G. s, errors are usually considered to be about . 1% of 1 machine unit but particular characteristics (e. g. offset error with both inputs zero) generally have rather smaller errors than this.

A1. 4   Hybrid interface units

Units used to provide communication between digital logic and analogue signals are grouped under two headings: (i) detection and control, (ii) data conversion.

(i)   Detection and control

(a)   Analogue comparator

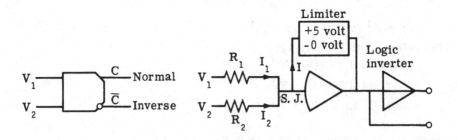

Fig. Al. 13

The circuit of a comparator is similar to that of a summer except that the feedback resistor is replaced by a limiter which causes the output to be restricted (bounded) to the range 0 to +5 volts (assuming DTL or TTL logic is being used). If the output voltage lies within this range, the feedback element has very high resistance so that the gain of the unit is very large. Thus if the total current $I(= I_1 + I_2)$ is positive (i. e. when $V_1 + V_2 > 0$ assuming $R_1 = R_2$) the amplifier output is driven to zero and C becomes logic HIGH. When I is negative the amplifier output is driven to +5 volts and C becomes logic LOW. The characteristic is shown below:

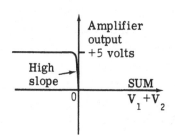

Normally the gain of the amplifier is chosen so that the output will switch between 0 and +5 volts for a change of a few millivolts in the input $V_1 + V_2$.

Fig. A1.14

Clearly the circuit can be extended to allow for any number of inputs. Some comparators also have a logic LATCH input. When this input is made HIGH the logic outputs will not change whatever the sign of the total analogue input. This characteristic is provided by adding logic gates (or a gated bistable) to the logic output shown.

(b) Relay switches

Switching of analogue signals can be achieved by mechanical relays driven by logic signals.

A joined to B if CONTROL HIGH.
A joined to C if CONTROL LOW.

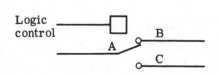

Fig. A1.15

Such devices have three major limitations:

    (a)   They are very prone to damage due to mis-patching.

    (b)   They can only be operated relatively slowly ($0.1 \rightarrow 1$ milli-second) and are not suitable for changing the analogue model within the compute period when operating at high speed.

    (c)   They may not present constant loads to devices connected to them. For example, the arrangement below might be used to change the gain of the integration process by a factor of 10:

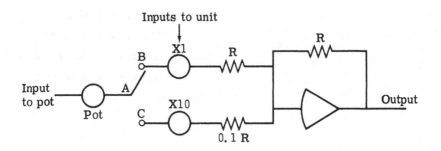

Fig. A1.16

However, the load on the pot and hence the coefficient by which it multiplies will depend on which input of the integrator is selected by the switch and thus the effective gain of the integration process will not change by the required factor as the relay is operated.

(c)   Electronic digital-analogue switches

These switches are essentially fast (< 1 microsecond operating time) switchable input resistors which must be joined to the summing junction of an integrator, inverter or summer. To the user a D/A switch provides an additional optional (by logic control) input to an amplifier unit (Fig. A1.17).

The switch itself is generally a field effect transistor which has a small resistance r when closed. A resistor of resistance $R - r$ is placed in series with the FET to give a total resistance R from input to summing junction (when closed) and thus provide a gain of 1.

304

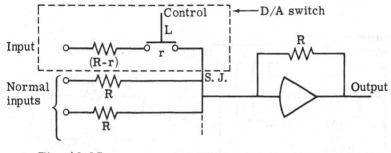

Fig. A1. 17

By using two FET switches operating in opposite phases the resistance into the D/A switch can be made constant irrespective of the state of the switch:

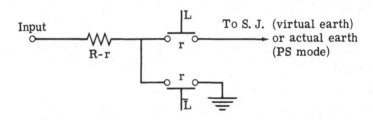

Fig. A1. 18

(ii) Data conversion

(a) Digital to analogue convertor (D. A. C.)

D. A. C. s usually employ a weighted resistor technique to convert a digital variable X into a current and then into a corresponding analogue variable (voltage) X. The technique is illustrated in Fig. A1. 19 for a 4 bit convertor.

Digital data is loaded in binary form into the 4 bit buffer register. Each data bit controls the state of an electronic switch, $0 \equiv$ LOW $\equiv$ OFF, $1 \equiv$ HIGH $\equiv$ ON. The total current I_T which flows through the bank of switches depends on which switches are closed, the reference voltage $-V$ and the values of the weighting resistors R, 2R, 4R, 8R. If R_{fb} is

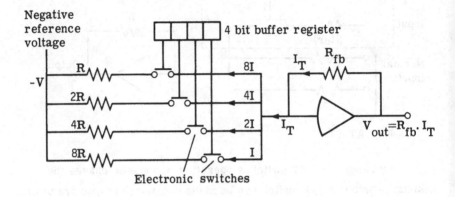

Fig. A1.19

made equal to R and V = 10 volts then the resulting output voltage for various digital data is shown below:

Data	Currents	Total	Output voltage
0 0 0 0		0	0
0 0 0 1	I	I	1
0 0 1 0	$2I$	$2I$	2
0 0 1 1	$2I\ I$	$3I$	3
0 1 0 0	$4I$	$4I$	4
$\vdots$		$\vdots$	$\vdots$
1 1 1 1	$8I\ 4I\ 2I\ I$	$15I$	15

Using modern switches and logic, new data can be input and switches set in less than a microsecond and the time for conversion is determined chiefly by the time it takes the amplifier to settle (5-10 μsec). Conversion time is independent of data word length (assuming the register is loaded in parallel).

With high precision convertors (12-16 BIT) the resistors R, 2R, etc. must be selected (or adjusted) with great care and have very stable characteristics in order for the device to have a 'smooth' linear digital data input/analogue output characteristic.

(b) Digital analogue multiplier (D.A.M.)

These devices are almost identical to D.A.C.s except that the voltage reference is replaced by analogue variable Y. Thus an analogue value Y is multiplied by a digital word X* to give an analogue variable YX. Sometimes these units may not contain an output amplifier but instead provide a current output which must be input to the S.J. of a unit in the analogue model. Such units are often called electronic pots.

(c) Analogue to digital convertor (A.D.C.)

A.D.C. devices are considerably more complex than D.A.C.s and it is usual to share one A.D.C. between many analogue input channels. The simplest type of A.D.C. is illustrated below:

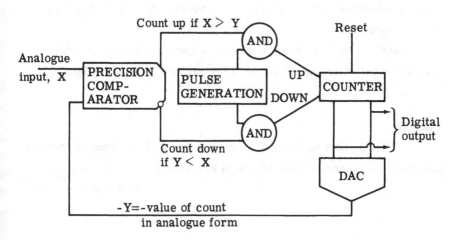

Fig. A1.20

Before conversion starts the counter is reset to mid scale. Once the analogue input is applied pulses are fed at very high frequency into the counter until the count matches the value of the analogue input variable.

The initial direction of count (UP/DOWN) depends on the sign of the difference between the analogue input and the mid-scale count as represented in analogue form by the DAC. The conversion stops when the comparator operates, i.e. when Y becomes equal to X.

Clearly to achieve a useful speed of conversion (~10 μsec) a very high frequency pulse generator and counter is required. E.g. if the convertor is a 12 bit device, reset to mid scale before conversion, a number of pulses between 0 and $2^{11} = 2048$ must be input before conversion is complete. To achieve 10 μsec conversion time (worst case) would involve use of a 200 MHz generator. The variable conversion time is also an adverse characteristic of this type of device.

More sophisticated convertors use bit comparison successive approximation techniques. Thus in a ±10 volt convertor the analogue variable is checked to see if it is positive or negative and the sign bit (i.e. the most significant bit) is set accordingly. The analogue variable is checked to see if it is greater or less than 5 volts magnitude and the next bit set. This process continues until the least significant bit is set. Conversion time is independent of input variable magnitude but depends on the word length of the convertor. Conversion rates of at least 1 bit per microsecond are achieved.

ADC systems contain extensive sample/hold and multiplexing (i.e. route selection) facilities and a typical system is described in §9.2.

Example

Write a short essay on 'The mode control of analogue integrators'. Use diagrams wherever they will be of assistance.

(BCS 1969)

Appendix 2 · Preparation and Checking

A2.1 Introduction

Problems which are studied by analogue/hybrid computer simulation are often complex and the process of problem preparation, i. e. scaling, patching, etc. , is very prone to error. Thus it is essential to carry out comprehensive checks, both static and dynamic, on the validity of the analogue/hybrid model before obtaining solutions to the simulated equations. Not only will these checks enable as much confidence as possible to be placed in the results obtained but are vital in getting some simulations working at all. In general the more thoroughly these checks are prepared and carried out the shorter will be the total time of the study. Inexperienced users are generally much too keen to get problems to run and skimp the checking phase. Sometimes they find that after many hours of taking 'production runs' they discover that some important feature was left out of the simulation and the results obtained are worthless.

Static checks should ensure that all the parts of the analogue model are connected together and working correctly at least initially.

Dynamic checks, in which solutions obtained with the analogue model are compared with those obtained by other means, should ensure that the equations are being solved correctly for at least one combination of coefficient and other values.

However, correct static and dynamic checks will not, unfortunately, guarantee that the results of the simulation trials will be correct. A computer model at best only approximates to the actual system under study as it is impossible to form model equations to completely and exactly represent and behaviour of the system. Thus in addition to the checks that can guarantee the conformity of the computer model to the model equations, the user must also perform checks to see if the computer solutions are of the general form expected, i. e. one must try to relate the solutions to the original system and check if they are reasonable. This is normally best done if the person with the problem also 'solves' it on the computer. However, when a problem is supplied to hybrid computer programmers, who then take responsibility to produce working simulations, it is vitally important that they obtain as much information about the problem as possible, e.g. likely maximum values, expected shape of solutions, etc., in order to check the validity of the solution. Ensuring that all measurements, e.g. graphs, made relate to the actual problem variables and not the computer variables helps in this type of checking. For example, the programmer may observe that the temperature of water in a tank in a computer model exceeds 100°C at some time in the equation solution. Checking back with the supplier of the problem shows that a limiter (to limit the temperature to 100°C) has been left out of the model equations and, consequently, from the simulation. Had the recordings been made in terms of machine units (or even volts) this error might well have gone undetected. Interaction between the problem supplier and programmer is essential at all stages of the study, particularly when first solutions are being made before any extensive parameter adjustment is attempted. The programmer must also become familiar with the problem so that the purpose and limitations of the study are clearly understood.

Another small practical point in validity checking is to record, by graph plotting or otherwise, every variable in the model whether it appears to be of interest or not. Odd faults, like a squarer working correctly for positive inputs but not for negative ones, can be detected this way.

A2.2 Static testing

The derivation of scaled equations, pot coefficients and static check pot, amplifier and derivative values has already been explained in §3. In these notes, some aspects, but not the basic method, of the process are discussed, particularly relating to errors that may be made even if the process is carried out carefully.

(i)   The first and most important point is that in many problems some (or all) of the initial condition values may be zero. A zero is no good for checking anything, e.g. in the set up below if the initial value of variable x is zero, very little can be deduced from checking that the

output of the squarer is zero. The two units may not be even joined together, the squarer may be set up to give + the square instead of - the

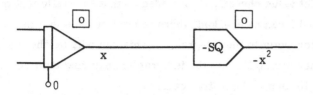

Fig. A2.1

square, etc. Consequently in problems of this type it is necessary to
perform a static test with conditions which are different to those used in
the normal I.C. mode.

In a number of large machines false test references of ±1 machine
unit are provided during the ST mode. These references automatically
become zero when the computer is switched from ST to I.C. Thus all
variables can be assigned non-zero initial values in the ST mode to check
out the analogue model. On a diagram these test references and values
can be indicated with a 'T'.

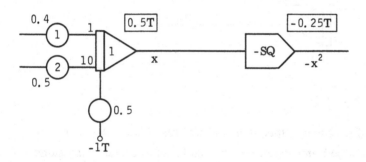

Fig. A2.2

Naturally enough it is very easy to use a true reference instead of
a test reference. Thus it is important to perform a separate I.C. check
as well as a ST check.

(ii)   Most small analogue computers do not provide facilities for

311

checking the output values of potentiometers or derivative inputs to integrators. Without these facilities it is impossible to check completely an analogue simulation. For example, with reference to the above diagram, even if pot value checking is provided so that the static test outputs of pots 1 and 2 can be checked, there is no guarantee that the pots are connected correctly to the integrator. This can only be checked by summing together the inputs into the integrator, including the effects of gains 1 and 10, to form a derivative value.

(iii) +1 and -1 test values at the outputs of amplifier units are of little use as they can easily be confused with each other or with reference values. For example, in the arrangement below, checking that the output of the squarer is -1 does not guarantee that the squarer input is joined to the output of integrator 1. The squarer input could be joined to integrator 2 output or to the +1 reference supply.

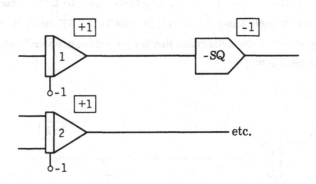

Fig. A2. 3

Equal test output values should also be avoided (e. g. +0. 5 at the outputs of both integrators shown) as these can lead to the same sort of trouble.

(iv) Amplifier units, particularly non-linear units, sometimes only work correctly over a limited range of their output values. Two particular faults commonly give trouble:

(a) An amplifier (integrator/summer) will limit when its output is large (+ or -) but work correctly otherwise.

(b)   A multiplier will work correctly over 2 quadrants (e. g.
      X + or - with Y > 0) but not over the other quadrants.

These types of errors can be hard to find.   The possibility of them occurring implies that all units should be checked for correct operation for a number of output values including extreme values.   These types of faults are best avoided by comprehensive daily maintenance in which units are tested under 'all' conditions.   Unfortunately this means that a number of expensive patch boards have to be permanently set up purely for maintenance checking.   However, it is better to try to avoid this sort of trouble than wait for it to occur in a complex simulation.

A2. 3   Dynamic checking

Dynamic checking can be divided into two areas, one of local testing and one of total problem testing.

Local tests

(i)   Many simulations contain sections which can be isolated and tested by themselves.   Naturally dynamic checks should be made on these sections prior to any solutions being obtained for the total problem.   In particular all function generators, both of the independent variable and of dependent variables, should be checked.   Functions of the independent computer variable, time, used either as forcing functions or variable coefficients can be checked by making pen recordings of them and comparing them with theoretical graphs.   Alternatively, in a hybrid set-up they can be logged and compared in tabular form with numerically calculated values.

Each function of a dependent variable in the analogue model should be checked over its total dynamic range by either of the methods suggested in §5.   This will generally mean that the normal input to the function generator circuit will need to be connected to a special test driving function of time (e. g. a timebase or a sinewave generator).   Functions generated within the digital computer, output to the analogue via D. A. C. s or D. A. M. s, should also be checked by graph plotting or by feeding the generated value back via an A. D. C. to the digital for comparison.

(ii)   Some problems simulated are non-linear extensions to well understood linear problems.   Naturally in these cases the non-linear ele-

ments can be removed and the solution of the linear problem compared
with theoretical predictions. An example of this type of problem is considered below. The equation concerned occurs in the study of the response of a non-linear mechanical system to a sinusoidal forcing function
and is known as Duffing's equation:

$$\frac{d^2y}{dt^2} + a\frac{dy}{dt} + b^2y + cy^3 = A \sin wt,$$

where a, b, c, A and w are all parameters. Clearly the solutions of
special linear cases (c = 0) of this equation are well understood and
thus these cases should be checked first. A possible test sequence could
be:

(a)   Make $a = c = A = 0$ so that the equation is one for S. H. M.
       Set up an initial condition in y, observe the oscillation pro-
       duced checking it for frequency and unwanted amplitude
       growth or decay. Compare the frequency with that predicted
       by $f = b/2\pi$.

(b)   For a special value of b^2 (e. g. $b^2 = 1$) introduce a certain
       amount of damping 'a' and observe the rate of decay of the
       amplitude of the oscillations. Again compare with theoretical
       predictions.

(c)   Set a to 0 and compare the frequency of the forcing func-
       tion term with the frequency of the waveform produced by
       the terms on the L. H. S. of the equation, e. g. make $b^2 = 1$,
       adjust the coefficients determining w so that w should also
       be 1 and record and compare sin wt and the solution of the
       equation $\frac{d^2y}{dt^2} + b^2y = 0$ (for $\frac{dy}{dt} = b$ and $y = 0$ at $t = 0$
       so that $y = \sin bt$).

(d)   Still with $A = 0$, $a = 0$ and $c = 0$ observe and check the
       output of the generator y^3 as y varies sinusoidally.

Once all these checks are done (and assuming a proper static check
has already been performed for a general set of values, a, b, c, A and
w) one can be confident about the validity of the solutions obtained. Clearly
more dynamic checks could be made on the linear model, e. g. checking
for forced harmonic motion, but this would involve use of rather more

mathematics and the amount of effort involved is probably not worthwhile (unless, of course, one was very familiar with the analytical solution of the linear equation).

Total tests

The best way to check dynamically a simulation is to compare the results obtained, for a particular but general set of parameter values, with results obtained completely independently by digital computer simulation.

The study of the problem on the analogue or hybrid machine involves a great deal of problem preparation (computer diagrams, reduction, scaling, patching) and errors are likely to occur at any one stage. Thus to be clear of these errors, the digital simulation solutions must be derived from the original set of equations relating to the problem and not from any reduced or scaled equations derived somewhere in the analogue/hybrid preparation. Of course for comparison purposes the digital simulation results could be scaled, using the same scaling factors as used in the analogue model. Alternatively, the analogue solutions could be interpreted in the terms of the problem variables and the comparison made with respect to the problem variables.

If differences are observed between analogue/hybrid and digital simulation solutions, the errors need not necessarily be attributed to the analogue/hybrid simulation. Some special types of problems are difficult to solve using digital simulation and it is always wise to run the digital simulation program using different integration procedures and demanding various accuracies before concluding that the analogue/hybrid set up is at fault. Should the errors be difficult to find it may be necessary to check out the simulation by comparing solutions obtained by both techniques for a number of particular and restricted cases, e.g. with some parameter values equal to zero.

Finally, when the analogue/hybrid simulation study is completed and optimum parameter values, etc., have been selected, it is a good idea to check the final results by digital simulation. Besides, hopefully, confirming their correctness, the digital simulation paperwork should provide a useful log of the problem and provide the results in tabulated form for those who prefer this type of output to graphical recordings.

315

A2.4 Computer aids

Computer aids to help problem preparation and checking are, unfortunately, not widely available. At Bradford we are fortunate to have available a very useful, but certainly not completely comprehensive, program called APSE[†] (Automatic Preparation and Scaling of Equations) which greatly assists problem preparation.

This package is primarily concerned with analogue (rather than hybrid) models. Equations, differential and algebraic, are input to the program and estimates of maximum values provided by the user. By user commands, the program generates scaled equations, potentiometer set-up and check lists, static check data, assignment data, etc. In fact, the computer output obtained enables the user to patch up and check out problems without drawing the usual computer diagrams. The package is simple to use as it demands a minimum of input data and commands. It does not necessarily produce the most compact simulation for the equations nor does it use the best method for generating functions [e. g. if a function $f(t) = \cos wt$ is required in the simulation, the method 'suggested' is to use a timebase to give wt and input this to a COS generator instead of introducing a 2 integrator inverter loop] but with a little careful planning and interpretation these limitations can be minimised [e. g. in the example above the user simply needs to introduce a differential equation to generate $f(t)$ rather than specify it as a function].

The package does, however, greatly reduce the amount of labour - particularly numerical calculation - associated with the preparation of analogue problems and provides a very useful log of the problem under study. Although for one off small problems (< 20 amplifiers) the amount of time and effort needed to prepare the problem by use of this package is probably as great as the effort to prepare the problem directly, changes can be very easily made (i. e. by adding or changing a number of punched cards) and new up-to-date output obtained. For example, the timescaling of the whole simulation may be changed by changing one instruction only. The effect of this on rerunning the package is to produce a new set of pot listings and static test data incorporating the effect of the timescale change. If the amplitude scaling of a variable is found to be incorrect when running

† Provided by the National Computing Centre.

316

the analogue/hybrid problem, this variable may be rescaled by changing the card specifying its maximum value, and new set-up and check-out data obtained.

The package can be made to produce an optimised static test in which static test pot values, for coefficients and initial integrator conditions, are chosen so as to make the unit output variables be as different as possible in amplitude thus avoiding the 'equal value' type of error discussed earlier.

Digital simulation solutions may also be obtained for the equations to aid dynamic checking. Clearly the solutions obtained this way cannot be regarded as completely independent (see previous section) as they use the same equations and data used in deriving the analogue model and therefore any errors in these details are common to both.

To simplify the use of the pot coefficient and check list data, the output from the package needs to be in a form in which it can be used as input data when setting up and checking out the analogue/hybrid simulation.

Examples

(1)   Describe how a static test and a dynamic check should be constructed for an analogue computer set-up. What features of the set-up will these checks omit to test? How accurately should the test results agree with the computer? To what extent is one justified in making all runs in parallel on another computer (e. g. digital) to ensure the correctness of the results?

(BCS 1970)

(2)   Describe the procedures to be adopted when setting up a problem on an analogue computer to reduce the probability that the results will be in error.

(BCS 1971)

Further Reading

Introductory books on analogue computation

1. Peterson, G. R. Basic Analog Computation, Macmillan (1967). (Good introduction and source of simple examples. However, does not use scaling method recommended in this text.)
2. Charlesworth, A. S. and Fletcher, J. R. Systematic Analogue Computer Programming, Pitman (1967).

More advanced texts on analogue and hybrid computing

3. E. A. L. Handbook of Analog Computation (1967). (Comprehensive text on analogue and simple parallel logic hybrid techniques.)
4. Bekey, G. A. and Karplus, W. J. Hybrid Computation (1968).
5. E. A. L. Analogue Computer Programming Manual Advanced Techniques, Ed. Smith, R. (1967).
6. E. A. L. Basics of Parallel Hybrid Computers, Ed. Hannaner, G. (1968).
7. Korn, G. A. and Korn, T. M. Electronic Analog and Hybrid Computers (2nd edition), McGraw-Hill (1972).

Hardware

8. Reeves, C. M. An Introduction to Logical Design of Digital Circuits, C. U. P. (1972).

Analogue - see Ref. 7 and:
9. Phillrick/Nexus Application Manual for Operational Amplifiers, Phillrick/Nexus Research (1968).
Hybrid Interface - see Refs. 4 and 7.

Software

10. Kemeny, J. G. and Kurtz, T. F. Basic Programming (2nd ed), John Wiley (1971).

318

HYBRID: see Refs. 4 and 5.

11.   Elzas, M. I. 'HL1 or towards a unique language for all continuous
       System Simulation', Proc. 7th A. I. C. A. Conference, Prague
       1973.

Digital simulation

12.   The SCi Continuous System Simulation Language (CSSL). Simula-
       tion, vol. 9, no. 6, Dec. 1967.

13.   Nilsen, R. N. and Karplus, W. J. 'Continuous System Simulation
       Languages. A State of the Art Survey', Proc. 7th A. I. C. A.
       Conference, Prague 1973.

14.   Martens, H. R. 'A Comparative Study of Digital Simulation
       Methods', SIMULATION, Feb. 1969.

Boundary value problems

THEORY:

15.   Fox, L. (ed.). Numerical Solution of Ordinary and Partial
       Differential Equations.

16.   Roberts, S. M. and Shipman, J. S. Two Point Boundary Value
       Problems Shooting Method, Elsevier (1972).

Optimisation

Parallel Logic Hybrid Methods - see Ref. 6.

General Methods - see Ref. 4 and:

17.   Dixson, L. C. W. Non-Linear Optimisation, E. U. P. (1972).

Index

Accuracy (see Errors)

Active units (see Analogue units)

ADC 181, 183, 307

Amplifier (see Operational amplifier)

Amplitude scaling 14, 32

Analogue computer 3 et seq.

    direct or special purpose 3, 8

    general purpose 5, 11

Analogue mode (see Mode)

    time scale (see Time scale)

Analogue units

    active 13

    amplifier (see Operational amplifier)

    comparator (see Comparator)

    differentiation 18, 279

    diode function generator (see D. F. G.)

    integrator (see Integrator)

    inverter (see Inverter)

    linear 11, 12, 289

    memory 7, 8, 89

    multiplier (see Multiplier)

    non-linear 12, 13, 299

    passive 13

    summer (see Summer)

AND gates (see Logic units)

Angular frequency 57, 259

A. P. S. E. 316

Backlash 286

Bang-bang 154

BASIC 132, 136, 144, 189

    HYBRID 177, 188, 196

Beam 68, 111, 224

BEDSOCS 144 et seq.

    control variable 151

    communication 150

    display 145, 146, 150

    dynamic region 145

    equations section 145

    EXIT 157

    function generation 154

    HIT 157

    initial region 150

    interaction 153

    PROCED blocks 154

    representation units 145

    terminal region 150

Bessel's equation of order zero 121

Bistable (see Logic units)

Block form languages (see Digital simulation language)

Boundary value problem 100, 160, 199, 223

Bucket brigade (see Memory pair)

Buffer 182

321